Sentence Repetition Testing for Studies of Community Bilingualism

Summer Institute of Linguistics and
The University of Texas at Arlington
Publications in Linguistics

Publication 104

Editors

Donald A. Burquest
University of Texas
at Arlington

William R. Merrifield
Summer Institute of
Linguistics

Assistant Editors

Rhonda L. Hartell

Marilyn A. Mayers

Consulting Editors

Doris A. Bartholomew
Pamela M. Bendor-Samuel
Desmond C. Derbyshire
Robert A. Dooley
Jerold A. Edmondson

Austin Hale
Robert E. Longacre
Eugene E. Loos
Kenneth L. Pike
Viola G. Waterhouse

Sentence Repetition Testing for Studies of Community Bilingualism

Carla F. Radloff

Principal Investigators

Daniel Hallberg
Charles Meeker

David Marshall
Carla F. Radloff

A Publication of
The Summer Institute of Linguistics
and
The University of Texas at Arlington
1991

© 1991 by the Summer Institute of Linguistics, Inc.
Library of Congress Catalog No: 91–68075
ISBN: 0–88312–667–2
ISSN: 1040–0850

All Rights Reserved

No part of this publication may be reproduced, stored in a retrieval system, or transmitted in any form or by any means—electronic, mechanical, photocopy, recording, or otherwise—without the express permission of the Summer Institute of Linguistics, with the exception of brief excerpts in journal articles or reviews.

Cover sketch and design by Hazel Shorey

Copies of this and other publications of the Summer Institute of Linguistics may be obtained from

International Academic Bookstore
7500 W. Camp Wisdom Road
Dallas, TX 75236

Contents

Foreword by Eugene H. Casad ix

Preface by John W. Oller, Jr. xi

Acknowledgments xv

1. Introduction 1

    1.1. The place of bilingualism testing in a sociolinguistic survey . . . 1
    1.2 Groundwork for second-language proficiency testing 2
    1.3 Selection of the instrument 3
    1.4 What is a sentence repetition test? 7
    1.5 How does an SRT assess second-language proficiency? 8

2. Use in Bilingualism Surveys 11

    2.1 Introduction 11
    2.2 Defining the population 11
        2.2.1 Obtaining a sample frame. 12
    2.3 Sampling 16
        2.3.1 Stratified random sampling. 16
        2.3.2 Stratified judgment sampling. 19
    2.4 Questionnaire 20
    2.5 Administering the SRT 22
        2.5.1 Personnel required. 22
        2.5.2 Equipment needed. 22
        2.5.3 Location for testing. 24
        2.5.4 Standard procedures. 24
        2.5.5 Recording responses. 25

	2.6 Scoring the test 25
	2.6.1 Defining an error. 26
	2.6.2 Encountering variant dialects. 28
	2.7 Interpreting SRT scores 28
	2.7.1 Calculating the test score. 28
	2.7.2 Determining the equivalent proficiency level. 29
	2.7.3 Extrapolating sample results. 33

3. Test Development Methodology 37

   3.0 Introduction 37
      3.0.1 Location. 39
      3.0.2 Personnel. 39
      3.0.3 Standard equipment. 41
   3.1 STEP ONE: Sentence elicitation and selection—preliminary form . 42
      3.1.1 Obtaining the sentences. 42
      3.1.2 Eliminating unsuitable or excessively long sentences. . . 43
      3.1.3 Tape recording the preliminary form of the test. 44
      3.1.4 Making an elaborated transcription. 45
   3.2 STEP TWO: Rating subjects 46
      3.2.1. Selecting the standard. 46
      3.2.2. Rating the participants. 48
   3.3 STEP THREE: Testing the preliminary form 49
      3.3.1 Determining who should do the testing. 49
      3.3.2 General guidelines for administration. 50
      3.3.3 Conducting the test. 52
      3.3.4 Scoring the test. 53
   3.4 STEP FOUR: Shortening and calibrating 55
      3.4.1 Applying the discrimination index. 55
      3.4.2 Figuring the difficulty level. 59
      3.4.3 Selecting the final fifteen sentences. 60
      3.4.4 Figuring the extracted final form score. 61
      3.4.5 Tape-recording the final form test tape. 62
      3.4.6 Calibrating with the external proficiency standard. . . . 63
      3.4.7 Figuring the line of regression. 64
      3.4.8 Figuring the standard error of estimate. 66
      3.4.9 Figuring the coefficient of correlation. 67
      3.4.10 Suggestions for improving the correlation. 68
      3.4.11 Control testing the final form. 69
   3.5 STEP FIVE: Training the test administrators 71
      3.5.1 Preparing the training materials. 71
      3.5.2 Training the test administrators. 72
      3.5.3 Maintaining interadministrator reliability. 73

Contents vii

    3.6 STEP SIX: Using the SRT in the field 73
    3.7 Summary of steps 74

4. Survey of the Literature 77

    4.1 Investigations into sentence imitation 77
    4.2 Second-language proficiency assessment in adults 81
    4.3 Different aspects of the test methodology 84
    4.4 Studies using sentence repetition in dialect testing 86
    4.5 Summary 88

5. Studies in Reliability and Validity 89

    5.1 Development of the Urdu SRT 91
        5.1.1 Urdu SRT calibration—first attempt. 91
        5.1.2 Natural conversation-style speed. 92
        5.1.3 Translation of the RPE proficiency criteria. 93
        5.1.4 Urdu SRT calibration—second attempt. 93
    5.2 Development of the Pashto SRT 96
        5.2.1 An early form. 96
        5.2.2 A new discrimination index. 97
        5.2.3 The final form. 97
        5.2.4 Calibration. 98
        5.2.5 Mother-tongue Pashto performance. 101
    5.3 Development of the revised Pashto SRT 101
        5.3.1 Using educated mother-tongue speakers. 101
        5.3.2 The preliminary form. 102
        5.3.3 Revised Pashto SRT calibration—first attempt. 103
        5.3.4 Revised Pashto SRT calibration—second attempt. . . . 103
        5.3.5 Selection of sentences for the final form. 106
        5.3.6 Discriminating between RPE levels 3+ and 4. 109
        5.3.7 Checking reliability. 112
    5.4-5.7 Other issues
    5.4 A screening test versus control testing 114
        5.4.1 Design of the vernacular screening tests. 114
        5.4.2 Difficulties with the vernacular screening tests. 115
        5.4.3 Control testing the SRT. 115
    5.5 Effect of two presentations on test score 120
    5.6 Interadministrator reliability 121
    5.7 Comparison with recorded text test 124

6. The Reported Proficiency Evaluation 127
  6.1 Introduction 127
    6.1.1 Mother-tongue raters use standard proficiency
          criteria in their evaluations. 127
    6.1.2 Trained fieldworkers conduct RPE interviews. 129
    6.1.3 RPE technique advantages. 130
  6.2 Support from the literature 131
    6.2.1 Untrained evaluators in second-language proficiency
          research. 131
    6.2.2 Calls for a new type of assessment technique. 134
  6.3 Methodology 135
    6.3.1 Personnel and preparation. 135
    6.3.2 Conducting the interview. 138
    6.3.3 Calculating the weighted score and equivalent
          RPE level. 143
  6.4 RPE as an independent measure of second-language
      proficiency 145
  6.5 Proficiency descriptions 146
    6.5.1 Accent proficiency descriptions 147
    6.5.2 Grammar proficiency descriptions 148
    6.5.3 Vocabulary proficiency descriptions 148
    6.5.4 Fluency proficiency descriptions 149
    6.5.5 Comprehension proficiency descriptions 150
  6.6 RPE level descriptions 151

7. Conclusion and Call for Research 155

Appendix A. Figures and Statistics 159

Appendix B. Sample Score Sheet 171

Appendix C. Elaborated Transcriptions 173

Appendix D. Sample Discrimination Index and Difficulty Level . . . 181

References 189

Foreword

Field research of any kind is a demanding task that carries a full panoply of challenges and renders a binful of rewards to those who do it well. And the present monograph, *Sentence Repetition Testing*, is the pleasing result of several years of diligent and careful work on the part of a well-qualified, thoroughly trained and genuinely dedicated team from the South Asia survey project.

The principal investigator, Carla Radloff, brings both the proper educational and professional background to the development of the SENTENCE REPETITION TEST: as a speech therapist, she had already used a type of sentence repetition test as a screening device. The other principal members of the team, Dan Hallberg, David Marshall, and Charles Meeker, have also been under the supervision of Calvin and Carolyn Rensch for their introduction to language surveys and have been thoroughly involved in the field testing and development of the sentence repetition testing. They have all been involved in the instruction of the field assistants, without whose willing and competent help Radloff and her team could never have accomplished their task. We all owe a deep debt of gratitude to these Pakistani colleagues.

Over the last several years, Radloff and her associates have been developing a screening test for evaluating an individual's proficiency in a second language. The test itself is a measuring device that is so designed as to allow, within a reasonable time frame, the testing of a sufficient sample of people so that the summary of their responses can be construed as a rough index of community characteristics of language proficiency. As Radloff is careful to emphasize repeatedly, the relative ease of field application does not mean that the test is easy to construct or that the field implementation of the method is simple: good results necessitate meticulous planning and implementation.

A major point that commends this work to all of us who are concerned with such surveys is the meticulousness and the care with which these researchers have carried out their work and the intellectual honesty that characterizes the public presentation of their work. They have shown some solid correlations between the sentence repetition testing and their method of REPORTED PROFICIENCY EVALUATION. Yet, they are clearly looking to other researchers in other areas of the world to replicate their studies.

And so we offer to our colleagues a field-tested method that they can employ in conjunction with other already developed methodologies. We do so with the sincere hope that subsequent researchers elsewhere will emulate the professional style and standards of the South Asia Sentence Repetition Test team.

Eugene H. Casad
September 1990

Preface

Probably there is no area of psychological or mental testing where we need empirical study more acutely or where there is a greater tendency to neglect it than in the assessment of language proficiency. We linguists especially—but nonlinguists too—legitimately consider ourselves quite expert in judging questions concerning language proficiency—our own in one or more languages and that of others as well. "What need, therefore," we are apt to ask, "for empirical investigation of questions concerning measures of language proficiency?" Why spend time, money, and energy in researching questions to which we already have solid, well-informed views about the outcomes? Wouldn't it make sense to expend resources on other matters? Why not just convene a panel of experts to decide the doubtful issues concerning language proficiency assessment?

The trouble is that experts are often mistaken in their opinions and consensus is rarely an adequate basis for deciding doubtful matters of fact. For instance, is elicited imitation (a sentence repetition task, say) a suitable basis for assessing degrees of language proficiency in illiterate, multilingual communities? Can it provide a satisfactory basis for certain kinds of decision-making regarding literacy projects of various sorts (including allocation of translation resources)? Or should such tasks as elicited imitation be rejected out-of-hand in favor of oral interviews or some other, perhaps more highly esteemed, alternative? How can reasonable judgments be made about such matters? Of course, one way would be to work from our best linguistic intuitions concerning the appearance of the procedures under consideration. We could even pool our resources and recruit the intuitions of others. By counting various opinions, and by determining which were the most commonly held, we might ensure at least a certain form of reliability in our judgments. Using this approach would result, at best, in what measurement people call FACE VALIDITY. Another approach would be to reason from pure theory—call it logic, semantics, or even a theological basis—to certain policies concerning language testing. For instance, the case can be made that every human soul is worth more than all the galaxies, therefore, no cost is too great for making the best possible judgments about literacy programs and translation projects. By this sort of a priori logic (which is irrefragable), a sort of transcendent validity would be required of any test actually employed in policy making. Between these two theoretical limits—the limit of mere appearance and that of ultimate truth—lie all of our difficulties in decision-making, and so long as we are standing on the ground, it will make sense not to lean too far either in the direction of mere opinion (based in appearances) or in the direction of abstract truth (which we can know only by faith to the extent that we can know it at all). It's the practical, pragmatic connection between the two that must concern us, and for which we are accountable. Here, therefore, we need empirical investigation.

The investigators for this research have chosen to address the middle ground between mere appearances (as judged by our best intuitions) and ultimate reality (known to us only by faith). Rather than making pronouncements independent of empirical evidences, they have devised a series of experimental/observational procedures. Their experiments involve a linking of fact with theory. The designs are replicable and the results of their study are open to public scrutiny. The fact that they have been able to demonstrate ways to improve validity coefficients markedly by adjustments in testing procedure (e.g., in chapter four from a correlation of .66 to .90 between their sentence repetition test (SRT) and their reported proficiency evaluation (RPE)) is, I believe, noteworthy. Informed readers will see that a validity coefficient of .66 shows a variance overlap of only .436 ($.66^2$) as against a variance overlap of .81 (nearly twice as much) for a coefficient of .90. By appropriate empirical research they were able to improve their SRT greatly by a few simple modifications. Now, it ought to go without saying that the improvement achieved was dependent upon appropriate empirical research. Neither the gain nor its achievement could have been assured by any amount of armchair reflection. Radloff notes in a recent letter that the SRT and RPE approaches have been applied in several previously uninvestigated languages in Asia yielding correlations of .82, .85, and .96 (with mother-tongue speakers functioning as raters for the RPE). It is unlikely that such results could be obtained by chance. Therefore, it seems that SRT-type tasks, as well as RPE-type tasks, have substantial promise as methods of assessing language proficiency in third-world contexts of low-to-nil-literacy. The SRT, of course, is preferred for most applications because of its cost-effectiveness. At the same time, neither of

Preface

these procedures is recommended as a final solution, but merely as practical steps toward informing decisions concerning literacy projects in such contexts. No doubt the research will find many other applications in educational settings as well.

The researchers and their sponsors are to be congratulated on the progress already achieved, and all of us are properly admonished by their work to have a long hard look at appropriate sorts of empirical evidence before venturing strong views on issues concerning which, as it turns out, we experts (of various stripes and persuasions, linguists included) are apt to know a good deal less than we thought we knew. Moreover, we find ourselves increasingly in debt to those who persevere in wrestling out a suitable, practical balance between that which merely appears to be and that which really is. Incidentally, I believe I speak for all of those who have been following the developing language testing research of the Summer Institute of Linguistics when I say that we are keenly awaiting publication of the currently ongoing Cameroon study on the relation between the SRT, RPE, and the Second Language Oral Proficiency Evaluation procedure piloted by SIL some years ago. May I join my own small voice with those who say thank you to all those researchers who persevere in such work? And, may I take an even bolder step and urge that everyone of us who participates in supporting such efforts and the worthy ends they seek to achieve should applaud the results achieved so far?

John W. Oller, Jr.
University of New Mexico

Acknowledgments

From its inception, this investigation of sentence repetition as a test of second language proficiency has been a team effort. At each stage, planning and discussion of results among the principal investigators has sparked creativity and sharpened ideas. Specific areas, however, have had the mark of individual contribution—innovation by Charles Meeker resulted in the discrimination index (described in chapter 3), and he also served as consultant for the much needed statistical analysis. David Marshall's insights and efforts applied to 'hometown' or screening tests for the sentence repetition test (SRT) resulted in greater credibility for the SRT (chapter 5). Both of these men brought the reported proficiency evaluation (RPE) to the point of initial field readiness (chapter 6), and each headed up the extensive fieldwork needed to develop the first two SRTs, Meeker for the original Pashto SRT and Marshall for the Urdu SRT. Daniel Hallberg joined the team in time for the revision of the Pashto SRT. He helped coordinate the extensive data collection process for the revised Pashto SRT and provided valuable input into the interpretation of the data. In addition, the entire membership of the SIL South Asia sociolinguistic survey team has participated in discussions on the various aspects of the SRT, providing necessary checks and balances in its development.

Field research was furthered by the efforts of Amjad Afridi, Nooran Afridi, and Ilyas Bhatti, with assistance in the earlier stages by Golab Shah and Zardad Khan. Special recognition is extended to Amjad Afridi who was responsible for all the data collection for the revised Pashto SRT, both the RPE interviews and the SRT testing.

The research reported in this manual was carried out as part of a wider sociolinguistic survey of Northern Pakistan, under the auspices of Lok Virsa, the National Institute of Folk Heritage, Islamabad.

This manual and field study report has gone through several editions. Special discussions on the content and editing of earlier versions with Calvin and Carolyn Rensch, directors of the South Asia survey, and Dan and Calinda Hallberg were most helpful. Dan also helped with the editing of the current version. Eugene Casad has been a great encourager since the survey preconference in Baguio, Philippines, in 1987, when the SRT first went public. He has kindly read through the current version of the manual twice, each time making many helpful observations. Positive response from many people to the SRT presentation at the International Language Assessment Conference at Horsleys Green, England, in 1989, spurred the publication of the research results. Gary Simons, in particular, served as most welcome catalyst for the reorganization and rewriting of this manual. Melinda Lyons and Melanie Mead have kindly helped search out pertinent literature. Special thanks and recognition go to Clare O'Leary for the hours of lively discussion on various aspects of SRT and RPE and for much crucial input during the rewrite of this manual. And many thanks to all the members of the team for their continued encouragement and help throughout the long days of writing and rewriting.

The development of the SRT and RPE techniques has been a team effort. The responsibility to communicate all the discoveries, insights, lessons, and recommendations which have accumulated as a result of the vast sum of man-hours invested in this effort, however, has fallen on me. The responsibility for the failure to communicate clearly also falls on me. Potential researchers, inquirers, and even those with casual interest are therefore invited to share their questions, comments, and complaints.

The principal aim in the presentation of this manual is that researchers and others faced with the need to do bilingualism testing will add SRT to their repertoire of tools. Another aim is that the SRT technique will actually be applied to other languages in other countries for the purpose for which it was designed—discovering patterns of second-language proficiency in communities.

11 October 1990
Carla Radloff
South Asia Sociolinguistic Survey Project
Peshawar, Pakistan

Correspondence:
  South Asia Survey Project
  South Asia Office
  Horsleys Green
  High Wycombe, BUCKS
  England HP14 3XL

1
Introduction

1.1. The place of bilingualism testing in a sociolinguistic survey

The scope of a sociolinguistic survey can be as broadly or narrowly focused as the number of goals the survey is designed to meet. Describing attitudes toward an official language or a neighboring dialect, noting patterns of language use in everyday activities, predicting language maintenance or shift, counting lexical similarity between geographical dialects, tracing use of linguistic forms across cultures, plotting boundaries of dialect differences—any or all of these, with many more variations—constitute possible foci of a sociolinguistic survey. Many times a single variable is studied, but often it is the interplay of variables, the effect of one on the other or both of them in relation to a third that is in focus. The goals within such studies reflect the researcher's interest, time, and ability to collect the pertinent data.

Community-wide bilingualism is frequently an aspect of study in a survey. Second-language proficiency is ultimately an individual matter, yet the aggregate of individual proficiencies produces a profile of bilingualism within that community. Community-wide bilingualism is usually not examined in isolation; rather, it is studied as it relates to language attitudes, or language use, travel patterns or other phenomena within a community. It is studied as a means by which language planners can make more realistic decisions. In a broad, comprehensive survey where lexical similarity, dialect intelligibility, language attitudes, and patterns of language use are all investigated, second-language proficiency is seen as only one part of the total picture. In studies of language maintenance and shift, second-language proficiency measurements can undergird the arguments for the predictions made.

1.2 Groundwork for second-language proficiency testing

If second-language proficiency testing is not the only component of a sociolinguistic survey, it is also not the first step of an investigation into bilingualism. Proficiency testing, even on a limited scale, can be a complicated undertaking. Considerable groundwork needs to be laid. It is necessary that the need for proficiency testing be established, the extent of testing be specified, the critical factors for sampling be identified, and the instrumentation for conducting the testing be selected.

If the effectiveness of schools in teaching the national language is the focus of the survey, proficiency testing would be most helpful. If the goal is to determine which languages should be used for radio broadcasting, perhaps a questionnaire would be more productive. If there is a NEED to know the different levels of proficiency at which different segments of a society function, testing is necessary.

The breadth of the goals of the survey determines the EXTENT to which proficiency testing is necessary. For example, if one narrowly-defined subgroup in a minority population is the focus of the study, then considerably less testing would need to be done than for goals which encompass the population of a large city, with all its social and linguistic complexity. Determining the percent of a population which functions at each of the different proficiency levels will require large-scale testing. Determining that the majority of a population has not attained a certain level of proficiency might require slightly less testing.

A study with very narrowly focused goals might require a person to meet a number of criteria before being selected for testing. In such a study the factors critical to the goal of the research are defined at an early stage. In other studies, the population may be sampled on the basis of general factors such as age, sex, or level of education. The results of the testing, then, would be analyzed to determine the influence of additional, more critical factors on second-language proficiency. For any study, though, no matter how many factors are deemed critical at the initial stages, the quality of the results and their interpretation rely on the care with which the SAMPLING of the target population is planned and the thoroughness with which that sampling is carried out.

Much has been written on language-related research objectives and research design. Introductory sociolinguistic textbooks such as those by Fasold (1984) or Wardhaugh (1986) cover research in a general sense. On the other hand, books such as those by Milroy (1987) and Hatch and Farhady (1982) are written specifically for designing and understanding language research. Milroy devotes an entire chapter to sampling, as do books on statistics for linguistics, such as Woods, Fletcher, and Hughes

Introduction

(1986). Grimes (1986; 1987) and Blair (1990) offer many practical suggestions for bilingualism surveys. In the following chapters on the use of sentence repetition tests, especially those chapters dealing with conducting proficiency testing and methodology, information pertinent to the discussion is presented on sampling, statistics, research design, etc. The reader is referred to works such as those mentioned here for further, more in-depth study.

1.3 Selection of the instrument

Once the need for and extent of proficiency testing is established, and critical factors for sampling identified, a research project still cannot move into gear for testing if adequate thought and preparation have not been devoted to the instrument or methodology to be used for the testing.[1] Primary considerations are that the instrument be both valid and reliable. Practical considerations are also important and will be examined in some detail.

In sociolinguistic surveys, two main areas of language proficiency are of interest (Grimes 1987). One is the inherent ability to understand structurally similar languages or dialects. The other is the learned ability to understand languages or dialects which are not similar. In determining how completely speakers of one dialect can understand a similar one, only a few individuals need to be tested (assuming contact factors have been controlled). This is because the ability to understand a structurally similar dialect or language is assumed to be relatively uniform throughout the speech community.[2] In order to determine the different levels of second-language proficiency in a population, however, it is necessary to test a much larger number of people, as was mentioned above. A second language is learned on an individual basis and the extent of that learning may be related to a number of language-contact factors, such as education, outside travel and its influence, marriage patterns, age, sex, etc. Therefore,

---

[1]Cartier (1980:14) enters a plea for "decision-referenced" testing, i.e., choosing the type of assessment instrument on the basis of the type of decision to be made from the results, rather than being guided by tradition or personal philosophy.

[2]Milroy (1987:21) notes that, in general, linguistic behavior is more homogeneous than many other types of behavior studied by general surveys, for example, dietary or television program preferences. Thus, large samples tend not to be as necessary for linguistic surveys as for other surveys. It is clear that she is referring, in this context, to the study of INHERENT aspects of language behavior, such as use of grammatical structures or specific phonetic variations, rather than LEARNED behaviors like second-language proficiency.

a population must be examined and a sampling must include an appropriate number of people in each subgroup of that population so that the results will reflect the weighting of the factors relevant for that group as a whole. Whereas testing ten people may be considered sufficient for determining inherent intelligibility between two languages or dialects, assessment of second-language proficiency of the people of a given language area may require testing two hundred. Therefore, it is necessary to have an instrument for measuring second-language proficiency that requires a minimum amount of time to administer and score, making the testing of large numbers of people possible.

A related concern is the limitation of the time available to conduct a given survey. Researchers have frequently found the time allotted to a certain area cut short because of circumstances beyond their control. In any type of survey, in order to ensure quality results, it is essential that time be taken to develop a proper network of personal contacts. The need to both develop contacts and test subjects points to the need for a test that requires a minimum amount of time to administer and score, thus maximizing the testing accomplished within the time available. Also related to this is the fact that in order to be acceptable to a wide variety of people, a test should not be overly demanding in terms of time and complexity or stress involved. If a test methodology is acceptable, people will more willingly give the time necessary for testing.

In this connection, the ORAL INTERVIEW technique should be mentioned. Originally developed by the Foreign Service Institute (FSI) for diplomatic trainees (see, for example, Jones 1975, Wilds 1975), the method concentrates on a subject's second-language performance during an interview conducted by a trained interviewer and/or linguist. The subject's performance is then evaluated according to the six FSI proficiency level descriptions. The technique was adapted by Educational Testing Service (1970) for training language-proficiency evaluators for Peace Corps volunteers and other educational applications. The Interagency Language Roundtable (ILR) has been responsible in recent years for further study and modification of the proficiency level descriptions and oral interview technique.[3] This oral interview technique has been found to be most helpful in obtaining an in-depth analysis of an individual's strengths and weaknesses in the second language, especially for more educated or sophisticated people who can function under the constraints of an interview of this type. This technique has limitations, however, when applied in a bilingualism survey

---

[3]The SLOPE (Second-language Oral Proficiency Evaluation) is also an adaptation of the ILR oral interview technique, designed for use in preliterate communities (SIL 1987). At the time of this writing it is in the field test stage of development.

of the type discussed here. Often bilingualism surveys are conducted in developing countries, frequently in rural areas where education is limited and free time is scarce. Isolating individuals, particularly women, for an in-depth interview may run counter to cultural norms. There is a need for a technique that will give results as reliably as the oral interview but allow for the exigencies of field conditions, and that will give comparably valid results, but be better designed for the large-scale testing that surveys require. A technique is also needed that will yield a valid general proficiency assessment, necessary for the goals of the survey, but not expend research time on unnecessarily detailed individual evaluations.[4]

Another area of concern in surveys which investigate community-wide bilingualism is the ability of a test to discriminate a wide range of second-language proficiencies. The standard method for dialect intelligibility testing described by Casad (1974) utilizes NARRATIVE TEXTS. Participants listen to the tape recordings of such texts and answer questions about their content. When extended beyond dialect intelligibility testing for use in second-language proficiency testing, this RECORDED TEXT TEST method becomes restrictive in that a given recorded text test may only test one level of general comprehension ability at a time, depending on the complexity of the text (Grimes 1987). If the text is too simple, it provides no challenge to people with middle- or upper-level abilities in the test language. On the other hand, if the content of the text is too complex or too literary, people with lower levels of proficiency have no success at all. The need, then, is for a test which discriminates a wide range of second-language abilities.

Two other difficulties arise in extending the use of recorded text tests beyond dialect intelligibility to bilingualism surveys, which point up additional requirements for an adequate test. One is the time required during the survey to modify an recorded text test at each test location. The questions for a text must be presented in the subject's own language. This means that each time a new dialect area is entered, the questions must be translated into that dialect and checked before testing can commence, which requires extra time at each location. The technique itself requires a significant amount of time from each subject, since he or she must first respond to the questions about a text in their own dialect (the 'hometown test', see Casad 1974) as well as the text(s) in the test language(s). The other difficulty lies in training test subjects to understand the recorded text test procedure itself. Researchers have noted a marked tendency for some

---

[4]"The validity, or lack of validity [of a test] has to be empirically demonstrated by comparison with a criterion.... Once the validity has been demonstrated, however, it is immaterial what type of test we are dealing with. If a test works for the purpose it was intended to, then that is all that matters" (Ingram 1978:12).

subjects to repeat a section of text and its related question, rather than to listen to the text and the questions and give an appropriate answer. This often eliminates otherwise qualified subjects or at the least increases the time needed to explain the test procedure. The need, then, is for an instrument which, once constructed, can be used without numerous modifications and whose test procedure is easy to understand and cost-effective in terms of administrative time.

Cultural and social constraints introduce further requirements for a proficiency test. If a test requires the tape recording of subjects' responses, its use will be limited in many cultures. For example, Muslim women have frequently declined to have their voices tape-recorded. Also, in many cultures it is difficult or inappropriate to isolate people in order to administer a test, especially women. The need therefore exists for a test whose results are valid even when the subject has already heard someone else's responses. Furthermore, in agrarian societies the demands of daily life are such that there may be little free time; this also is probably especially true of women. These factors underline the need for a test which requires little time for administration.

Finally, the situation frequently arises in which it is not possible to have a mother-tongue speaker of the test language do the test administration and scoring. There are situations where political, social, or cultural constraints in an area or even time constraints for a given survey or survey location make it impossible. The need, then, is for a test whose administration and scoring are not dependent upon the test administrator's being a mother-tongue speaker of the test language.

The present field study investigation into sentence repetition as a measure of second-language proficiency has demonstrated that SENTENCE REPETITION TESTS (SRTs) used in the field fulfill all these requirements and more. From the outset, efforts were made to design the SRT methodology so that researchers who do not speak the language being tested or have only rudimentary proficiency are able to oversee and partake in the development of such a test. Also, the training for test administrators should allow even those with minimal proficiency to administer and score a test reliably (although, of course, use of a mother-tongue or fluent speaker of the test language would be more expedient). The SRT also meets the need for a test with short administration and scoring time—a fifteen-sentence SRT with three practice sentences can be administered in approximately five minutes. The SRT procedure is easy for people to understand; indeed, it follows the natural tendency of people to repeat what they hear. The SRT is so designed that once developed and calibrated it is ready to be used without further modification wherever bilingualism in that particular language is a question. The tape recording of participants' responses is optional once an SRT is developed and the test administrators are trained (see chapter 3), thus minimizing the cultural problems mentioned earlier. Furthermore, since a 'correct answer' for an SRT is dependent upon the verbatim repetition of an entire sentence, there is little that an onlooker can 'learn' from another person's performance.[5]

Once trained, the same test administrator can give that SRT in all locations. When necessary, one administrator alone can give the SRT, although it is easier if a technician is also present to operate the tape player and help in other ways. Also, an administrator can train him- or herself to give the SRT, when provided with the elaborated transcription of the test and the training tape (see §3.5.2). It should be noted that 'complete' mastery of the phonology of the test sentences by the administrator is not required—only an awareness of the crucial differences as pointed out by the elaborated transcription (§3.1.4). This is true because a 'heavy accent' or mispronunciation is acceptable up to the point where a word is garbled. Then it is an error. (See §2.6 for further discussion.)

In the field study described in chapter 5, the Urdu and original Pashto SRTs were found to discriminate among all the lower and middle levels of the proficiency standard they were calibrated with; the revised Pashto SRT is able to discriminate between the higher levels as well. Thus the SRT meets the requirement for a test that discriminates the wide range of proficiency levels. The low demands of an SRT on administrative time and personnel coupled with the simplicity and non-threatening nature of its methodology result in a testing tool that is very productive in helping to assess second-language proficiencies in a community-wide survey.

1.4 What is a sentence repetition test?

An SRT, as designed for large-scale assessment of second-language proficiency, consists of a series of tape-recorded sentences in the second language. The individual being tested listens to the sentences one by one and repeats each sentence immediately after hearing it. These sentences are not related in meaning, but their sequence and content reflect increasing levels of complexity and length. For maximum credit the individual must repeat each sentence verbatim, although some credit is given if a repetition includes only one or two mistakes.

---

[5]In the geographical area of the SRT field study it has proved to be practically impossible to test village women in isolation. There have been situations where up to six women have taken the test in one household, each listening to the others' responses, but with no noticeable effect on scores.

An SRT is an indirect, correlated test. It has no inherent standard for categorizing second-language proficiency; rather, its results have meaning because they refer to another, external proficiency standard. Each SRT must be calibrated separately with such a standard: a score of twenty-four points on an SRT in one language, for example, does not necessarily reflect the same proficiency level as a score of twenty-four on an SRT in another language. But once those SRTs are calibrated with a standard, conclusions can be drawn about performance across the tests because reference is to a certain proficiency level on the common standard. In the assessment of second-language proficiency the most commonly recognized standard is that set by the Foreign Service Institute (FSI) with its description of six levels of proficiency (see, for example, Jones 1975, Wilds 1975). If a specific SRT would be correlated with that standard, then, a twenty-four-point score could be said to refer to a specific FSI proficiency level.

The type of SRT described in this manual is a screening, as opposed to a diagnostic, type of test. It is used to obtain an objective, general assessment of a person's proficiency in a second language, fitted for the purposes of a sociolinguistic survey. It does not 'diagnose'; it is not used for an in-depth analysis of one person's strengths or weaknesses in that second language, as would be required, for example, in a foreign language classroom. It is best used when the survey goals encompass obtaining an overall profile of the second-language proficiency levels of an entire community. Administration of an SRT requires only a few minutes, but since its development is a somewhat involved process, it would probably be most economically used to investigate second-language proficiency in a language of wider communication or other language with many second-language speakers. It is a tool designed to be used to meet the needs of the research project, according to the information desired.

1.5 How does an SRT assess second-language proficiency?

"The number of unconnected words that we can hold in immediate memory is about the same as the number of unrelated digits, even though a word contains much more information than a digit." Thus Stevick (1976:16) describes the adult memory span (with reference to mother-tongue English speakers). The number he refers to is seven, plus or minus two (Norman 1976), but the capacity of that seven increases greatly with CHUNKING, the non-conscious loading of meaning. The phenomenon of chunking means that each of the seven chunks can carry its own load of information.

Syntax is a means for chunking verbal information. A sentence three, four, or even five times seven words can be easily remembered and repeated because of this phenomenon of chunking meaning along syntactic lines. This is the heart of the sentence repetition test for second-language proficiency: as people become more familiar with a second language and more confident in manipulating its syntax, they are more and more able to pack the chunks full of information; and the more they control the morphology the better able they are to organize within the chunks of syntax; and the more vocabulary they know the better able they are to hold on to the meaning until they can repeat the sentence.

Memory, per se, affects the SRT performance when sentences are too short or too long. A sentence is 'too short' if it has only seven (plus or minus two) words in it (referring to the English standard); a person totally unfamiliar with the syntax of that language could repeat such a sentence (if he has been trained to imitate unfamiliar sounds). Because no chunking may be required, the number of words is within the normal adult memory span for unconnected words or digits. Such sentences may be useful for practice purposes or if one wishes to include a few extremely easy sentences in a SRT, but for assessing second-language proficiency the sentences must be longer.

However, the sentences should not be 'too long'. A sentence is too long when even an educated mother-tongue speaker of that language is unable to repeat it. There is a point where automatic chunking ceases to be adequate and the use of mnemonic strategy enters in. But there is no time, opportunity, or even need for utilizing strategy in a sentence repetition test. What is being assessed is a person's ability to use a second language automatically, without pondering.

Testing the ability of a person to repeat sentences in a second language touches on several aspects of proficiency. An SRT measures comprehension ability inasmuch as chunking can occur only where meaning is understood. People can repeat only what their control of the syntax, morphology, and vocabulary of a language enables them to understand.[6] The SRT is also a test of speakers' production skills since they must correctly repeat all the pertinent forms for person, tense, register, etc.[7]

In the pilot study that examined the feasibility of sentence repetition tests for bilingualism surveys (Radloff and Marshall 1986) and again in the field study, SRTs have shown a high correlation with the proficiency

---

[6]Indeed, the most common response participants make when unable to repeat a test sentence is, "I didn't understand that".

[7]Mastery of phonological production is not assessed other than where 'accent' distorts a word beyond recognition.

standards utilized. In other words, the higher people were rated according to the other standard, the better their performance on the corresponding SRT. (Specific data on the field study versions are discussed in chapter 5.) Thus, the sentence repetition test appears to meet the theoretical requirements of a test for second-language proficiency when correlated with an appropriate standard, and its usefulness is greatly enhanced by its ability to meet the practical requirements of testing in field situations.

In this chapter the SRT technique was placed into the wider context of sociolinguistic surveys. In the next chapter, the practical know-how for using an SRT in a bilingualism survey is given as well as case studies of how the technique has been applied. Chapter 3 details the methodology for developing an SRT and for calibrating it. An extensive review of literature pertinent to the SRT technique is included as chapter 4. Chapter 5 presents the history of the development of SRT as a technique (and thus the rationale for many of the steps recommended in Chapter 3), along with reliability and validity studies. The reported proficiency evaluation, a calibrating instrument for SRTs developed in field situations (called Other Evaluation or OE in earlier drafts), is described in chapter 6. Readers concerned only with methodology may refer to chapters 2, 3, and 6.

2
Use in Bilingualism Surveys

2.1 Introduction

This chapter discusses the preparation for and use of sentence repetition tests (SRTs) in bilingualism surveys. It is assumed that finding out the percentage of the community at each of the proficiency levels is one of the primary goals of the survey. It is, therefore, assumed that the need for bilingualism testing has already been established. Crucial points for designing and carrying out the bilingualism testing are presented and illustrated through examples from different surveys where an SRT was the instrument chosen for second-language proficiency assessment.

2.2 Defining the population

The first step in any survey is to delineate the boundaries of the community in which the research will be focused (Milroy 1987:23). This is done through preliminary investigation of published sources, interviews with knowledgeable people or officials in the area, use of questionnaires with a variety of people, etc. (Grimes 1987).

As an example, the Torwali Kohistani language in the Swat valley (of northern Pakistan) was the focus of a sociolinguistic survey reported by Rensch (1987). The research team defined the boundaries encompassing that language to include the village of Behrain and its environs and part of the Chail side valley by drawing on published sources and interviews with people in that area. The most recent government census was also consulted. In addition to defining the boundaries of the Torwali speaking area, from the information thus gathered it was determined that bilingualism in both Urdu, the national language of Pakistan, and Pashto, the predominant language of wider communication in that area, should be studied. SRTs in both of those languages had previously been developed (see chapter 5).

2.2.1 Obtaining a sample frame. Defining the population to be studied and seeking out an adequate SAMPLE FRAME go hand in hand. "The most common type of sampling frame is a list (actual or notional) of all the subjects in the group to which generalisation is intended" (Woods, Fletcher and Hughes 1986:52). Subjects are then randomly selected from the sample frame for inclusion in the study. Milroy (1987:19) mentions electoral registers or telephone directories as examples, but notes biases in such lists since they include only part of a population.

Woods, et al. (1986:53) describe STAGEs of sample frames. The first stage, for example, would examine the entire geographical area of the language group being surveyed and randomly select the regions to focus on—the number of regions (and subsequent divisions) being dependent on the scope of the resources available for the survey. Each region is subdivided, and sub-regions would again be randomly selected for the second-stage sample frame. Villages would then be chosen within each subregion for the third-stage sample frame and their populations listed for random selection of test subjects. The sample frame mediates between the population of interest and the sample, and allows generalization from the sample values to those in the population of interest.

For the purposes of bilingualism surveys, where—as in all sample-based studies—the quality of sampling determines the quality of results, the sample frame at the village level must be as detailed and complete as possible. Where official sources for such detailed information are not available, it is encumbent upon the research team to be responsible for its collection. Rensch (forthcoming) describes a COMMUNITY PROFILE or demographic profile of a community, where, in census-taking fashion, information about every household in a community is gathered (cf. Blair 1990). Simple information pertinent to the language group in question such as the number of males and females living in each household, and the (approximate) age and level of education for each is probably enough for many bilingualism surveys. This is especially true when the results of the testing will subsequently be analyzed to determine the influence of different factors on bilingual proficiency. However, in a study where specific factors are already known to affect second-language proficiency, such as membership in an ethnic sub-group, for example, or seasonal migration for work, such information should be gathered as part of the demographic or community profile.

In the Torwali survey introduced above, members of the research team personally interviewed representatives of the different households. However, the research team for the survey of the Hindko language, centered in the nearby Hazara district of northern Pakistan, found another source for their sample frame (Rensch 1988). Detailed house-to-house surveys were conducted by graduate students from the anthropology department of a national university as part of the fieldwork for their master's theses. As part of the research team's cooperation with the programs of that university, they were able to obtain the necessary information from those anthropological surveys about numbers of males and females in each household, with their ages and levels of education, in the Hindko-speaking communities under study. Chart (1) shows the results of this demographic profile for Singo di Garhi, a Hindko-speaking village.

(1) Educational levels of Hindko-speaking adults in Singo di Garhi (data from Rensch 1988)

MEN

Age	No Formal Education	1-5 years	6-10 years	11+ years	Total	Percent
13-19 yrs.	1	1	10	0	12	23.0
Percentage	1.9	1.9	19.2	0		
20-29 yrs.	4	4	4	1	13	25.0
Percentage	7.7	7.7	7.7	1.9		
30-39 yrs.	5	4	3	0	12	23.1
Percentage	9.6	7.7	5.8	0		
40-49 yrs.	4	2	2	0	8	15.3
Percentage	7.7	3.8	3.8	0		
50 + yrs.	6	0	1	0	7	13.4
Percentage	11.5	0	1.9	0		
All age groups	20	11	20	1	52	99.8
Percentage	38.4	21.1	38.4	1.9		

WOMEN
Educational Levels

Age	No Formal Education	1–5 years	6–10 years	11+ years	Total	Percent
13–19 yrs.	12	1	0	0	13	29.6
Percentage	27.3	2.3	0	0		
20–29 yrs.	15	0	0	0	15	34.1
Percentage	34.1	0	0	0		
30–39 yrs.	6	0	0	0	6	13.6
Percentage	13.6	0	0	0		
40–49 yrs.	3	0	0	0	3	6.8
Percentage	6.8	0	0	0		
50 + yrs.	7	0	0	0	7	15.9
Percentage	15.9	0	0	0		
All age groups	43	1	0	0	44	100.0
Percentage	97.7	2.3	0	0		

An interesting use was also made of voter registration lists by the Hindko survey research team. Although such lists are exhaustive, in that all men and women of voting age are included, they are biased in that very respect because other age groups are not represented. They also provide no further breakdown for level of education. However, the Hindko survey team was able to utilize the registration lists as a check on the information taken from the demographic profiles as gathered from the anthropological surveys.

The percentage of men and women for each of four age groups was calculated from the voter registration list for Sherpur, a Hindko-speaking village. These percentages were compared with those for the same age groups of two other Hindko-speaking villages, Jammun and Singo di Garhi. Since these villages were all reported to be typical of the area, it was assumed that the percentage of population in each of the age categories should be roughly similar. As can be seen in (2), the percentages are very close, lending credence to the comprehensiveness of the Jammun and Singo di Garhi demographic profiles, since the voter registration lists are presumed to be exhaustive.

(2) Percentages of population in four age groups, comparison of voter registration lists, and demographic profiles (data from Rensch 1988)

Age	Sherpur registration, complete		Jammun demographic, complete		Singo di G. demographic, complete		Sherpur demographic, incomplete	
	Men	Women	Men	Women	Men	Women	Men	Women
20–29	30.7	39.3	29.8	39.0	32.5	48.4	36.1	33.3
30–39	31.3	24.5	29.2	24.1	30.0	19.4	24.1	15.7
40–49	16.6	15.5	16.4	16.4	20.0	9.7	9.6	23.5
50+	20.9	20.4	24.6	20.5	17.5	22.6	30.1	27.5

The demographic profile obtained for the village of Sherpur itself, however, was not comprehensive; only a portion of the Hindko-speaking men and women in that village were counted. Chart (2) shows that the percentages in each age category for the incomplete demographic profile of Sherpur are somewhat different. By having the age group percentages for the voter registration lists and the more complete demographic profiles to compare with, appropriate extrapolations could be made, so that, ultimately, interpretation of results for Sherpur was possible.

Finally, one more innovative example of obtaining a demographic profile as a sample frame should be mentioned. The sociolinguistic survey of the settled Gujari language speakers in the upper Swat valley is reported by Hallberg and O'Leary (1991). The community under study is located in a narrow part of the valley, with rather steep mountain slopes on either side of the river. To obtain the demographic profile, the researcher went to the opposite side of the river from the community with a young man from the village. This young man was one of the schoolteachers and a native of the village and thus was personally acquainted with all the families of the village. From the opposite side of the valley, the two men could easily see every house in the village. Indicating each house in turn, the young man was able to give the researcher detailed information on whether each household was Gujari-speaking, and the numbers of males and females in each, with their approximate ages and levels of education. Any information he was unsure about was later checked in the village.

These examples from actual bilingualism surveys which ultimately used SRTs as the assessment instruments, are presented as illustrations of different ways that sample frames, in these cases, demographic profiles, have been obtained. It is worth mentioning again that the more confidence the researchers can place in their definition of the boundaries of the language community to be surveyed and the listing of the members of that community, the more confidence they will be able to have in their sampling, and, ultimately, in the results of the testing.

2.3 Sampling

The confidence with which the results of a bilingualism survey can be interpreted is in direct proportion to the degree of care taken to ensure that the subjects tested represent the community of which they are members. Thoroughness in sampling will have a greater impact on results than choice of the assessment instrument, provided the researchers choose among instruments that truly measure a wide range of proficiencies.

Second-language proficiency is learned behavior. It is therefore incumbent upon the researcher to test a large enough sample to illuminate the different factors influencing the degree of learning in the various segments of the community under study. Age, sex, and level of education are frequently determining factors in second-language proficiency. Other factors, such as participation in seasonal migration for work, religion, occupation, or ethnic subgroup, however, may prove to be more significant in certain surveys. If the research team is aware of potentially significant factors through presurvey investigations, the sampling procedure should take these factors into account from the beginning. Often, however, the process of analyzing the data brings these other, significant factors to light.

2.3.1 Stratified random sampling. It is necessary for the research team to know a great deal about the total population under study in order to make sure that the sample is representative of the population in every possible way and still random (Hatch and Farhady 1982:9). If it is known, for example, that age, sex, and level of education are potentially significant variables in second-language proficiency, subjects for testing would be chosen randomly within the various subgroups defined by these categories. This is called a STRATIFIED RANDOM SAMPLE. Such sampling could include different villages or ethnic subgroups as necessary 'strata' to be taken into account.

The characteristics chosen as significant define the number of CELLS of a matrix. These, in turn, determine the number of subjects that need to be tested. For example, a bilingualism survey which determines that five age groupings and four levels of education for both sexes are necessary to adequately represent the population will need to fill 40 cells. If a minimum of five people are tested in each cell, as recommended by Grimes (1987) for ensuring a reasonable statistical treatment of the data, the researchers will need to test 200 people.

This number of cells, however, is only theoretical. The actual number of cells to fill in such a matrix is determined by the demographic profile of that community. As an example, reference to (1) shows that three of the four categories for education are basically irrelevant for the Hindko-speaking women of Singo di Garhi, since women do not receive education in that community. Also, one of the age categories includes fewer than five women, according to the demographic profile.[8] So, instead of needing to fill twenty cells with the results of testing for five women each (100 subjects), the test administrators needed to administer the SRT to five women in only five age and education categories, for a total of twenty-five subjects. The data in (3) gives again the percentages from (1) for age and education categories for the Hindko-speaking women of Singo di Garhi. The number of Urdu SRTs administered to the sample of these women is given as well as the corresponding RPE proficiency levels[9] for the scores obtained. Due to circumstances beyond the researchers' control, testing was cut short in this village and only thirteen of the desired twenty-five women could be tested.

If stratifying the sample to increase representativeness is both obvious in its need and accomplishable within a bilingualism survey, ensuring the RANDOMNESS of that sample is probably not. "Random sampling implies that the appearance of one subject in the sample is in no way affected by the appearance of any other subject. That is, random sampling implies the independence of the selection of subjects in the sample" (Shavelson 1988:10). If a bilingualism survey is, for example, carried out under the auspices of the federal government with the authority to test people in every third house, randomness in the selection of the sample may be achieved. However, in most bilingualism surveys potential subjects are contacted, not by any rigorous process of randomization, but rather through networks of social relationships. Whether introduced by friends or friends of friends or employers or leaders of organizations or uncles or

---

[8]Approximating age levels for women can often be difficult in societies where birth records are not kept and women are not educated. In several of the studies reported here, women were asked the age of their oldest child. That number was added to the typical age for marriage in that culture to arrive at an approximation of the woman's age.

[9]RPE proficiency levels are determined from the Reported Proficiency Evaluation, the external proficiency standard used for calibration of SRTs during the field test of the SRT. These levels range from 0+ or very minimal proficiency in the language to 4+ or proficiency approaching that of a native speaker. Chapter 6 describes this technique in detail and offers support from the literature. Chapter 5 traces its development and application through the field study stage. Section 6.6 provides level descriptions helpful in evaluating test results.

cousins-twice-removed or shopkeepers or through the people sitting in the same tea shop as the test administrators, potential subjects are generally brought to the research team through some kind of personal contact.

(3) Singo di Garhi women: percent of population in age and education categories, number of Urdu SRTs given; Urdu RPE levels derived from USRT scores. (data from Rensch 1988 and Radloff 1991)

	Educational Levels					
Age	No formal education	1–5 years	6–10 years	11+ years	Total	Percent
13–19 yrs.	12	1	0	0	13	29.6
Percentage	27.3	2.3	0	0		
No. of SRTs	5					
(RPE levels)	(1+, 1, 0+, NA, NA)					
20–29 yrs.	15	0	0	0	15	34.1
Percentage	34.1	0	0	0		
No. of SRTs	5					
(RPE levels)	(1, 1, 0+, 0, NA)					
30–39 yrs.	6	0	0	0	6	13.6
Percentage	13.6	0	0	0		
No. of SRTs	0					
(RPE levels)						
40–49 yrs.	3	0	0	0	3	6.8
Percentage	6.8	0	0	0		
No. of SRTs	2					
(RPE levels)	(0+, 0+)					
50+ yrs.	7	0	0	0	7	15.9
Percentage	15.9	0	0	0		
No. of SRTs	1					
(RPE levels)	(NA)					
All ages	43	1	0	0	44	100.0
Percentage	97.7	2.3	0	0		
Total SRTs	13					

NA = Subject interviewed but not tested due to low Urdu proficiency

This social network process of obtaining subjects is good and works toward ensuring their full cooperation in the actual testing process. Although not random in the strict sense of the word, it also need not detract from the representativeness of the sample thus obtained.

2.3.2 Stratified judgment sampling.
Milroy argues for what she terms JUDGMENT SAMPLING in which, on the basis of specifiable and defensible principles, the judgment of the investigator is relied upon for sampling rather than on any principle of random selection.

> The principle underlying judgement sampling is that the researcher identifies in advance the TYPES of speakers to be studied and then seeks out a quota of speakers who fit the specified categories. A good judgement sample needs to be based on some kind of defensible theoretical framework; in other words, the researcher needs to be able to demonstrate that his or her judgement is rational and well-motivated. (Milroy 1987:26, emphasis hers)

The type of matrix resulting from a demographic profile, as illustrated in (1), is one example of the type of defensible principle upon which judgment samples can be selected. The potential subject is introduced through a social contact. The researcher then makes a judgment of how well that person fits the categories chosen. The person, for example, who is indeed a Hindko speaker from Singo di Garhi and is of the age and level of education needed can then be included in the sample and have the SRT administered to him.

Judgments are made at all levels, not just in the selection of an individual subject. An example is taken from the Hindko bilingualism survey, introduced above (Rensch 1988). The Hindko language is spoken over a wide geographical area, encompassing several districts. The research team for the Hindko bilingualism survey, on the basis of government census figures, judged that the highest concentration of Hindko speakers live in the Hazara district; thus, the bilingualism survey was focused there. The team traveled to different areas of the district and interviewed people in each one. On the basis of this preliminary investigation the further judgment was made to confine bilingualism testing to two representative villages. One village represented more isolated villages, without access to the facilities of modern-day Pakistan. The other village selected had good access to these facilities. A demographic profile was then prepared for these two villages and bilingualism testing with an SRT was carried out in each. Selection of subjects for administration of the SRT was then done on the basis of the demographic profile.

Milroy points out the relationship between goal and method, where the objectives of a research study to a very large extent dictate the methods of subject selection. For research among a population whose characteristics are definable by objectively specifiable dimensions, judgment sampling may be preferable to random sampling (1987:27–28). Shavelson echoes Milroy's cautions to use specifiable and defensible principles, in pointing out that when samples other than random samples are used, inferences from the sample should be made to the population of subjects like those observed in the study, taking care to point out the limitations of the generalizations made (1988:209). Woods, et al. add that it is the "inescapable duty" of researchers to describe carefully how their experimental material—including subjects—was actually obtained (1986:56).

2.4 Questionnaire

At the point, then, where a potential subject has been selected as part of the sample, a questionnaire should be administered. Items on this questionnaire should cover the basic demographics for this person, confirming that he or she is indeed the type of subject required for the study. Other questions may cover additional variables that might influence second-language learning. General information should be gathered on such things as the subject's village of residence, age, level of education, profession, language spoken in the home, name, clan, etc. Additional information, pertinent to the goals of the survey, should be gathered, such as places traveled to, including frequency of travel, the general purpose for such travel and the language(s) spoken while there, relatives who are speakers of the test language, patterns of exposure to the test language, patterns of use of the test language, preferences for language use and other questions which would approximate language attitudes, etc. (see Showalter 1991).

The subject's responses to these questions are analyzed together with his or her score on the SRT. If the sampling is representative of the basic categories chosen, then the influence of these other, potentially significant variables can be discerned. The graphs in (4) show the profiles of second-language proficiency in Urdu and Pashto for Torwali Kohistani speaking men (from Rensch 1987). The first graph compares the equivalent REPORTED PROFICIENCY EVALUATION (RPE) levels in Urdu for educated versus uneducated men. The second graph compares the RPE proficiency levels for the same groups of men for Pashto proficiency. (See §6.6 for descriptions of the RPE levels.)

The profound effect of education on learning Urdu, the national language of Pakistan, can be seen in the first graph in (4). The majority of uneducated men scored on the Urdu SRT at the equivalent RPE proficiency level of 0+, which indicates a very minimal proficiency in the language. Those uneducated men who have greater proficiency in Urdu have traveled more widely and/or worked in other areas of Pakistan where Urdu

(4) Comparison of RPE proficiency levels in Urdu and Pashto (from SRTs) for educated (E) and uneducated (N) Torwali-speaking men (data from Rensch 1987)

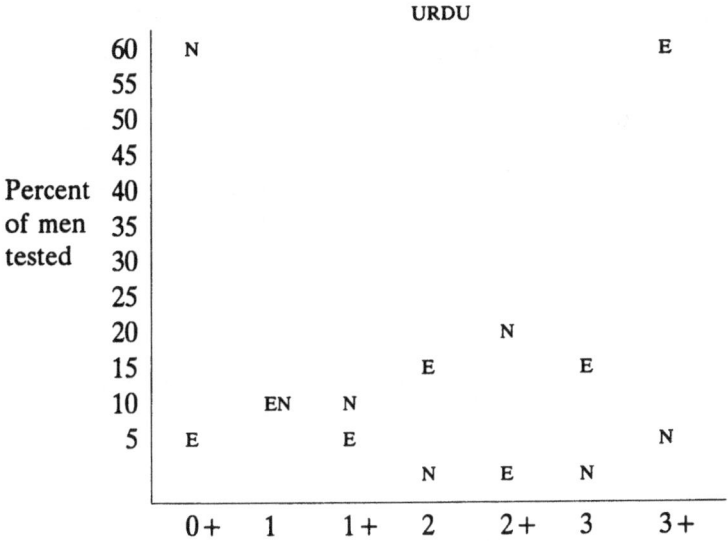

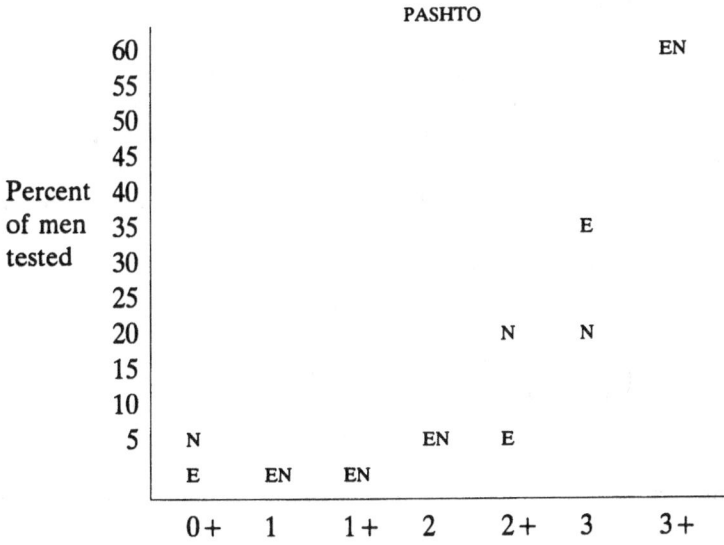

is the language of wider communication, according to their responses to the questionnaire given at the time of testing.

A sharp contrast is seen in the second graph in (4), listing RPE proficiency levels in the Pashto language for educated and uneducated men. The proficiency profiles of the two groups are almost parallel, illustrating that factors other than education are critical in the acquisition of Pashto. Pashto is the language of wider communication of the Swat valley and of the larger Northwest Frontier Province as well. Behrain village is located on the main road of the valley. On the questionnaire that was administered with the SRT, the Torwali-speaking men reported much contact with people from other areas and thus much exposure to Pashto.

2.5 Administering the SRT

The advantages of using an SRT as the test instrument in a bilingualism survey are best realized in actual field use. Administration time is short, approximately five minutes for a fifteen-sentence test, and the simplicity of its methodology allows all subjects, sophisticated or unsophisticated, to participate.

Once the subject has been selected through the sampling process and any accompanying questionnaire completed, the trained test administrator may begin the administration of the test.

2.5.1 Personnel required. For administration of an SRT in a bilingualism survey, the only personnel required are the subject and the trained test administrator. The greater the test administrator's fluency in the test language, the greater the ease with which the training for test administration and the actual scoring of tests can be accomplished. However, an administrator with only minimal fluency in the test language should still be able to obtain reliable and valid results if fully trained. It is possible, and has been done under field conditions, for the administrator to operate the tape player and mark the subject's responses on the scoresheet by him- or herself. If a technician is present to run the tape player, however, that will help in the efficiency of the testing process. The administrator and the technician should practice how they will divide responsibilities and who will set up which part of the equipment before actually beginning to test. The training for test administrators should be completed before initiating the data collection for the survey. See §3.5 for training procedures.

2.5.2 Equipment needed. The necessary equipment includes a tape player, two or three sets of headphones and one or two Y-adaptors. The

Use in Bilingualism Surveys

Y-adaptor allows two sets of headphones to be used with the one tape player. Both the subject and the test administrator need to hear the test stimuli. If a technician is present to help, a third set of headphones is needed. The second Y-adaptor is inserted into one arm of the first Y-adaptor, thus making three branches and so enabling three sets of headphones to be used with the one tape player. A schematic of such an arrangement of the equipment would be as follows:

(5)

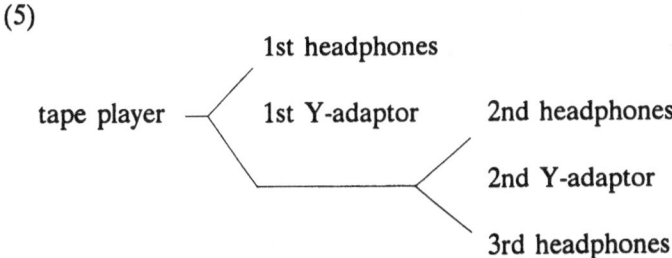

A good quality tape player should be used so that the transmission of the sound of the test sentences is clear and free from background noise. It is very helpful if the tape player has a pause button, since the tape needs to be stopped after every test sentence for the subject to reply. It is also helpful if the player has no built-in speaker. This precludes playing the tape any way but through the headphones, the recommended procedure.[10]

The headphones should also be of good quality so that the full spectrum of sound is transmitted to the subject. Small, lightweight headphones are the best, since they are easy to transport and are comfortable to wear. Also, they allow a certain amount of outside noise to still be heard, which is helpful if the subject is afraid that he or she will be cut off from the outside. The type of headphones that rests on the ear is preferable to the type that sticks into the ear, since many different people will be using them; it is more sanitary.

---

[10]The subject must repeat the test sentence verbatim for maximum points. The use of headphones allows the subject maximum concentration and the quality of the sound reproduction is also higher through headphones. The test administrator may sometimes be tempted to use a built-in speaker for test administration rather than taking time to set up the headphones arrangement. If the player has no speaker, this forces the administrator to follow the proper procedures. Also, occasions arise where a group of people gather around the subject. They might pressure the test administrator to play the test tape through the speaker, "so everyone can hear". This, of course, would place the subject at an unfair disadvantage, since he or she would not be able to hear the sentences optimally. So, using a tape player with no built-in speaker has definite advantages.

2.5.3 Location for testing. The best location for testing is, of course, one that is away from the noise of traffic or children or animals, etc. However, the exigencies of the field situation frequently preclude such luxury. This highlights the advantage of playing the test tape through headphones, which allows the subject to concentrate in the midst of potential distraction.

It is also best to have few people around to lessen distraction of the subject. On-lookers should be encouraged to wait quietly and should be requested to not speak to the subject during the administration of the test. For example, in using SRTs in various bilingualism surveys, it has occurred that upwards of eleven women with assorted children have been present during the test administration, waiting their turns at the headphones. However, because they were quiet throughout the testing, the subjects had no trouble concentrating on the test sentences. And, as has been mentioned in the introduction, since maximum scoring for an SRT requires verbatim repetition of entire sentences, on-lookers cannot 'learn' enough from hearing other subjects' responses to make any noticable difference in their scores, a distinct advantage in the SRT technique.

2.5.4 Standard procedures. The test administrator should explain the procedure to the subject, or have it explained if the administrator does not share a common language with the subject. The administrator (or the one describing the procedure) should refrain from calling it a "test" or saying that this will find out "how much you know" about the test language. Rather, the procedure should be introduced as an opportunity to help the researchers, for which they will be very grateful. The test tape should also contain a brief introduction in the subject's mother tongue, such as the following:

> This cassette contains some sentences that we would like you to repeat. Some of the sentences are easy, some are difficult. You will hear the sentences in [Pashto]. Please repeat them just as you hear them. Repeat them in [Pashto].

The test administrator should place the headphones on the subject, taking care that the earpieces are on the subject's ears. Alternately, the administrator could put on his or her own headphones first to demonstrate how it is done. The introduction tape should then be played. The volume should be preset to a comfortable listening level. Following the introduction and before playing the practice sentences for the test, the administrator should inquire of the subject if the volume is acceptable.

The test tape should then be started. Pause the tape after each stimulus so the subject can reply without being rushed by the next sentence. The tape may be rewound to replay the three practice sentences as many times as needed. It has been the experience of test administrators in bilingualism surveys using SRTs, however, that subjects quickly catch on to the methodology of repeating what they hear. The tape should not be rewound to replay the test sentences, or if it is necessary to rewind, the first repetition of the sentence should be scored.

The test administrator should not comment on the correctness of the subject's repetition. If he or she feels that some response is necessary, then a neutral comment should be given, such as, "You're doing fine." Likewise at the end of testing sessions, the subjects should be reassured that they did "just fine", and agree with them that some of the sentences were very long. Special care should be taken to not compare the performance of one subject with another. Rather, a subject could be complimented that he or she "understands a lot" of the test language.

2.5.5 Recording responses. Scoresheets should be made so that each subject's responses can be marked separately and easily scored. A simple design for a scoresheet is to write out all the sentences in the local script or phonetic notation (whichever is preferred by the test administrator), leaving some space between each line for noting the errors. Blanks may be included at the top of the form for noting pertinent information on each subject, such as name, age, mother tongue, test identification number, etc. This sheet can then be photocopied and a separate copy used for scoring each subject's responses. A simple mark can be made on or below the word where each error occurs. A sample scoresheet with the type of errors marked is included in this manual as appendix B.

The test administrator should take care to position the scoresheet in such a way that the subject cannot see what is written on it. It is also better if on-lookers are not allowed to read the sentences, especially if they will be taking the test later. The administrator should attempt to make a similar number of marks (of some sort) for sentences successfully repeated as for sentences with marks for errors made. In other words, an attempt should be made to mark errors on the scoresheet in an unobtrusive manner. This is especially true when the subject has made many errors in a sentence.

2.6 Scoring the test

A mark should be made on the scoresheet for every word where the subject has not repeated the test stimulus verbatim. The sum of these marks for a sentence is subtracted from the possible three points for that sentence. Three or more errors on a sentence result in zero points for that sentence.

2.6.1 Defining an error. An error is any deviation from the sentence as it is tape-recorded, even if the deviation retains the original meaning. Errors fall into the following main categories: omission, substitution, change of word order, significant distortion of pronunciation to garble a word, repetition (such as restarting), and addition. Deviations in pronunciation attributable to 'foreign accent' are not counted as errors.[11] Three points are possible for each sentence; each time an error of any type or magnitude occurs in a sentence, a point is subtracted.

This verbatim scoring convention, counting any deviation as an error, is widely used in educational testing and other applications of second-language proficiency assessment (see Oller 1979:265; Hendricks, et al. 1980; Prutting, et al. 1975).[12] Such a strict standard is also needed for an SRT since one is never sure why the error occurred. For example, one particularly difficult form may have challenged the person to the extent that he/she forgot the rest of the sentence and so repeated the difficult part verbatim, but erred on the remaining easy forms. Additionally, field study test administrators noted that, for example, errors of substitution (including synonyms) occurred as the person was being stretched to the limit of his/her ability to repeat a sentence. In other words, the substitution was a signal that the

---

[11]'Foreign accent' intrusions into pronunciation of test words are acceptable up to the point where a word is garbled. Indeed, the Foreign Serivce Institute proficiency levels allow an "obviously foreign" accent through level three and note its presence even in level four proficiency (reproduced in Hendricks et al. 1980). Support for this standard also comes from other sources: "Purely phonological substitutions or deletions [in school-age children's repetition of sentences] were cited with great frequency and consistency by [trained] evaluators, but the relative importance of such features in overall language development was disputed" (Natalicio and Williams 1971:62). In discussing standards for scoring dictation tests, which he considers the written type of repetition tests, Oller suggests that spelling errors "which do not indicate difficulties in perception of distinct sounds of the language or which do not affect the lexical identity of a word should not be counted ... spelling errors are probably not at all correlated with other types of errors in dictations or with language proficiency" (1979:299). Extrapolating from dictation, then, to oral repetition, Oller's statements could be extended to provide additional rationale for not counting pronunciation errors unless they reflect total nonunderstanding by garbling the word.

[12]"Two scoring procedures are suggested for elicited imitation: a word-by-word (verbatim) scoring is suggested to determine which language or language variety a child (or group) prefers to speak (and simultaneously how well they can produce it); and a more lenient content scoring is recommended to determine how well a child (or group) comprehends a text in a given language (or language variety)" (Oller 1979:300).

sentence was almost too difficult; perhaps in a simpler sentence he/she could have repeated the test word correctly.

The following chart summarizes the scoring system and suggests ways to mark the different types of errors for descriptive marking (see also appendix B for a sample application of these scoring conventions). In an actual test situation where responses are not tape-recorded, there is not sufficient time to mark the specific type of error committed. Merely placing a simple mark on the word upon which an error occurred would be sufficient to score the test.

(6) Scoring key for an SRT

Scoring range
- 3 points   perfect, no errors in sentence
- 2 points   one error in sentence
- 1 point   two errors in sentence
- 0 points   three or more errors in sentence

Types of errors
- o   word omitted from sentence
- s   word substituted for another
- \> or <   any change of word order (counts as one error)
- ~ ~   word garbled so as to lose meaning
- +   word or phrase added to sentence
- R   word or phrase repeated (counts as one error)
- w   wrong word or word ending (grammatical error)

There should be no more than one error marked for each word. For example, if a subject substitutes one verb for another and changes the tense while doing so, still only one error is counted on that word. Errors of repetition occur when the subject begins the sentence, stops, then begins the sentence again. This counts as one error, no matter how many words were repeated a second time. The rest of the sentence is scored according to the accuracy of the second attempt. For example, if the subject makes an error, backs up and corrects that error and then completes the sentence correctly, only one point (for the restarting) is subtracted.

A change of word order counts as one error even if several words are affected. Of course, all the original words must be retained in such a case. If a word is omitted or added, then an additional point is subtracted. Errors of substitutions are generally counted along the lines of the part of speech. For example, for the stimulus sentence "The teacher repeated the sentence to the students," the subject replies, "The teacher is saying sentence to the students." This would generally be counted as three errors and zero points would be awarded for this sentence. "Saying" would be considered as substituted for "repeated," and "is" is an addition and "the" an omission.

The most important principle to follow in scoring SRTs is that there be agreement among the test administrators concerning what constitutes an error. In the training of administrators, which prestages any actual use of an SRT in a bilingualism survey (see §3.5), the scoring of practice tests should acquaint the trainees with different types of potential errors. The scoring of different error types should be agreed upon for each survey.

2.6.2 Encountering variant dialects. It is important to mention that sometimes, in a given area, a dialect variation of the test language is spoken which does not significantly impede communication with the standard dialect of the language under investigation. The effect of such dialect variation can show up through consistent patterns of error on the SRT responses across participants in that dialect area. Minor phonological dialect differences, such as *wakat* for *waqt* (Urdu for 'time') are rather common and according to standard scoring procedures are not counted as errors (see §2.6.1). Occasionally, though, there are lexical changes that a mother-tongue speaker of the standard dialect of the test language can identify as words used in the non-standard dialect commonly spoken in the test area. Upon entering a new general area for testing, where the test language dialect might differ, the research team may decide to obtain permission from the first ten or so subjects to tape-record their test responses. Such lexical dialect differences could then be listened for by comparing these tape-recorded tests. For example, only one such possible consistent lexical dialect difference was encountered in the field study of the SRT—*wesa* for *yosa* (Yusufzai Pashto for 'take away'). In the scoring procedure, such consistent, identified dialect differences were specially marked. For the particular purposes of the bilingualism survey of that language area, it was decided not to count that difference as an error. A different survey with different purposes might decide otherwise.

2.7 Interpreting SRT scores

2.7.1 Calculating the test score. Calculating the score for a given subject on an SRT should be done apart from the testing situation. It is not within the purposes of most bilingualism surveys to inform individuals of their test scores, since the goal is a profile of community-wide second-language proficiency. If the procedure has been introduced to the subject as an opportunity for him or her to help the researchers, then when the SRT is finished the administrator can thank the subject for his/her help and procede to the next subject.

The calculation of a subject's SRT score, then, is accomplished by adding the number of points correct on each of the fifteen test sentences. With three points possible for each sentence, the maximum score on an SRT is forty-five points.

2.7.2 Determining the equivalent proficiency level. The process of developing an SRT is described in a step-by-step fashion in chapter 3. The end result of this development process is the chart of the ranges of scores, exemplified by those presented in (7). The history of development for both these SRTs and also that for the revision of the Pashto SRT is presented in chapter 5.

(7) Score ranges on the Urdu and original Pashto SRTs corresponding to RPE levels.

Urdu		Original Pashto	
SRT score	= RPE level	SRT score	= RPE level
37 & up	= 3+ & up	37 & up	= 3+ & up
31–36	= 3	33–36	= 3
25–30	= 2+	28–32	= 2+
19–24	= 2	23–27	= 2
13–18	= 1+	18–22	= 1+
9–12	= 1	14–17	= 1
2–8	= 0+	10–13	= 0+

The point score on an SRT for a given subject is compared to the results of the calibration of that SRT in order to determine the equivalent proficiency level for that score. The calibration process was completed with the development of the SRT, prior to its use in the field project. This calibration or validation process is described in chapter 3 and results in statistically derived ranges of scores equivalent to the specific proficiency levels of the external proficiency standard used. Once an SRT is developed in a given language, it can be used in any location for providing a general assessment of second-language proficiency suitable for obtaining the community-wide profile necessary in bilingualism surveys. The SRT score obtained for each subject is compared to the ranges of scores corresponding to the different proficiency levels. The range of scores that each subject's score falls within gives the level equivalent for his or her performance. Then the percentage of subjects at each proficiency level is calculated.

In the field test of SRT, the RPE was used as the calibrating standard (see chapters 5 and 6). Thus, the ranges of scores for the SRTs developed are equated to what are called RPE LEVELS OF PROFICIENCY. The lists in (7) show the ranges of scores for both the Urdu SRT and the original Pashto SRT which correspond to the different RPE proficiency levels. It should be noted that for different SRTs, different score ranges will correspond to the same RPE proficiency level. In the same way, the same numerical score on tests in two different languages will often correspond to different RPE proficiency levels. For example, a total score of twenty-six on the original Pashto SRT is equivalent to RPE proficiency level 2, whereas a score of twenty-six on the Urdu SRT is equivalent to RPE level 2+. Conversely, a score on the Urdu SRT of fouteen and a score on the original Pashto SRT of twenty-one both are equivalent to the same RPE proficiency level, 1+, in those respective languages. Although different in number, both scores refer to the level of proficiency where the person has a limited, basic ability to function in the language in question. This is because the ranges are statistically derived from the data which is collected separately for the calibration of each SRT. The actual test scores may be the same or different between two SRTs; that does not make the crucial difference. The crucial difference is that those scores have been statistically calibrated with the external proficiency standard. The reader is referred to chapter 3 for the methodology of test development and calibration, and to §6.6, for a description of the RPE levels.

The following three graphs, (8) through (10), illustrate the profiles obtained for three communities through second-language proficiency testing. Each community represents a different vernacular language group. Proficiency testing in the standard dialects of both Urdu (the national language) and Pashto (the language of wider communication) was accomplished in each community through the use of the Urdu and original Pashto SRTs. Only the scores for educated men are utilized for these particular graphs since their purpose is to illustrate the influence of factors other than education which are critical to second-language acquisition in these communities. These figures nicely illustrate some of the advantages of using SRTs in bilingualism surveys. Since the SRTs in both languages were calibrated against the same standard, the RPE (see chapter 6), results describing second-language proficiency can be compared across languages. Since an SRT can be immediately used at a test site, without further modifications, the same test can be given no matter what the vernacular background of the subject or community happens to be.

Use in Bilingualism Surveys

There is a great emphasis on education in Sherpur, a Hindko-speaking village with good access to all the facilities of modern-day Pakistan. Indeed, in the test sample, all but one of these educated men had five or more years of schooling. It is interesting, though, to compare their performances on the Urdu and original Pashto SRTs, as can be seen in figure (8). Urdu, the national language, is the medium of instruction in the government schools for all subjects; thus it is understandable that level of education and proficiency in Urdu go hand-in-hand. On the other hand, proficiency in Pashto is obtained in informal, social situations, as the Hindko-speaking people of Sherpur have contact with their Pashto-speaking neighbors. In Sherpur, the Hindko speakers are the landowners, thus having a higher social status than the Pashto speakers. These educated men have developed a rather high proficiency in Urdu, but, for the main part, only a basic conversational ability in Pashto. One can see how the second-language proficiency profile reflects sociolinguistic realities in this community.

Different sociolinguistic situations are reflected in the two other figures. Second-language proficiency profiles for Urdu and Pashto show a much more similar profile for educated Gujari speakers in Peshmal (9) and

(8) Comparison of RPE proficiency levels in Pashto (P) and Urdu (U) for educated Hindko-speaking men of Sherpur (from SRT scores) (data from Rensch 1988)

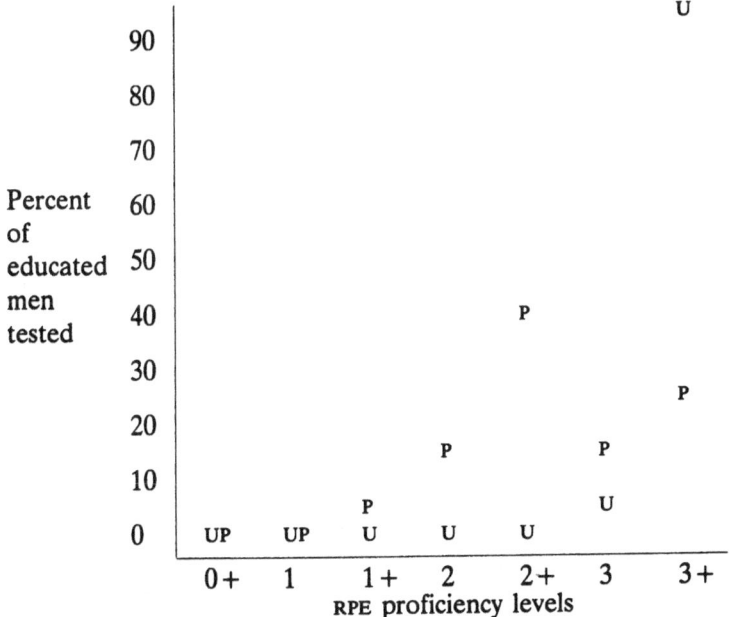

educated Torwali speakers in the Behrain area (10). In both areas, Pashto is the language of wider communication and is even taught as a subject in the primary grades in some schools. The prestige of Pashto is enhanced by its utilitarian value—proficiency in Pashto opens the door to many job opportunities. Yet, for educated people, the prestige and utilitarian value of Urdu, the national language, remains high.

In both of these studies the education level of participants covered a much wider range than in the Sherpur Hindko study. In both of these studies most of the test participants displayed a language proficiency greater than just basic conversation in both Urdu and Pashto. And in both these studies, the educated participants' proficiencies in Urdu and Pashto more closely paralleled each other than was the case in the Sherpur Hindko study.

The comparison of these three studies highlights some of the advantages of the SRT. The fact that it is quick to administer allows the researcher to include more people in the study, thus developing a more representative profile. The fact that an SRT needs no further modification after it is calibrated allows the trained administrator to give the test in any community

(9) Comparison of RPE proficiency levels in Pashto (P) and Urdu (U) for educated Gujari-speaking men of Peshmal (from SRT scores) (data from Hallberg and O'Leary 1991)

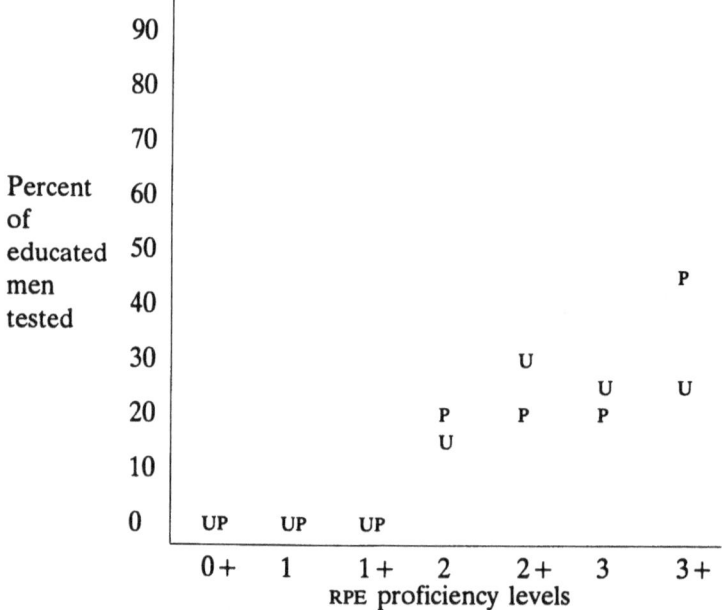

(10) Comparison of RPE proficiency levels in Pashto (P) and Urdu (U) for educated Torwali-speaking men of Behrain (from SRT scores) (data from Rensch 1987)

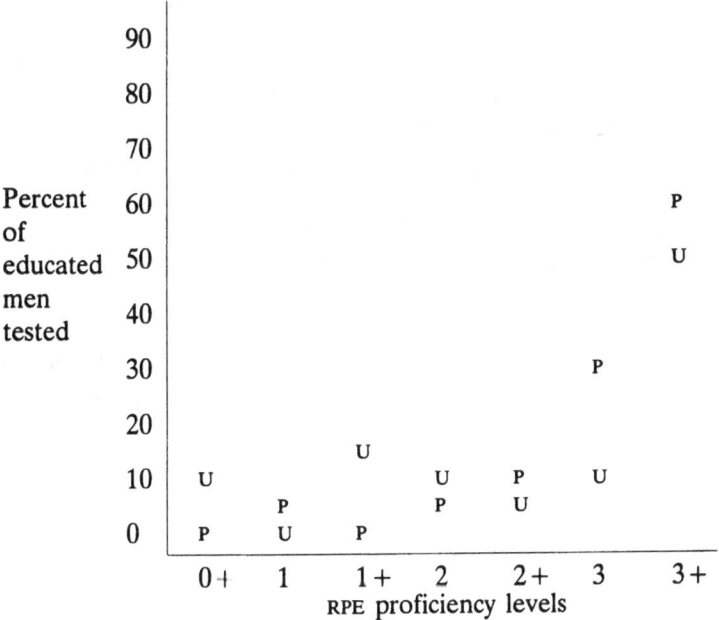

where proficiency in the test language is a question, regardless of the mother tongue of the population. Furthermore, the fact that SRTs are calibrated with a single descriptive instrument, in this case, the reported proficiency evaluation, allows the results of a test in one language to be directly compared with the results in another language or with those of another community.

2.7.3 Extrapolating sample results. There are many different ways that the results from testing the sample of subjects can be extrapolated to predict or approximate the profile of proficiencies in the community. The specific method used, whether statistical or nonstatistical, depends on the goals of the survey, the variables deemed critical in the sample selection, and other such survey-specific qualifications. Hatch and Farhady (1982:39), as an example resource, present the principles of inferential statistics which allow the researcher to expand the findings of the sample to make predictions about the population as a whole. Those statistics, which are based on theories of probability, tell the researcher how confident he or she can feel in generalizing the findings from sample subjects back to the total population the sample represents. The important aspect to consider in any extrapolation is that it is only as representative of the population as the sample is. In other words, the care taken in obtaining as representative a sample as possible is directly proportional to the confidence the researcher can ultimately have in the extrapolations from the sample data to the population.

An example of a simple extension of testing results to the population, using percentages, can be seen with data from the Hindko language survey (reported by Rensch 1988). The demographic profile of Singo di Garhi, a Hindko language speaking village, was judged to be complete (see (1)). Therefore, making predictions from the sample to that population can be done with relative confidence. Charts (11)–(13) illustrate one way that the data obtained regarding Urdu proficiency could be extended to the whole village.

Chart (11) shows the percentage of educated and uneducated males of school-age and above in Singo di Garhi, calculated from the demographic profile (1). It also shows the percentage of both groups which scored at the highest level on the Urdu SRT, that is, RPE proficiency level 3+ and above. These percentages were calculated by figuring the percentage of test subjects in each group who scored at the highest level on the Urdu

(11) School-age and older male population of Singo di Garhi, percent of population and percent projected at RPE 3+ and above in Urdu (data from Rensch 1988)

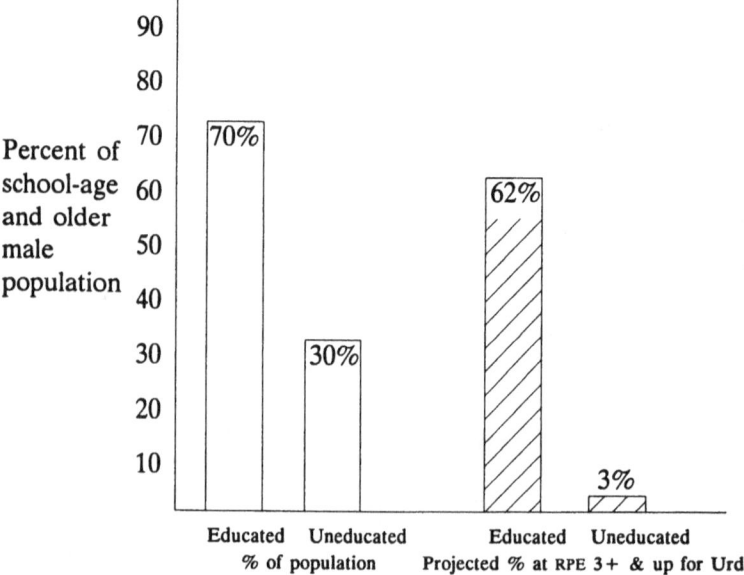

Use in Bilingualism Surveys 35

SRT and then extrapolating it to the whole school-age and above male population of Singo di Garhi. The educated and uneducated groups were taken as a whole because education had been found to be the key factor in determining level of proficiency in Urdu, the national language.

Chart (12) does the same for the school-age and above female population of Singo di Garhi. Probably because no women have been educated in that village (nowdays a few girls have started attending school), there were none who scored at the highest level on the Urdu SRT. In fact, none of them scored as high as RPE level 2. This results in zero percent of the women for the village projected to be RPE level 3+ and above in Urdu.

Chart (13) combines charts (11) and (12) to give a projected total for the whole village with RPE proficiency level 3+ and above in Urdu. As can be seen, the relative percentages are quite different from those of (11), where only the proficiency of the men was considered. A total of thirty-eight percent of the population of Singo di Garhi is projected to have RPE proficiency level 3+ and above in Urdu if the projected percentages of educated and uneducated people are combined. This is significantly less than half of the population of that village. If the primary channel for

(12) School-age and older female population of Singo di Garhi, percent of population and percent projected at RPE 3+ and above in Urdu (data from Rensch 1988)

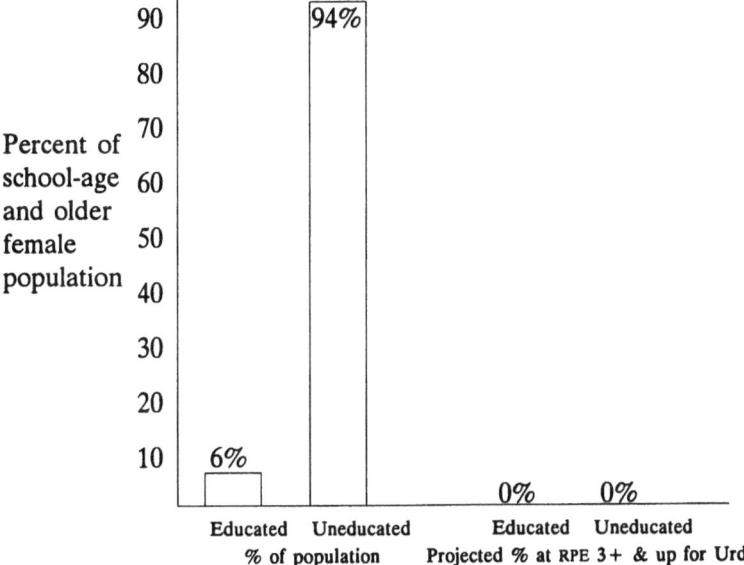

developing proficiency in the national language, Urdu, is through education, then increasing trends in that village of educating both boys and girls should make a difference in a similar projected proficiency profile in a future survey.

These charts have been offered as an example of how test sample results can be projected onto the population from which that sample was drawn. As was mentioned above, there are many different ways that extrapolations can be made, both statistical and non-statistical. The extrapolations made should obviously be fitted to the characteristics of the population sampled and the results obtained.

In this chapter the actual use of an SRT in a bilingualism survey has been presented. The next chapter outlines the procedure the research team would go through to develop an SRT, the procedure which actually precedes using it in the field.

(13) Male and female total school-age and older population of Singo di Garhi percent of population and percent projected at RPE 3+ and above in Urdu (data from Rensch 1988)

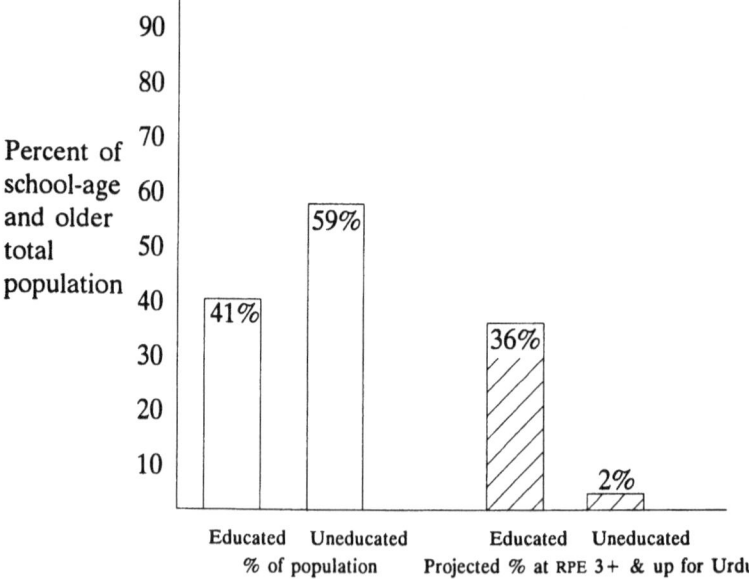

3
Test Development Methodology

3.0 Introduction

The methodology for constructing, calibrating, and administering a sentence repetition test (SRT) is outlined in six major steps. The first step is to elicit a sample of sentences in the target (or test) language and select some forty to fifty sentences from that sample to be tape recorded (and transcribed) as the PRELIMINARY FORM of the SRT. Step two consists of evaluating approximately fifty second-language speakers of the test language on an external proficiency standard. In step three, those people are given the preliminary form of the SRT and adjustments are made in the content of the SRT (where necessary and possible) to extend its range of difficulty. By applying a series of statistical formulas and processes, described in step four, the preliminary form of the SRT is shortened to the FINAL FORM and is calibrated against the external proficiency standard. (See chapter 6 for a detailed explanation of one standard, the reported proficiency evaluation.) The calibration equates raw score performances on the SRT with equivalent proficiency levels of the external standard. (Once an SRT is calibrated, there is no need to keep administering the external proficiency standard for that purpose.) Step five suggests ways to train SRT administrators and step six offers recommendations for SRT use in the field. Figure (14) shows the relationship of these steps.

It is well worth the effort to make sure that these steps are carried out with the highest degree of care possible. The results obtained from the actual use of the SRT in the field may be used to help draw conclusions and/or make recommendations that affect entire populations. The confidence with which those results can be interpreted depends upon the confidence which can be placed in each separate aspect of the test as it is developed. For example, it is worth taking extra care to locate the right educated mother-tongue speakers of the language to assist in the development of the test. It is also worth taking the extra time to have the recommended number of people rated before moving to the next step. Finally, it is worth the extra time and effort to obtain a fully elaborated transcription of the sentences (see example in appendix C). For most of the steps, taking the extra time at the beginning will not only insure higher quality results, but will also save time later.

(14) Relationship of the six steps of SRT development

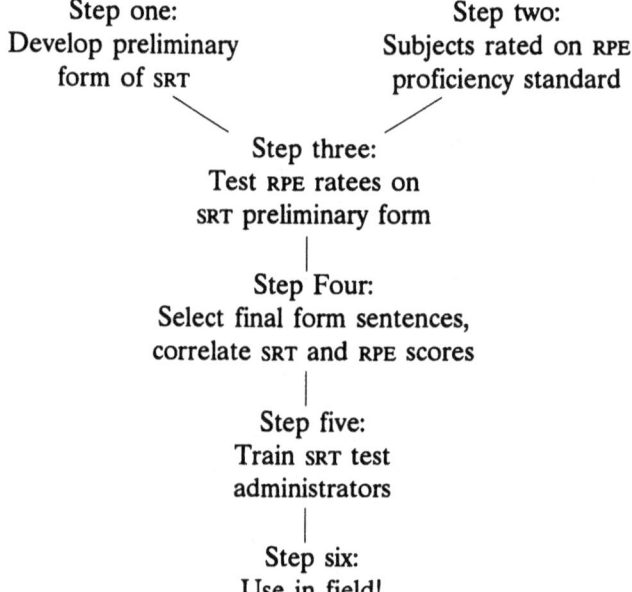

The recommended steps for SRT construction have been developed through the pilot study of the SRT and the field study reported in this manual. They are based primarily on the development of the revised Pashto SRT, the most finely-tuned and discriminative test developed in the field study (see chapter 5). However, every step (and almost every substep) is the result of lessons learned through the entire process of development. Rationale for some substeps is given in the text, that for others is apparent through the history of the development of SRT as described in chapter 5. Research teams intending to develop an SRT in a language for use in

Test Development Methodology

second-language proficiency testing in a sociolinguistic survey are encouraged to follow closely the steps as outlined.[13]

3.0.1 Location. The entire process of developing and calibrating an SRT is much easier if it is done in an area where the language in question is the common language of wider communication. It should also be an area where the test development personnel have good personal contacts or where good contacts can easily be developed. This will especially facilitate finding the right people for calibrating the test, both mother-tongue speakers of the language of wider communication and a pool of second-language speakers of the language of wider communication. Effort expended to carry out the test development and calibration in such an area will be well worth while in terms of the ultimate efficiency of the development process and the quality of the test developed.

3.0.2 Personnel. The main categories of personnel involved in the test development include the researcher, educated mother-tongue speakers, a pool of second-language speakers, and the test administrator.

The researcher. The methodology for test development has been designed so that a researcher with only minimal proficiency in the test language will be able to oversee and be involved in the development process. Naturally, the greater his or her knowledge of the language, the easier the whole process will be. It is also possible to learn things from published grammatical sketches and phonological descriptions that will be of great assistance, especially in establishing the standards for scoring.

If there are two researchers, the work can be divided. For example, one researcher can work on step one, eliciting and selecting sentences, while the other begins having second-language speakers rated on the external proficiency standard, as in step two. If there are more researchers on the team, the work can be appropriately divided. Reference will be variably made to the 'researcher' or 'research team' in this chapter.

Educated mother-tongue speakers. The minimum number of educated mother-tongue speakers required for test development is three: one (or

---

[13]If the reason for a certain step is not clear, researchers are urged to follow it anyway and to write to the South Asia Sociolinguistic Survey team. The rationale for the procedure will gladly be provided. If it proves necessary for the research team to deviate from these recommendations, it will be important and helpful to make careful note of all such deviations, their rationale, and the results obtained, and to share these observations with the South Asia team. Any other comments or suggestions will also be appreciated.

more) for sentence elicitation, two (or more) for initial sentence selection. The educated mother-tongue speaker chosen to record the sentences may be one of these people or someone else. Educated mother-tongue speakers will also help to set scoring standards based on the results of the first ten people tested.

The term 'educated' is specified in order to set a standard of difficulty for sentence content and to help ensure the use of a prestige form of the language. The end result of being able to discriminate the widest range of second-language abilities possible through the SRT depends on setting this initial standard high enough to challenge speakers at higher levels of proficiency. It is assumed also that an educated person will be more aware of his or her language. The definition of educated will, of course, vary with the culture. In areas where formal schooling is common, the ideal helper would be a college graduate. If, for some reason, that much education is not available, a person with matriculation or a high school equivalent, who is recognized as having much experience in language-related matters may be just as helpful. For a language with no educated standard, a person who is recognized as a fluent or persuasive speaker or a good story teller or who is 'language aware', etc., would be just as qualified. For the purposes of explanation, this latter category of helper will also be labeled educated mother-tongue speaker. The important point is to be able to set the standard of difficulty necessary to adequately represent the higher levels of proficiency in the test language, a goal which is most likely to be attained by an educated speaker of the language.

It is essential that the educated mother-tongue speakers share a common language with the researcher. This will make adequate communication of what is required at each step possible and will facilitate a good translation of the sentences.

A pool of second-language speakers. The second-language speakers of the test language need to be of varying proficiency levels from very high to very low. They do not have to be from any particular language group; they can have any combination of languages as their mother tongues. For step two, the calibration of the SRT with the external standard, several persons at each level of proficiency should be rated. For the final selection of sentences for the final form of the test, it will be necessary for approximately fifty people, representing the full range of performance be given the preliminary form of the test.

Possible sources for this pool of people could include a neighborhood, employees of a local college or business, a social or religious organization or group, friends of friends, relatives of friends, etc. For example, for the calibration of the Urdu SRT, the subjects were either students or employees of a local university.

Test administrator(s). The test administrator can be anyone who has completed the training as outlined in step five (§3.5) and who demonstrates satisfactory consistency in scoring as compared with other administrators. Administrators do not have to be mother-tongue speakers of the language in question; indeed, the methodology is so designed that an administrator with minimal proficiency in the test language can be trained to score SRTs reliably. The greater the fluency in the test language, though, the greater the ease with which the training process and test scoring can be accomplished. Administrators should share a common language with the researcher. If circumstances dictate, however, that there is no common language, much care must be taken to ensure good understanding of all aspects of training, administration, scoring, and reporting of results.

3.0.3 Standard equipment. The equipment needed for the testing process are tape recorders and microphone, as well as headphones and Y-adaptors.

Tape recorders and microphone. Two tape recorders, or one tape recorder and one tape player are necessary. The tape recorder will be used for preparing the test tapes. For the preparation of training tapes for the test administrators (see step five), the tape player can be used for playing the test stimuli whereas the tape recorder can be used for recording the subject's responses. A good quality microphone, preferably the clip-on style, is necessary for recording the test sentences. Such features as noise-reduction and tape counter are very helpful on both tape recorder and player. Also, for dubbing purposes, a pause button on both tape machines and an attenuating patch cord are needed.

Headphones and Y-adaptors. Three sets of headphones will be needed. Small, lightweight headphones are preferred for portability. They are also less threatening to participants unfamiliar with sound equipment.[14] In the test situation, one set will be worn by the subject, one by the test administrator, and one by the researcher or technician, if present, who is

---

[14]As mentioned in chapter 2, the use of headphones is required to ensure that the subject is able to concentrate and to hear the test sentences clearly. In this respect, the use of a 'play only' tape player is also helpful, because this type of player does not usually have an external speaker, thus forcing the use of headphones. It may be that the test administrator will have to free one ear from the headphones so that he can accurately hear the subject's response.

running the tape recorder. Two Y-adaptors are also required to enable all three people to listen to the test stimuli at the same time. It is essential that the adaptors and headphones are compatible with the tape recorder/player, whether stereo or monaural. The set up for the headphones and adaptors is described in §2.5.2.

3.1 STEP ONE: Sentence elicitation and selection—preliminary form

The goal of step one is to obtain a tape recorded sample of forty to fifty sentences which are well-formed and natural and represent a wide range of difficulty, from simple to very difficult.

3.1.1 Obtaining the sentences. It is necessary to work closely with one (or two) educated mother-tongue speaker(s) for gathering the sample. The researchers must obtain fifty to sixty sentences either from that educated mother-tongue speaker or in collaboration with him or her. Some sources that have proven useful include:

- tape recording a text of the educated mother-tongue speaker's response to a given topic
- selecting sentences from a newspaper or advanced textbook in the language under investigation (be sure sentences are natural)
- requesting the educated mother-tongue speaker to create a sentence emphasizing a certain feature of grammar, etc.

Some topics for elicited texts which have proven useful in obtaining sentences with a wide range of complexity include:

- a description of the working of the government (or of a local government worker)
- a defense of personal beliefs against criticism (using timely cultural or country-related topics)
- a similar request made of three or more people of differing status to obtain varying degrees of politeness, formality, etc.

It is necessary to elicit some very difficult sentences which use complex grammar (e.g., embedding, dependent clauses, etc.) and/or advanced vocabulary. Also needed are some sentences of medium difficulty and some easy ones. Simple, short sentences (five to nine words) are useful, too, as practice sentences. Questions are not used in an SRT; they might confuse the respondent. Sentences beginning with connectors or other

Test Development Methodology

discourse markers are acceptable.[15] It is advisable to have a wide variety of content in the sentences, for example, not too many descriptive as opposed to action sentences. Also, a variety in content prevents people from guessing words based on the context of other sentences.

The researchers should have the educated mother-tongue speaker write in the local script all the sentences obtained, whether originally from a tape recorded text or from a book. This will be used in step one, §3.1.3 for the tape recording of the preliminary form of the SRT. Ask the educated mother-tongue speaker to leave space between each sentence so that later the sentences can be cut apart and their order rearranged for tape recording.

The research team should make an initial phonetic transcription of the sentences at this time to make the later sections of the test construction easier.

The educated mother-tongue speaker should then tape-record (with natural speed and intonation) all sentences selected, whether from written sources or from oral texts, so that in the next substep the educated mother-tongue speakers can try to repeat them. Each sentence should be presented individually on the tape, separated by a three-second pause.

3.1.2 Eliminating unsuitable or excessively long sentences. The research team needs to work with two other educated mother-tongue speakers at this stage since it is necessary to have more than one opinion about the sentences obtained; also it is often difficult for a person to be able to critically examine his or her own work. It may be helpful to work with one educated mother-tongue speaker at a time.

The researchers must then examine the sentences that the first educated mother-tongue speaker has written down and ask the opinion of the second two educated mother-tongue speakers of the sentences: Are these things people would say? Are they too controversial? Too political? Do they 'sound funny'? Are these good examples of the language? Are they too similar to some other sentences? Careful note of their comments on each sentence should be made and sentences eliminated that they believe are inappropriate. It is important to check with people not originally

---

[15]Indeed, sentences beginning with connectors or other discourse markers are useful for separating people with greater proficiency from those with lesser. It has been noted that people with greater proficiency in the language will repeat such words without difficulty, whereas people with lesser proficiency often omit them.

involved in the elicitation of the sentences so that there can be an unbiased opinion on the sensitivity or potential offense of a sentence.[16]

After checking the general appropriateness of the sentences, the team should play the tape recording of the selected sentences as recorded by the first educated mother-tongue speaker for these two educated mother-tongue speakers to repeat. This should be done with one person at a time. Stop the tape recorder after each sentence and have the educated mother-tongue speaker repeat the sentence. Make careful notes on their responses using the phonetic transcription of the sentences (§3.1.1) as a guide. Discard any sentences that are clearly too long for them to be able to repeat, but keep those sentences that they both can ALMOST repeat or that one can repeat and the other almost repeat. (Such sentences may be good for discriminating the upper levels of proficiency.) If desired, this tape could be played for several other educated mother-tongue speakers, which would provide just that much more input into the suitability and length of the sentences.

Following this, the team should examine the sentences that remain. There should be forty to fifty sentences that reflect a wide range of difficulty, and a greater number of more difficult sentences than easy ones. If there are too few sentences or not enough in a certain range of difficulty, the researchers must elicit more sentences (or select some from an advanced textbook) to fill in what is lacking. These, too, should be tape-recorded and presented to the educated mother-tongue speakers so that they can repeat them to check the length. (Note that in all stages of SRT preparation and administration, listening through headphones increases concentration and improves the test environment.)

3.1.3 Tape-recording the preliminary form of the test. The following sequence should be followed in recording the preliminary form of the test.

Order the sentences from shortest to longest. The research team should cut apart the written sentences (§3.1.1), discarding the eliminated sentences. The forty to fifty sentences that have been chosen (§3.1.2) should be placed in order from shortest to longest. If two sentences are the same length, put the simpler one first. If there is uncertainty about where word

---

[16]For example, idiomatic expressions, double entendre or marginally taboo topics may cause sentences to be embarrassing or ridiculous to subjects. Male and female reactions may be different, so it could be helpful to have the opinion of both. It also occurs that in some cultures women are less concerned about 'saving face' and will, therefore, give a more honest opinion of the appropriateness of a sentence. For that reason it may be helpful to have at least one female educated mother-tongue speaker.

breaks should occur, order the sentences by number of syllables. This step may go faster if done with one of the educated mother-tongue speakers. The three shortest sentences can be considered as PRACTICE SENTENCES, that is, in the actual testing process they can be played more than once and they will not be scored, per se. Otherwise, include three other short sentences at the beginning to function as practice sentences.

Record the sentences. Once these forty to fifty sentences are selected and put in order, it is necessary to select an educated mother-tongue speaker to tape-record them for the preliminary form of the test. Be sure this person is a mother-tongue speaker of the standard dialect chosen for the test and uses the standard pronunciation or 'accent' for that dialect. (In many cultures a man's voice will be more widely acceptable for an SRT than a woman's.) The tape recording should be done in a quiet place using the highest quality recording equipment available. Special care should be taken that there are no background interfering noises and that no hiss or static is introduced by the equipment. The educated mother-tongue speaker should read the written sentences one by one in the order determined in the previous substep. He should first read each sentence, then practice it out loud once, then record it. A three-second silence should be left between each sentence (long enough to be able to stop the tape player and restart it without cutting off any sound). Record each sentence only once. The person doing the recording should not speak too slowly or too quickly; rather, a normal, conversational speed should be used.[17] He should use normal intonation for the types of sentence used and be careful not to pause during the sentence. If the sentences sound 'wooden' or the person sounds like he is reading a list, start the recording process again. It is good to have the quality of the recording checked with one or more other educated mother-tongue speakers.

A copy of this test tape should be dubbed, using the highest possible quality sound equipment. The original will be the tape to use for testing this preliminary form of the test (the forty to fifty sentences); the other will be a backup.

3.1.4 Making an elaborated transcription. When making an elaborated transcription, the sentences should be translated word-for-word and transcribed phonetically in three- or four-line format.

---

[17]"For advanced [language] students, there is the gap between understanding rapid but clearly enunciated speech . . . and rapid telescoped speech" (Valette 1977:114).

Transcribe the sentences phonetically and check them. To make an elaborated transcription of the preliminary form of the test, the team must make a phonetic transcription of the forty to fifty sentences just recorded (or revise and reorder the previous phonetic transcription, §3.1.1). Check each sentence word by word with an educated mother-tongue speaker to make sure no critical sound distinctions were missed.

Translate word-for-word; note key points. The educated mother-tongue speaker needs to give both a word-for-word translation and also a free translation of each sentence. This will be of great help in setting the scoring standards for the test sentences.

As much as is possible at this stage, try to find out which tense markers, person inflections, etc., depend on a single sound change or some other such minimal difference that will require special attention in scoring the test; make note of these. A grammatical write-up of the language will help identify such points. More key points will emerge as the first subjects take the test and begin making errors (see §3.3.4).

Transcribe the sentences. For the final form of the elaborated transcription, each sentence is written in a three- or four-line format. This elaborated transcription will be used in §3.3.4 for setting the scoring standards for the tests and in step five for training administrators. The optional first line, the sentence written in local script, would probably be of greatest benefit to the test administrators who are not familiar with phonetic notation. A sample elaborated transcription is given in appendix C. The format for this transcription is as follows:

(15)   Line 1—the sentence written in local script (optional)
       Line 2—a phonetic transcription of that sentence
       Line 3—a word-for-word translation of that sentence
       Line 4—a free translation of that sentence

3.2 STEP TWO: Rating subjects

The goal of this step is to assess the level of proficiency of approximately fifty second-language speakers of the test language who will represent the full range of proficiency levels.

3.2.1. Selecting the standard. At this point it is necessary to have second-language speakers rated on an external proficiency standard. These same speakers will also be tested on the preliminary form of the SRT in step three. Results from that testing on these subjects will be used in step four to determine the range of SRT scores which corresponds to each level on the standard.

The field study of the SRT has used the RPE as the external proficiency standard, and this step is explained with that as the standard. The RPE method is described in detail in chapter 6 along with instructions on how it can be used during this step. With the RPE, mother-tongue speakers of the test language evaluate second-language speakers whom they know personally according to a set of standard criteria. The letters assigned by this evaluation process are converted to numbers and the resulting total score conforms to a certain 'RPE level' of proficiency. RPE proficiency levels are from 0+ (very minimal proficiency) to 4+ (approaching the proficiency of a native speaker).[18]

In the field study, the RPE has proved to be a practical method for obtaining an apparently reliable and valid assessment of people's proficiencies in a second language, which is necessary for calibrating the SRT. The procedure requires one trained fieldworker to guide the untrained mother tongue speakers in their evaluations. The network of personal contacts made by the fieldworker provides the necessary raters and ratees within the community where the SRT is being developed. An advantage of using the RPE to calibrate an SRT is that the mother-tongue raters evaluating their acquaintances are part of the wider community which communicates with the second-language speakers being evaluated on a real-life, day-to-day basis.

There are other assessment tools that could be used for rating second-language speakers. The one chosen should conform to the standard that explains the final SRT scores in the way most meaningful to the research team and the people who will act upon the conclusions and recommendations of the survey.

One method is the ORAL PROFICIENCY INTERVIEW pioneered by the Foreign Service Institute (see, for example, Jones 1975 or Bruhn 1990). The result of the interview is an evaluation of the individual's second-language proficiency at one of the FSI levels. Individuals are assessed as being at levels 0 (no proficiency) to 5 (native proficiency). The Educational Testing Service (1970) developed training procedures for language testers of Peace Corps volunteers, which allows FSI levels to be assigned on the basis of oral

---

[18]The numbering system for the levels and proficiency criteria for the RPE have been adopted from the original FSI skill level descriptions and weighting scale, presented in the Educational Testing Service (1970) *Manual for Peace Corps Language Testers* (see chapter 6). The RPE levels (§6.6) have not yet been correlated with Foreign Service Institute proficiency levels.

interview performance. Another field version of the FSI-type oral proficiency interview, designed for use in pre-literate communities, is the SECOND-LANGUAGE ORAL PROFICIENCY EVALUATION (SLOPE), now in the field test stage of development (SIL 1987). Use of the SLOPE technique results in a level rating for an individual similar to the FSI proficiency levels.

Batteries of tests in major languages have been developed by institutions around the world. Cartier (1980) mentions one such battery and Carroll and Hall (1985) introduce the nine levels of proficiency identified by the general tests of the Pergamon Institute of English. As the researchers have access to such facilities, the calibration of an SRT in these languages could be completed using results from the appropriate battery as the standard. Care should be taken that the tests measure the type of oral proficiency assessed by the SRT. In other words, tests of written skills or probably even formal speech-making would not be appropriate standards against which to calibrate an SRT.

Again, the standard chosen to calibrate an SRT should be one which expresses most clearly to the research team and their audience the different levels of proficiency identified through administration of the SRT. In the next section on procedures for ensuring the inclusion of subjects at each level of proficiency, appropriate modifications should be made for standards which do not state their results in terms of levels, per se. The important point is to make sure that the wide range of proficiency is represented in the sample.

3.2.2. Rating the participants. The goal of this step is to assess the level of proficiency of approximately fifty second-language speakers of the language under investigation, who represent the full range of proficiency levels. It is necessary to keep evaluating until there are approximately five people identified at each of the half-levels of the RPE, that is, 0+, 1, 1+, 2, 2+, 3, 3+, 4, and 4+. Chapter 6 gives step-by-step instructions for administration of this technique. If a different standard has been chosen, then appropriate numbers of subjects should be found at each proficiency level of that standard.

Finding subjects at certain levels of proficiency is often easier than finding those at others, depending on sociolinguistic factors operating in the community. Therefore, it is good to keep current records of the ratings on the subjects and to administer the preliminary form of the SRT to them as soon as possible (step three). By regularly plotting the RPE rating scores and SRT preliminary form scores on a scattergram, the research team can determine if all the proficiency levels are being included in the rating. Also they can monitor the configuration of the scores and discern if the current form of the test is difficult enough to discriminate among the higher proficiency levels and easy enough for people with lower proficiency levels to score. (See also §3.3.2 on testing higher level speakers and §5.3.6 regarding the importance of monitoring the configuration of the scattergram.).

It is important that each proficiency level be represented in the calibration, especially those at the two extremes. Since the calibration of an SRT is statistically determined, it is necessary that the full range of proficiency levels be present in the calculations so that the results can be fully applied. In other words, if there are no subjects rated at level 4 or above, no statement can be made about the ability of that SRT to discriminate between levels 3+ and those above. Likewise, if no subjects at levels 0+ or 1 are identified, that SRT will not be able to discriminate below level 1+.

As soon as approximately five people at each half-level of proficiency have been identified through the RPE evaluations, for a total of approximately fifty people, this step is complete. However, if it is possible to evaluate more, that should be done. The more people that have been rated, the greater the confidence in the calibration of the SRT.

3.3 STEP THREE: Testing the preliminary form

The goal of step three is to test the approximately fifty people rated at varying levels of proficiency from step two, on the preliminary form of the SRT in preparation for calibrating the test and shortening it to its final form (step four).

3.3.1 Determining who should do the testing. The test administrator may be one of the researchers or another person trained to administer an SRT. If the RPE has been chosen as the calibrating standard (step two), it would be helpful for one fieldworker to be trained in both methodologies. Then he or she could easily follow up the people rated in step two and give them the SRT. If a different person is trained for the SRT administration, he or she should work closely with the RPE fieldworker, in order to maximize the personal contact with the mother-tongue raters in finding the people they have rated.

It is recommended that a single administrator score all the tests at this stage. This is for consistency since at this point the scoring standards have not yet been set and other administrators cannot be trained. If more administrators are needed/desired for testing the preliminary form, the first administrator should test enough people to establish the scoring standards (see §3.3.4 below). Then training tapes and other training materials should be prepared as outlined in step five (keep all the forty to fifty sentences of the preliminary form at this stage) and the training of the additional administrators completed.

The test administrator should be trained in the proper procedures for giving a test as described in §2.5. Additionally, he should listen to the preliminary form test tape as many times as necessary to become completely familiar with the sentences and be able to follow along with the stimulus at the same rate it is said on the tape.

3.3.2 General guidelines for administration. The following guidelines should be followed for administering the preliminary form.

Tape-record the responses. Permission should be obtained from the the first ten or so people who are tested to tape record their responses to the test. These taped responses are necessary in order to establish the scoring standards (as described below in §3.3.4). This tape will also be used in step five for training new test administrators (§3.5) along with additional taped responses obtained later in the testing process. If desired, of course, all the subjects' responses could be recorded if they are willing. The more recorded test responses available, the easier the establishing of scoring standards and the training of new administrators.

An easy way to tape record the responses is to set up two tape machines. The tape recorder that is recording the subject's responses can be left running throughout the administration of the test. That leaves the technician free to turn the tape player on and off for the test tape itself. Subsequent use of such tapes for scoring or training would also require the use of two tape machines.[19] Figure (16) illustrates a possible arrangement of the equipment.

Begin with higher-level speakers. If possible, testing should begin with those speakers whose second-language proficiency has been rated at the higher levels (step two). This will allow the research team to discern as soon as possible whether or not the preliminary form of the SRT they have constructed contains sufficiently difficult sentences to discriminate among these higher proficiency levels. As preliminary form SRT scores become available, they should be plotted on a scattergram against the RPE rating

---

[19]Alternatively, if it is desirable to record both the stimulus and the subject's response on one tape, the following suggestion may prove helpful: fasten a miniature clip-on microphone into the foam covering the earpiece of the headphone; this will pick up the stimulus as it comes through the headphones and also pick up the subject's voice. Tape the lead wire of this microphone onto the lead wire of the headphone. This way there is only one wire and one piece of equipment on the person being tested.

Test Development Methodology 51

scores obtained in step two. An example of this type of scatterplot can be seen in (37) (chapter 5).

(16)

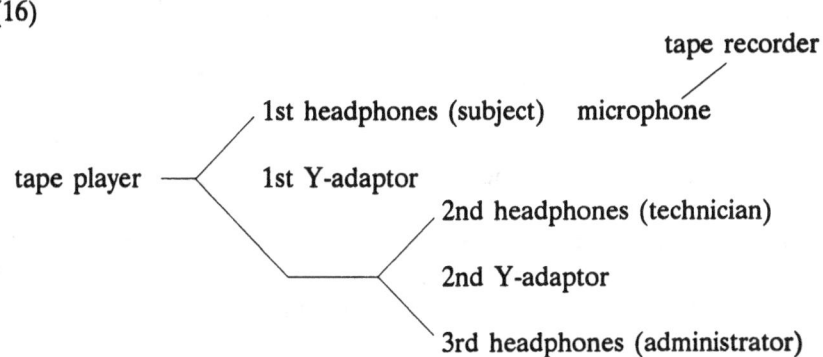

If no difference is found in the SRT performances of the speakers who have been rated at the upper levels, it is necessary to go back to the educated mother-tongue speaker and elicit some more difficult sentences. The new sentences should be checked by another educated mother-tongue speaker for length and acceptability and transcribed and translated (as described in step one). These new sentences should then be tape-recorded onto the end of the preliminary form test tape by the same educated mother-tongue speaker who recorded the other sentences, using the procedures outlined in §3.1.3.

This amended version of the preliminary form should then be given to the same higher-level speakers tested previously. If still no difference is found to discriminate the performances of these higher-level subjects, the methodology of the proficiency standard used to calibrate the test should be reexamined. Perhaps there has been some irregularity in application of the procedures. Perhaps that particular standard does not correlate as highly with the SRT as the RPE does, and therefore more data will have to be gathered before a discrimination among these levels can be observed (see further discussion in §3.4.10).

At any rate, if it is not clear whether or not a discrimination has been made among these higher levels, continue on with the testing. The statistical calculations in step four will indicate the range of scores that correspond to each level. (A similar procedure would be followed if the preliminary form were found not to be discriminating between the lowest proficiency levels.)

Administer to fifty people. If only some of the higher-level subjects have been administered the preliminary form of the SRT up to this point, the test should be given to all the rest of the people who have been rated in step two. Permission should be obtained from two or three subjects at each of the proficiency levels to tape-record their responses to the test. At least ten additional subjects' responses should be tape-recorded. These tapes, combined with the tapes of the first ten subjects (for a total of at least twenty subjects' responses), will be used as training tapes for administrators (see step five, §3.5.1). It is recommended that the SRT preliminary form be administered to approximately fifty people in order to give a sufficient spread of performance for the discrimination index (step four).

3.3.3 Conducting the test. This section is a summary and brief repetition of the procedures for administering an SRT presented in more detail in §2.5. The researcher is referred to that presentation for a more in-depth explanation of the testing process.

Equipment needed for testing. The minimum equipment needed for testing is a tape player, two sets of headphones, and a Y-adaptor which allows two headphones to be plugged into the same jack. If a technician will be operating the tape player, a third set of headphones and a second Y-adaptor will be needed. The second Y-adapter is plugged into one arm of the first Y, giving a total configuration of three branches (see (16) for detail).

Select a quiet text location. The setting for the test should be a quiet enough place that the subject will not be distracted and can hear the tape through the headphones, and the administrator can easily hear the subject's responses.

Follow standard procedures. Standard procedures for test administration should be followed, such as:

- BEING PROPERLY INTRODUCED TO THE SUBJECT: administrators should take advantage of social networks wherever possible to be introduced to a potential subject rather than approaching people 'cold'. They should introduce themselves honestly and not try to 'trick' subjects into participating by making themselves out to be something they are not nor by making empty promises about the benefits of participating.

- INTRODUCING THE PROCEDURE AS AN OPPORTUNITY FOR THE SUBJECT TO HELP THE RESEARCHERS: administrators should avoid such terms as "give you a test" or "find out how much of the language you know" and similar intimidating statements. Rather, the administrator should introduce the process as an opportunity to

Test Development Methodology

help, and should describe the task not as a test, but as merely listening to and repeating sentences in another language.

- EXPLAINING THE PROCEDURE TO THE PERSON BEFORE STARTING: the subject is told that he will hear some sentences through the headphones and is requested to repeat the sentences just as they are heard, e.g., Pashto in Pashto, Urdu in Urdu, etc.

- PUTTING THE TAPE PLAYER ON 'PAUSE' AFTER EACH STIMULUS: this allows the subject to give the response without being rushed by the next stimulus sentence. The tape may be rewound to replay the first three practice sentences as often as necessary until the person understands the procedure. The tape should not be rewound to replay test sentences. Rather, the administrator should indicate to the subject that 'everything is okay' and proceed to the next test sentence.

- NOT COMMENTING ON THE SUBJECT'S PERFORMANCE: The administrator should not say or indicate by his or her expression how well the subject has repeated the test sentence. If the test administrator feels that encouragement is needed, he or she may give a non-evaluative response such as, "You are doing fine."

Record each subject's responses. Scoresheets should be made so that each subject's responses can be marked separately and easily scored. A simple design for a scoresheet is to write all the sentences in the local script or phonetic notation (whichever is preferred by the administrator), leaving some space between each line for noting the errors. Blanks may be included at the top of the form for recording pertinent information on each subject, such as identification number, age, mother tongue, name, etc. This sheet can then be photocopied and a separate copy used for scoring each subject's responses. A mark can be made on or below the word where each error occurs. (A sample scoresheet is included as appendix B in this volume.)

3.3.4 Scoring the test. In scoring the test, it is necessary to first define what constitutes an error on the SRT, and then to establish the scoring standards for each SRT.

Definition of an error. An error is any deviation from the sentence as it is recorded, even if the deviation retains the original meaning. Errors fall into the following main categories: omission, addition, substitution, change of word order, repetition or false start, and distortion of the pronunciation of a word to the point that it is garbled. Three points are possible for each sentence; each time an error of any type or magnitude occurs in a sentence, a point is subtracted. The following chart summarizes the scoring system and suggests ways to mark the different types of errors. It is helpful to use a more descriptive marking system while scoring standards are being set. As mentioned above, during actual field administration a simple marking system is more feasible. (See also appendix B for a sample application of these scoring conventions and §2.6 for more elaboration).

(17) Scoring range
      3 points perfect, no errors in sentence
      2 points one error in sentence
      1 point   two errors in sentence
      0 points three or more errors in sentence

    Types of errors
      o   word omitted from sentence
      s   word substituted for another
      > or <   any change of word order (counts as one error)
      ~ ~   word garbled so as to lose meaning
      +   word or phrase added to sentence
      R   word or phrase repeated (counts as one error)
      w   wrong word or word ending (grammatical error)

Establish the scoring standards. It is necessary for the researcher and the administrator to establish scoring standards for each SRT. These standards define what constitutes an error for the particular language in which the SRT is developed. This should be done after the first ten subjects have taken the test and tape recordings have been made of their responses and before this prelimininary form of the test is administered to the remainder of the necessary fifty subjects.

Using the tape of the responses of these first ten people who took the preliminary form test (from §3.3.2), the researcher and/or administrator should go over it sentence by sentence with an educated mother-tongue speaker and score the responses with his or her help. While the administrator should be able to identify mistakes such as omission, change of order, etc., the educated mother-tongue speaker will be able to help identify all those more language specific errors, such as a vowel change which alters the tense, or plural markings, etc. For example, in the Urdu language gender agreement is marked by a vowel change and plurality is often marked by nasalization.

At this stage, the administrator should note every deviation from the test stimulus for each person on the individual scoresheet, using the suggested

Test Development Methodology

descriptive marking system for identifying each error made. This process helps determine what constitutes an error, where errors are likely to occur, etc. It is also essential for subsequent use of these test results in training administrators (step five). Administrators will need to be able to identify the different types of errors encountered in scoring tests without the aid of an educated mother-tongue speaker.

The researcher and/or administrator should also make careful notations on the elaborated transcription (from step one, §3.1.4) about the areas of potential error pointed out by the educated mother-tongue speaker, such as plural markings, tenses, etc. These notes will also be helpful for reference in training other administrators (step five) to score the tests. By drawing the attention of the prospective administrators to these fine points, a more accurate scoring of tests is possible. Such notations (shown by underlining) on an elaborated transcription are presented in appendix C.

3.4 STEP FOUR: Shortening and calibrating

The goal of step four is two-fold: (1) to shorten the preliminary form of the SRT to the fifteen sentences which best distinguish speakers with respect to their second-language proficiency and to arrange them in order from easiest to most difficult for the final form of the SRT, and (2) to correlate the performance of the people tested on the preliminary form (step three) with the rating they received in step two to determine what range of SRT scores on the final form corresponds to each level of the external proficiency standard, in this case, the RPE.

There are many ways in which the most discriminating sentences can be selected and ordered. The DIFFICULTY LEVEL (DL) and the DISCRIMINATION INDEX (DI) formulas are offered as effective methods for these two functions. Similarly, the statistical formulas in §§3.4.7–9 are offered as means for determining the range of scores corresponding to each proficiency level and the confidence with which they can be used. Other methods might also prove satisfactory.

An attempt has been made to present the formulas in such a format that the researcher can use them and understand their application without needing the assistance of a statistician. The usefulness of any SRT will be extended manyfold by knowing statistically which SRT scores correspond to which levels on the proficiency standard.

3.4.1 Applying the discrimination index. The discrimination index (DI) is a measure that shows which sentences are most effective in discriminating among performances of subjects displaying the varying levels of proficiency.

The lower the discrimination index, the more discriminating the sentence. This discrimination index technique was developed specifically for the purpose of selecting sentences for an SRT. It was inspired by analogy to the Kendall W correlation coefficient described by Casad (1974:177). The more discriminating sentences should be in the final form of the SRT. It is recommended that the scores from approximately fifty respondents be utilized in order to improve statistical accuracy in application of this formula.

Arrange the data. The data are obtained from testing the preliminary form on the approximately fifty people from step two whose proficiency levels are known. It is recommended that the sentence selection process be based on the performance of these people. There is a risk of skewing the results of the difficulty level and discrimination index by including people for whom no proficiency level has been ascertained. See §5.3.6 for further discussion.

These data are arranged in the manner described below and illustrated by the hypothetical example in (18). This hypothetical example shows the scores of fifteen people on a test consisting of seven sentences, with a maximum total score of twenty-one points. Using a large sheet of graph paper is the most convenient way to do the DI by hand. However, if most of these calculations can be done on a spreadsheet program on a computer, it will go faster.

First, the SUBJECTS ARE ARRANGED according to their total scores, that is, the total number of points they received on the forty to fifty sentences of the preliminary form of the SRT. The subjects are entered in successive positions across the top of the page, starting with the person who had the lowest score and ending with the person who had the highest score ('Subject Total Score' in (18)). For example, hypothetical subject A had the lowest total score of the group, with only one point out of the possible twenty-one points. Subject L had the highest score with twenty out of twenty-one possible points.

Next, the SENTENCES ARE ARRANGED according to their total score ('Sent. Tot.' in (18)), i.e., the total number of points scored by all the subjects on each individual sentence. The sentences are entered down the side of the page in order from the easiest (highest number of points) to the most difficult (lowest number of points). It is important to leave three blank lines after each sentence for subsequent rearranging. For example, sentence 6 was the easiest with a total number of thirty-two points scored by all the subjects together. Sentence 2 was the hardest sentence with a total of fourteen points.

Test Development Methodology 57

Then, the POINTS RECEIVED BY EACH SUBJECT on each sentence are filled in, taking care to be accurate. For example, subject N scored two points on sentence 6, one point on sentence 3, etc.

(18) Hypothetical example of preparation for DI and DL calculations; arrange subjects and sentences according to the preliminary form SRT scores (see §3.4.1 for explanation)

Sent. No.		A	E	I	M	B	F	J	N	C	G	K	O	D	H	L	Sent. Tot.
						Participants											
6.	Actual	1	1	1	2	2	2	2	2	2	3	3	3	3	3	3	32
	Rearr.																
	Diff.																
3.	Actual	0	0	0	1	0	1	1	1	2	2	2	2	2	3	3	20
	Rearr.																
	Diff.																
7.	Actual	0	0	1	0	0	1	1	1	2	2	2	3	2	2	3	20
	Rearr.																
	Diff.																
4.	Actual	0	0	0	0	0	0	1	1	0	3	2	3	3	3	3	19
	Rearr.																
	Diff.																
1.	Actual	0	0	0	0	0	0	0	1	1	2	3	1	3	3	3	17
	Rearr.																
	Diff.																
5.	Actual	0	0	0	0	1	1	1	1	1	1	1	1	2	2	3	15
	Rearr.																
	Diff.																
2.	Actual	0	0	0	0	0	1	1	1	1	1	1	2	2	2	2	14
	Rearr.																
	Diff.																
Subject Total Score (out of 21)		1	1	2	3	3	6	7	8	9	13	14	15	17	18	20	

Calculate the discrimination index. The discrimination index is then calculated by following these steps as illustrated in (19).

In (19) the rows containing the ACTUAL scores by each subject for each sentence are labeled 'Actual'. This is the actual score for each subject (in order from lowest to highest total score) on that particular sentence.

In (19) the next row for each sentence is labeled 'Rearr.' All the numbers in the actual row have been REARRANGED so that the numbers are in order: all the 0s, then the 1s, then the 2s, then the 3s (note that for sentence 2 no one scored 3 points). This rearranged row is the ideal order one would predict for the scores should that sentence discriminate perfectly among all the different proficiency levels. (Note that the correspondence between the score and the individual subject is no longer kept.) For example, on sentence 7 four subjects scored 0 correct, four scored 1 correct, four scored 2 correct, and two scored 3 correct. The numbers in the actual row have been permuted so that all the like quantities are together in the rearranged row.

(19) Hypothetical example of calculations for the DL and DI; rearrange sentence scores and subtract from actual scores (see §3.4.1 for explanation).

Sent. No.		A	E	I	M	B	F	J	N	C	G	K	O	D	H	L	Sent. Tot.	DL*	DI (Tot. Diff.)
6.	Actual	1	1	1	2	2	2	2	2	2	3	3	3	3	3	3	32	.29	
	Rearr.	1	1	1	2	2	2	2	2	2	3	3	3	3	3	3			
	Diff.	0	0	0	0	0	0	0	0	0	0	0	0	0	0	0			0
3.	Actual	0	0	0	1	0	1	1	1	2	2	2	2	2	3	3	20	.56	
	Rearr.	0	0	0	0	1	1	1	1	2	2	2	2	2	3	3			
	Diff.	0	0	0	1	1	0	0	0	0	0	0	0	0	0	0			2
7.	Actual	0	0	1	0	0	1	1	1	2	2	2	3	2	2	3	20	.56	
	Rearr.	0	0	0	0	1	1	1	1	2	2	2	2	2	3	3			
	Diff.	0	0	1	0	1	0	0	0	0	0	0	1	0	1	0			4
4.	Actual	0	0	0	0	0	0	1	1	0	3	2	3	3	3	3	19	.58	
	Rearr.	0	0	0	0	0	0	0	1	1	2	3	3	3	3	3			
	Diff.	0	0	0	0	0	0	1	0	1	1	1	0	0	0	0			4
1.	Actual	0	0	0	0	0	0	0	1	1	2	3	1	3	3	3	17	.62	
	Rearr.	0	0	0	0	0	0	0	1	1	1	2	3	3	3	3			
	Diff.	0	0	0	0	0	0	0	0	0	1	1	2	0	0	0			4
5.	Actual	0	0	0	0	1	1	1	1	1	1	1	2	2	3		15	.67	
	Rearr.	0	0	0	0	1	1	1	1	1	1	1	2	2	3				
	Diff.	0	0	0	0	0	0	0	0	0	0	0	0	0	0				0
2.	Actual	0	0	0	0	0	1	1	1	1	1	1	2	2	2	2	14	.69	
	Rearr.	0	0	0	0	0	1	1	1	1	1	1	2	2	2	2			
	Diff.	0	0	0	0	0	0	0	0	0	0	0	0	0	0	0			0
Subject Total Score (out of 21)		1	1	2	3	3	6	7	8	9	13	14	15	17	18	20			

*DL = 1.00 − Total/45

Test Development Methodology

The third line for each sentence in (19) is labeled 'Diff.' This is the absolute DIFFERENCE between the actual score for each person for that sentence and the rearranged or ideal sequence of scores. For example, in sentence 7 there were four instances of the actual score and the rearranged score being different. These four instances are reflected in the four 1s that appear in the difference row. Also, note that there is a two-point difference between the actual and rearranged scores at one place in sentence 1.

Once these steps have been completed, the numbers in the difference row for each sentence are added together. This sum represents the discrimination index for that sentence. For example, the discrimination index for sentence 7 is 4 because there were four instances of difference between the actual and the rearranged scores. The discrimination index for sentence 3 is 2 since there were only two instances where the actual score was different from the rearranged score. Since 2 is less than 4, sentence 3 with its lower discrimination index is a more discriminating sentence; the way the subjects scored on it is closer to the ideal, which is represented by the rearranged scores.

An example of the application of the discrimination index technique and arrangement of the scores to obtain the discrimination index is given in appendix D, which lists all the scores of subjects on the preliminary form of the revised Pashto SRT. For this revision there were only twenty-nine total sentences, whereas for the development of a new SRT there should be forty to fifty sentences that the discrimination index will help choose among. Section 5.3.5 describes how the discrimination index was taken into account in the selection of sentences for the final form of the revised Pashto SRT.

3.4.2 Figuring the difficulty level. The difficulty level (DL) measurement is actually just a description of the percent of INCORRECT responses obtained for a particular sentence. It is useful for ordering sentences from easiest to most difficult since one then takes the sentence with the smallest difficulty level as the easiest and the largest difficulty level as the most difficult. The difficulty level is obtained by dividing the total number of correct points for that particular sentence, as scored by all the subjects, by the total number of points possible for that sentence (the number of subjects times the three possible points) and subtracting the resulting number from one (1.00).

(20) $$\text{Difficulty Level} = 1.00 - \frac{\text{(Number of correct points for that sentence)}}{\text{(Total possible points for that sentence)}}$$

The total number of points for sentence 6 in (19) is 32. There are fifteen subjects, each of whom could have scored three points for a possible total of forty-five points for that sentence. Thirty-two divided by forty-five is .71 and subtracting that from 1.00 results in a difficulty level of .29 for sentence 6. The fact that sentence 6 has a low difficulty level, shows that it is a relatively easy sentence for subjects to repeat. Sentence 5 has a higher difficulty level (.67); it is more difficult for subjects to repeat. However, since both sentences also have a discrimination index of 'zero' (theoretically perfect discrimination) they are good choices for the final SRT which should contain sentences with low discrimination indexes and a range of difficulty levels.

3.4.3 Selecting the final fifteen sentences. Considering the discrimination index numbers for all the sentences, select fifteen sentences with the lowest discrimination index scores.[20] The range of possible discrimination index scores will depend on the number of subjects included in the calculations. It is unlikely that any sentence will have the perfect discrimination index of 0, but it may be that some sentences have a discrimination index as low as ten. This would certainly separate these more discriminating sentences from less discriminating sentences that might have a discrimination index of over forty.

The sentences selected should also represent the full range of difficulty levels. For example, in the hypothetical example in (19), sentences 6 and 2 both have the 'perfect' discrimination index of 0 and are at the two extremes of difficulty. They would both be included in the final form of an SRT. If three sentences were to be selected from the hypothetical example, sentence 3 would also be included since it has a low DI (2) and represents the mid-range of difficulty with a difficulty level of .56 (see (21)). The upper, middle, and lower ranges of difficulty levels should be represented in the fifteen sentences selected.

In actual practice, these calculations are based on more subjects than in this hypothetical example (about fifty rather than fifteen), and on more sentences (forty to fifty rather than the seven given in (18) and (19)), and the resulting shortened test would have fifteen sentences rather than the three that have been discussed. Additional factors are, of course, also considered in the final selection of sentences, along with the discrimination index and difficulty level. The quality of the tape recording of an individual sentence might preclude its inclusion, the content of a sentence may ultimately be judged as not desirable, the configuration of the scattergram

---

[20]If a slightly longer test is desired twenty sentences could be selected, although in the field study of SRT a test length of fifteen sentences has proved satisfactory.

Test Development Methodology

(see §3.2.2 and §5.3.6) may indicate that there are insufficient difficult sentences or easy sentences to discriminate between the higher or lower levels. Experimenting with selecting different sentences can change the configuration of the data on the scattergram, pulling in some of the outliers and decreasing the margin of error (SEE). Also, sentences with difficulty levels above .95 should probably be avoided as being too difficult; often the difficulty of the test can be raised by including more sentences in the difficulty level .70 to .80 range and fewer below difficulty level .20. (§5.3.5 provides an example of including these different factors in the sentence selection process.)

Taking all these factors into account, then, fifteen sentences are selected. These fifteen sentences are ordered according to their difficulty level scores, from low to high, for the final form of the SRT. Three short practice sentences are also added (see §3.4.5).

3.4.4 Figuring the extracted final form score. In order to calibrate the final, fifteen-sentence form of the SRT, an extracted score for each person previously tested is calculated. This is done by removing the rows and sentence totals for the sentences that were not selected for the final set of fifteen. The total score for each subject based on the fifteen sentences that remain is then recalculated. It is assumed that this extracted score represents how the subject would have done had he been given the shortened, final form of the test.[21] Table (21) illustrates the extracted scores for the hypothetical three-sentence test resulting from the example given in (18)–(19).

The extracted scores for all fifteen hypothetical subjects are listed at the bottom of (19). For example, subject G originally scored thirteen total points on the seven-sentence form of the hypothetical example (see (18)). On the three sentences selected for the final form of this hypothetical test, he had a total of five points, his extracted score.

Extracted scores for the revised Pashto SRT are listed for all subjects in (59), appendix A. The total scores for each subject on the preliminary form of that test are also given.

---

[21]In the field study of the SRT, it was never possible to give the final form of an SRT to the same subject who had taken the preliminary form. That is, it was never possible to make that type of test-retest check on the similarity between a subject's EXTRACTED SCORE on the final form of the SRT and what his ACTUAL SCORE would have been. It is hoped that this type of reliability check would be accomplished in the development of a future SRT. See §5.4.3, however, for a different type of reliability check on an SRT and also chapter 4, review of the literature, for studies on reliability in related research.

(21) Hypothetical example of extracted scores (see §3.4.4 for explanation)

							Participants									Sent.		DI (Tot.
Sent. No.		A	E	I	M	B	F	J	N	C	G	K	O	D	H	L	Tot.	DL	Diff.)
6.	Actual	1	1	1	2	2	2	2	2	2	3	3	3	3	3	3	32	.29	
	Rearr.	1	1	1	2	2	2	2	2	2	3	3	3	3	3	3			
	Diff.	0	0	0	0	0	0	0	0	0	0	0	0	0	0	0			0
3.	Actual	0	0	0	1	0	1	1	1	2	2	2	2	2	3	3	20	.56	
	Rearr.	0	0	0	0	1	1	1	1	2	2	2	2	2	3	3			
	Diff.	0	0	0	1	1	0	0	0	0	0	0	0	0	0	0			2
2.	Actual	0	0	0	0	0	1	1	1	1	1	1	2	2	2	2	14	.69	
	Rearr.	0	0	0	0	0	1	1	1	1	1	1	2	2	2	2			
	Diff.	0	0	0	0	0	0	0	0	0	0	0	0	0	0	0			0

EXTRACTED
Subject
Total Score   1 1 1 3 2 4 4 4 5 5 6 7 7 8 8
(out of 9 possible) = (3x3)

3.4.5 Tape-recording the final form test tape. If equipment which will maintain high sound quality is available, these fifteen sentences selected for the final form of the SRT should be dubbed from the master copy of the preliminary form test tape (§3.1.3) onto another tape. This dubbed tape would then be the test tape for the final form SRT. If high-quality equipment is not available, it will be necessary to have them re-recorded by the educated mother-tongue speakers, making sure he uses the same conversational speed and intonation as before.

Three practice sentences should be recorded at the beginning of the tape. These sentences are selected from the preliminary form sentences remaining after the selection of the fifteen. The practice sentences should have low discrimination indexes and low difficulty levels. The first practice sentence should be quite short, the next a bit longer. It is important that the third practice sentence be the SAME LENGTH as the first test sentence, so that people are not taken by surprise.[22] This, then, is the tape for the final form of the SRT.

---

[22] In both the pilot study and the field study of SRT this 'surprise factor' has proved to be important. It was observed that a sudden large increase in length between test sentences would often startle subjects to the point that they were unable to remember the longer sentence. This could occur even though the second was less than twice the length of the first. The fact that they were subsequently able to repeat much longer sentences with no difficulty showed that it was the sudden increase in length that was the problem, not their second-language proficiency, nor their short-term memory.

3.4.6 Calibrating with the external proficiency standard.

Once the extracted scores are figured, the final form of the SRT can be calibrated. This consists of correlating these extracted final form scores with the raw scores of the external proficiency standard which were obtained in step two, above. As described above in §3.2, the RPE has been used as the external proficiency standard during the development of the SRT technique and will be used in the examples in this section. If a standard other than the RPE has been chosen by the research team for calibrating an SRT, the scores from that standard should be used in the following formulas in place of the RPE scores.

In the scoring of an RPE evaluation, points are awarded for performance in relation to each of five skill areas (see chapter 6). The total of these points (sixteen to ninety-nine possible) is termed the raw score and is converted into an RPE proficiency-level rating. The numerical raw scores are used for the following statistical formulas rather than the equivalent proficiency-level rating. The scores for subjects from steps two and three will be used in the statistical analyses described below, that is, the approximately fifty subjects for whom both the raw score from the proficiency rating and the extracted SRT score are available.

The relationship between subjects' EXTRACTED SCORES for the final form SRT and their RATING on the external proficiency standard is most easily visualized by plotting both sets of scores on a scattergram. With the raw scores from the RPE as the vertical (Y) axis and the extracted scores from the SRT as the horizontal (X), the resulting pattern illustrates the relationship between performance on the two tests. While a qualitative or visual examination of the scattergram allows one to make a preliminary estimate of how closely the two measures vary together, a statistical analysis provides a quantitative assessment of the results and allows the survey team to interpret subsequent survey field results with greater confidence. See (39) for an example of such a scattergram.

Three different statistical measures provide insights into the relationship between SRT scores and the proficiency rating scores—in other words, between performance on an SRT and proficiency in that language as measured by RPE or another standard. The LINE OF REGRESSION (or estimation) is the most helpful in understanding the results of SRT testing in actual field application since it allows one to estimate or predict what a person's proficiency rating should be, given their performance on the SRT. If an SRT has been calibrated with the RPE, then the estimates of proficiency would be expressed in terms of RPE proficiency levels. The standard error of estimate measures how well the line of regression explains the relationship between the SRT and the RPE—in other words, the degree of confidence one can place in the results of the predictions made. The

COEFFICIENT OF CORRELATION determines the ratio of explained variation to the total variation—in other words, how much of an increase in an SRT score can be explained by an increase in measured proficiency in that language and how much is due to other, unidentified factors. Another way to explain this is that the coefficient of correlation measures the amount to which an SRT score varies in the same direction as the proficiency (RPE) score, i.e., how much one increases when the other increases.

3.4.7 Figuring the line of regression. The results of calculating the regression line allow one to predict the score on the external proficiency standard, in this case RPE, from a subject's SRT score. By figuring the regression line for the scores of the people who were rated on RPE, one can determine the range of SRT scores that corresponds to each proficiency level on RPE. Then that SRT can be used in a field situation and the results stated in terms of equivalent RPE proficiency levels. Once an SRT is calibrated, there is no need to keep administering the external proficiency standard for that purpose.

Since the goal is to ESTIMATE the proficiency level from the SRT score, the SRT is the independent variable 'x' and the proficiency level is the dependent variable 'Y'. The actual formula for the least squares regression line is seen in (22) (Spiegel 1972:220).

(22) $Y_{est} = a_0 + a_1 * x$, where

$$a_0 = \frac{(\text{sum Y})(\text{sum X}^2) - (\text{sum X})(\text{sum XY})}{N(\text{sum X}^2) - (\text{sum X})^2}$$

$$a_1 = \frac{N(\text{sum XY}) - (\text{sum X})(\text{sum Y})}{N(\text{sum X}^2) - (\text{sum X})^2}$$

Determining the regression line for the particular SRT, then, consists of substituting the values of the SRT and RPE scores for the variables of the formula. For purposes of illustration, the least squares equation is presented again, with the experiment related variables substituted into the formula. In explanation, 'N' refers to the number of subjects for whom both scores are available. 'Sum SRT' refers to the total extracted scores (zero to forty-five points possible) from the final form (fifteen sentences) of the SRT for all the subjects combined. 'Sum RPE' refers to the total of the raw scores (sixteen to ninety-nine points as opposed to the level equivalent) from the RPE for all the subjects. To obtain '(sum SRT^2)', square each subject's SRT score and add those squares. To obtain '(sum SRT)^2', add the SRT scores for all the subjects and square the result. '(Sum SRT*RPE)' is obtained by multiplying each subject's

Test Development Methodology

extracted SRT score by his/her RPE raw score and totaling the results for all subjects.[23]

(23)   Estimated RPE score = $a_0 + a_1$*SRT score, where

$$a_0 = \frac{(\text{sum RPE})(\text{sum SRT}^2) - (\text{sum SRT})(\text{sum SRT*RPE})}{N(\text{sum SRT}^2) - (\text{sum SRT})^2}$$

$$a_1 = \frac{N(\text{sum SRT*RPE}) - (\text{sum SRT})(\text{sum RPE})}{N(\text{sum SRT}^2) - (\text{sum SRT})^2}$$

Table (59) in appendix A gives an example of how the raw scores for the revised Pashto SRT were multiplied and/or squared and the resulting sums figured. The appropriate sums from (59), then, would be substituted into the formula as illustrated in (24).

(24)   Estimated RPE score = $a_0 + a_1$*SRT score, where

$$a_0 = \frac{(3460)(40414) - (1392)(93544)}{58(40414) - (1392)^2} = 23.6723$$

$$a_1 = \frac{58(93544) - (1392)(3460)}{58(40414) - (1392)^2} = 1.49929$$

To plot the regression line itself on the scattergram, a 'high' and a 'low' point should be calculated and then a line can be drawn between the two. To figure where these points should be placed, two SRT scores are substituted for 'SRT' in the above formula. Any of the possible range of SRT scores can be used (one to forty-five possible points), but one should be from the higher range and one from the lower. For example, an SRT score of thirty-seven is substituted into the least squares equation, yielding an estimated RPE score of seventy-nine, as in (25).

(25)   Estimated RPE score = $a_0 + a_1$*SRT score
       79.146 = 23.6723 + 1.49929*37

The same process is repeated for a lower SRT score. For example, an SRT score of nineteen substituted into the equation yields an estimated RPE score of fifty-two. These two points (high and low) are plotted on the scattergram and a line is drawn through them. This is the line of regression for the calibration of the final form of the SRT. Table (39) in chapter 5

---

[23]In this discussion of statistical formulas, the asterisk (*) means to multiply the numbers on either side of it.

shows a scattergram with the line of regression drawn in, connecting the high and low marks as calculated by this process (the high and low points are marked by a '+').

By permuting the above formula, the range of SRT scores that correspond to each RPE proficiency level can be figured. When the final form of the SRT is subsequently used in the field situation, these ranges can be consulted to figure the RPE proficiency equivalents for the SRT scores obtained in a given community. The permutation of the formula is in (26).

(26) $$\text{SRT} = \frac{(\text{RPE} - a_0)}{a_1}$$

For example, RPE raw scores from forty-three to fifty-two equal RPE proficiency level 2. By substituting first forty-three and then fifty-two in the 'RPE' position in the above equation, the lower and upper limits of the range of SRT scores on a given test corresponding to RPE proficiency level 2 can be determined. Using the above figures from the revised Pashto SRT as an example, the lower and upper limit revised Pashto SRT scores that correspond to RPE proficiency level 2 are thirteen and nineteen, respectively. See (40) in chapter 5 for the complete range of revised Pashto SRT scores equivalent to the different RPE levels.

(27) $$12.89 = \frac{(43 - 23.6723)}{1.49929} \qquad 18.89 = \frac{(52 - 23.6723)}{1.49929}$$

Once these calculations are completed for determining the SRT score range for all the corresponding proficiency levels, the calibration of the SRT is completed. The following two sections outline other formulas which are also helpful in interpreting the calibration data: standard error of estimate and coefficient of correlation.

3.4.8 Figuring the standard error of estimate. The standard error of estimate (SEE) is analogous to the standard deviation. Just as sixty-eight percent of a population are within one standard deviation of the mean, so sixty-eight percent of the actual measured values are within one standard error of estimate of the value estimated from the regression line. SEE lines parallel to the regression line can be drawn to show how much the actual value of RPE (Y) could be expected to differ from the estimated RPE value (Y_{est}). In other words, it illustrates the number of points on the RPE raw score scale that equals the 'margin of error' for predicting RPE proficiency scores from SRT scores.

Test Development Methodology

Plotting the points for the SEE line using numbers on the Y axis (where Y still represents the RPE scores and X represents the SRT scores) is done by means of the formula in (28) (Spiegel 1972:243).

(28) $$S_{y,x} \text{(SEE)} = \sqrt{\frac{(\text{sum } Y^2) - a_0(\text{sum } Y) - a_1(\text{sum } XY)}{N}}$$

The resulting number represents the number of points on the RPE (Y) axis that should be marked off on either side of a given point on the regression line. By doing this at a high and low point, the SEE lines parallel to the regression line can be drawn. For the revised Pashto SRT, the SEE is 7.68, as noted in (59) in appendix A. The scattergram presented as (39) in chapter 5 shows how lines were drawn eight points on the RPE scale from either side of the regression line to graphically illustrate the margin of error for the revised Pashto SRT. (The right SEE points are marked with '<' and the left SEE points are marked with '>' on the scattergram.)

3.4.9 Figuring the coefficient of correlation. The coefficient of correlation determines the extent to which the abilities measured by RPE and SRT vary in the same direction in the subjects tested. In other words, it determines the degree to which people who score high on an SRT are also rated high on the RPE. Fasold (1984:104) quotes an interpretation system for coefficients of correlation shown in (29).

(29) 0.01–0.20 slight; almost negligible relationship
0.20–0.40 low correlation; definite but small relationship
0.40–0.70 moderate correlation; substantial relationship
0.70–0.90 high correlation; marked relationship
0.90–0.99 very high correlation; very dependable relationship

Again keeping RPE scores as Y and SRT scores as X, the coefficient of correlation is calculated using the formula in (30) (Spiegel 1972:245).

(30) $$r = \frac{N(\text{sum } XY) - (\text{sum } X)(\text{sum } Y)}{\sqrt{[N(\text{sum } X^2) - (\text{sum } X)^2] * [N(\text{sum } Y^2) - (\text{sum } Y)^2]}}$$

Substituting the values for the revised Pashto SRT from (59) in appendix A, the correlation coefficient for this test is seen to be $r = .91$. This can be interpreted, using the above system, as a very high correlation, a very dependable relationship.

(31) $$r = .906350 = \frac{58(93544) - (1392)(3460)}{\sqrt{[58(40414) - (1392)^2] * [58(225578) - (3460)^2]}}$$

3.4.10 Suggestions for improving the correlation. The calibration of the original Pashto SRT and the revised Pashto SRT have demonstrated that a coefficient of correlation as high as $r = .90$ between scores on the SRT and RPE can be achieved and replicated. The question arises, then, about what to do when the calibration of an SRT in another language does not attain that high correlation.

The procedures for the proficiency standard used to calibrate the test should be reexamined. As was seen in the first attempt to calibrate the revised Pashto SRT (§5.3.3) irregularities in the administration of the RPE, the external calibrating standard, accounted for a lower initial correlation with the SRT ($r = .65$). When the calibration was done again with proper procedures for the RPE, the correlation with the preliminary form of the revised Pashto SRT rose to $r = .90$.

The procedures for administration of the SRT should be reexamined. Care should be taken that the administration of the SRT conforms to the guidelines as presented in step three, §3.3.3.

The content of the SRT should be reexamined. If subjects at several different proficiency levels are scoring in the same range on the SRT, the test may contain too many 'easy' sentences. Another way to describe this is by the scatterplot; a 'flattening out' of the scatter of scores at either the high or low end would indicate that more difficult sentences need to be included in order to discriminate among the various levels of proficiency. (This was found in the Urdu SRT and the original Pashto SRT, see §5.1.4 and §5.2.4).

It is possible that another external calibrating standard will not correlate as highly with the SRT as the RPE does. The type of SRT used in bilingualism surveys, as described in this manual, has not been calibrated with any other standard than the RPE. The very high correlations found between the Pashto SRTs and the RPE indicate that the second-language skills assessed by an SRT are very close to the second-language proficiency levels evaluated by mother-tongue speakers, those who are most closely associated with the actual daily use of the test language by their acquaintances. It may be that other types of standards chosen for calibrating an SRT will not evidence such high correlations.

Clark (1980:19) suggests that verbatim repetition of heard sentences of increasing length and complexity could be one of several testing techniques which would correlate at a high level with external criterion measures used in a validation study. However, whereas in the field study correlations of $r = .90$ have been found for the SRT with the RPE, examination of the

Test Development Methodology

literature seems to suggest that techniques other than the RPE may produce correlations lower than found with the RPE, but still considered 'high' in terms of general interpretation (see §3.4.9). Cartier notes that "correlations with [oral proficiency] interview ratings above $r = .70$ are quite respectable" (1980:8). In reference to a taped battery of second-language Spanish proficiency tests, he reports correlations with FSI-type interviews of $r = .74$ and $r = .72$ for two forms of the test battery. Hendricks, et al. (1980) found a correlation of $r = .70$ between the FSI-type interview and the repetition task they used. Henning (1983) reported a correlation of $r = .72$ between an FSI-type interview and an imitation test. Showalter (1989) found a correlation of $r = .69$ between a sentence repetition test and an FSI-type oral interview. Carrow (1974) obtained a correlation of $r = .79$ for children between a repetition task focusing on grammatical items and their measurement in a standardized method for sampling spontaneous speech.

Other types of testing techniques have also been correlated with oral proficiency interview ratings. Clark reports a study where "can do" questionnaires were found to correlate at a level of about $r = .60-.65$ with actual speaking proficiency as measured by the FSI technique (1980:20). Quakenbush (1986:204) noted a correlation of $r = .56$ between responses to a self-test questionnaire and oral interview scores, while Kamp (1987:8) obtained a correlation of $r = .54$ between a similar questionnaire and oral interview scores. Bachman and Palmer (1983) found correlations between FSI oral interviews and "can you" self-rating questionnaires of $r = .51-.56$ and between the interviews and oral translation tasks of $r = .72-.77$. Showalter (1989) obtained $r = .70$ between an oral cloze test and an FSI-type oral interview. Henning (1983) reported a correlation of $r = .68$ between an FSI-type interview and a completion task.

Results from a wide variety of studies such as these suggest that use of the oral proficiency interview to calibrate an SRT may not result in the very high correlations that have been found with using the RPE. If this proves to be the case, that does not mean that the calibration is any less valid, just that results obtained in the field from using an SRT so calibrated will have to be interpreted with greater caution. It may be that control testing the SRT, as described in the next section, would provide the reconfirmation of the cutoff point for 'successful' test performance that would allow actual survey field results to be interpreted with greater confidence.

3.4.11 Control testing the final form. Control testing the final form of an SRT consists of administering the test to mother-tongue speakers of the dialect of the test language chosen as the standard for that particular SRT.[24] These mother-tongue subjects should represent a wide range of age and educational levels as well as other factors that the research team sees as significant, such as sex, social class, rural versus urban residence, etc. By including subjects from a wide range of such factors, the research team can be assured that such factors exercise no significant influence over mother-tongue (MT) performance on the test. Standard testing procedures should be followed, as outlined in step three, §3.3.3.

By conducting control testing of the final form of the SRT, researchers can confirm the calibration of the test with the external proficiency standard. Also, if the correlation with the calibrating instrument is found to be lower than desired (see §3.4.10), control testing will more sharply define the cutoff level for the upper proficiencies. Control testing will also confirm that proficiency alone determines performance on the SRT.

As an example of this type of testing, control testing of the original Pashto SRT revealed that performance of mother-tongue speakers on the test was uniformly high, eighty-four to one hundred percent correct for subjects with good personal contact with the test administrator. (See discussion in §5.2.5 and §5.4.) Control testing also showed that such factors as age and level of education made no significant difference in the performances of mother-tongue speakers on the test. Both findings confirmed the integrity of the Pashto SRT, underscoring its ability to challenge higher-level proficiency speakers and thus discriminate a wide range of proficiency levels. The cutoff point for second-language speakers with an equivalent RPE proficiency level of 3+ and above on that test is the same as the lower range of performance by the mother-tongue speakers. This confirms that second-language speakers scoring above that level can be said to function at an 'adequate' proficiency. Also, since proficiency was, by definition, held constant in these mother-tongue subjects, and age and education factors made no significant difference on their performances, differences in performance by second-language speakers on this test can be interpreted as revealing their proficiency, and, by extension, the influence of different factors on their learning of the Pashto language.

---

[24]This type of control testing has been widely done in other studies that demonstrate the integrity of the SRT technique. For example, Gallimore and Tharp (1981) compared the performance on a repetition test of children who were native speakers of standard English with children who were native speakers of nonstandard dialects or codes. The standard English group performed significantly better ($p < .002$) than the nonstandard group. Hamayan, Markman, Pelletier, and Tucker (1978) found that monolingual French-speaking children performed consistently better than second-language children on a repetition task.

Test Development Methodology

3.5 STEP FIVE: Training the test administrators

The goal of this step is to provide materials and practice for training SRT administrators and maintaining interadministrator reliability and consistency. Each trained test administrator should be able to listen to a subject's responses and score them accurately and reliably. He or she should be able to do this on the spot, under field conditions, since the tape recording of subjects' responses in an actual survey is the exception rather than the rule.

3.5.1 Preparing the training materials. The following steps should be used in preparing the training materials.

Elaborated transcription. The elaborated transcription prepared for scoring the preliminary form of the SRT needs to be shortened for use with the final, fifteen-sentence form of the test. It should be edited so that the three practice sentences and the fifteen test sentences appear in the same order as on the final test tape. See appendix C for a sample elaborated transcription.

Training and interadministrator reliability tapes. The next step is to make two tapes, one for training test administrators, the other for interadministrator reliability purposes.

In step three, §3.3.2, tape recordings were made of a total of at least twenty subjects' responses to the SRT stimuli sentences on the preliminary form of the SRT. These tapes have the subjects' responses to all forty to fifty sentences of the preliminary form of the SRT. Since the test administrators will be trained for the fifteen sentences of the final form of the SRT, each subject's responses should be shortened so that only responses to the fifteen sentences of the final form remain. Dubbing the responses to these fifteen sentences onto another tape so that they are in correct order according to the final form of the test would be nice, but to do such for all the subjects would be time consuming. Since these tapes will only be used for training and checking, it is probably sufficient to just dub the final-form fifteen sentences for each subject onto another tape in whatever order they occurred in the original preliminary form of the test. Ten subjects' responses should be dubbed onto one tape to be used for training administrators (§3.5.2). The other ten subjects' responses should be dubbed onto a second tape to be kept for interadministrator reliability purposes (§3.5.3). An effort should be made to have a range of proficiency levels on each tape. An identifying phrase should be recorded before each subject's responses, e.g., "Training tape, test six" or "Interadministrator reliability tape, test nine".

Sample scoresheets. Scoresheets for each subject's tape-recorded test should have already been prepared in step three, when these tests were scored with the help of the educated mother-tongue speaker. These need to be edited so that only the fifteen sentences on the SRT final form (plus the three practice sentences) remain. These scoresheets will be used for training purposes and so should contain more than just a mark on words where an error occurred (simple marking like that, though, is acceptable for field use). Detailed notations of the specific types of errors (omission, substitution, change of order, etc.) which were made on a particular word or words by each subject should be noted. This way the administrators being trained can more thoroughly understand the nature of possible errors they must learn to listen for (see appendix B for a sample scoresheet).

3.5.2 Training the test administrators. Each prospective administrator should receive a copy of the final fifteen-sentence elaborated transcription (§3.5.1), the SRT final form test tape (step four, §3.4.5), the training tape with sample scoresheets filled out for each tape-recorded test (§3.5.1), and a quantity of blank scoresheets to practice on.

Familiarization. The first step is for the prospective administrators to familiarize themselves with the elaborated transcription, making sure that they can read the phonetic or local script transcription and can understand the notes regarding scoring standards (key points to listen for, etc.), whether provided in a separate summary or noted by underlining on the elaborated transcription. They should also become familiar with the techniques of test administration. Suggestions are given in step three §3.3.3.

The administrator should listen to the SRT final form test tape many times and practice saying all the sentences while following the transcription. They should practice until they are able to say the sentences with the tape and follow along visually at the same speed as the tape. Only when this is possible should the prospective administrators proceed to the next substep, i.e., practicing the scoring.

Practice scoring. The prospective test administrators should then listen to the training tape (prepared above in §3.5.1) and score the recorded tests themselves. Then, using the sample scoresheet for each test, they should compare their marks with the sample and learn to recognize the errors that each subject has made. The administrators should listen to this tape over and over until able to identify the errors and come up with the same scores as the sample scoresheet but without looking at it. When this stage of confidence is attained, the administrators should complete the following step on interadministrator reliability before beginning to test in the field situation.

Test Development Methodology

3.5.3 Maintaining interadministrator reliability. For the purposes of monitoring interadministrator reliability, each trained test administrator should be given the tape prepared for this purpose, discussed above in §3.5.1, and an appropriate number of blank scoresheets for the tests recorded on the tape. This reliability checking should be completed before a newly trained administrator begins testing in the field. It should also be periodically done for all other administrators, to maintain reliability.

The trained test administrator should listen to the interadministrator reliability tape. In order to simulate an actual test situation they should score the tests WITHOUT referring to the sample scoresheet and without rewinding the tape. The average of the scores they assign should be within five points (out of 45) of the scoring standard set when the recorded tests were first scored with the help of the educated mother-tongue speaker.[25] If the average of an administrator's scores is too much higher or lower than the standard, this administrator should obtain some additional practice, perhaps scoring some tests together with another trained administrator.

Each trained test administrator should also periodically follow this same procedure: listen to the interadministrator reliability tape and score the tests without referring to the original sample scoresheet or replaying the recorded responses to the test stimuli, in order to simulate an actual test situation. The administrator should check his or her scores with the score originally assigned by the educated mother-tongue speaker and also the scores assigned by other administrators. This will provide a check to maintain a high level of consistency in scoring standards between administrators. Additional tapes for this purpose should be made at intervals to ensure that administrators do not become too familiar with one tape. Periodic checks and discussions on scoring standards will help maintain good interadministrator reliability.

It is also important to have periodic checks and discussions on the actual procedures used in administering tests in order to ensure that test administrators are consistent. Some general guidelines have been given in step three, §3.3.3, and also in §2.5.

3.6 STEP SIX: Using the SRT in the field

The administration of an SRT in the field will involve the same procedures outlined in §2.5 (also above in step three, §3.3.3, except that the final

---

[25]Scorers for the research in elicited sentence imitation reported by Gallimore and Tharp (1981:376) were trained to a criterion agreement of 80 percent or more with expert scorers.

fifteen-sentence form of the SRT will be used). Selection of people to be tested depends on the results of community profile studies and sampling procedures previously completed. Chapter 2 describes an outline for using an SRT in a bilingualism survey and the reader is referred to that chapter for further information.

It has proved helpful to tape-record a few translated sentences of explanation in the local language and play it prior to the administration of a test. This is in addition to direct face-to-face explanation of the SRT procedures when the test administrator is introduced to a prospective participant. An example of such a tape recorded explanation could be:

> Listen carefully to each sentence and then repeat it. Some sentences are easy to say and some are hard. Repeat the sentences exactly as you hear them—Pashto sentences in Pashto, Urdu sentences in Urdu.

It has also proved helpful to prepare scoresheets ahead of time. A convenient type of scoresheet consists of a photocopy of the test sentences to be used for each subject. Each person's errors, then, can be noted directly on that sheet for ease of scoring. Such photocopies can be in either the local script or a phonetic rendering of the test sentences, depending upon which is most easily followed by the test administrator. See appendix B for a sample scoresheet in phonetic notation.

It is always helpful to tape-record the responses of the first five or ten subjects (even more if only the more bilingual people are tested first) when beginning to test in a new area.[26] This is particularly true if it is suspected that the test language is spoken slightly differently in that location. Scoring the first tests from the tape recording has a number of advantages: It points up any dialect differences in the test language that will be consistent across second-language speakers in that particular area (and therefore possibly be allowed as permissible deviations from the standard). It gives an opportunity to verify the on-the-spot scoring of the test by allowing one to listen again later. It also reveals any new and different error patterns that need to be watched for.

3.7 Summary of steps

The following outline summarizes the development of an SRT utilizing the RPE technique as a calibrating instrument. Detailed explanation of the RPE methodology is given in chapter 6.

---

[26]Such tapes can be used as new interadministrator reliability tapes as well.

Test Development Methodology

Step one—Develop preliminary form of SRT
- Obtain initial sample of sentences from educated mother-tongue speaker
- Review for naturalness, etc. with educated mother-tongue speaker
- Tape-record forty to fifty sentences by educated mother-tongue speaker for preliminary form
- Make an elaborated transcription of the sentences

Step two—Obtain RPE ratings (see chapter 6 for details; modify accordingly if using other standard)
- Translate proficiency criteria into language of mother-tongue raters
- Interview mother-tongue raters
  - Administrator introduces and explains proficiency criteria
  - Mother-tongue rater ranks second-language acquaintances for first factor
  - Mother-tongue rater rates each ratee for first factor
  - Mother-tongue rater ranks and rates ratees for other factors in turn
- Calculate numerical equivalent of ratings
- Assign RPE level equivalent for each ratee's score

Step three—Administer preliminary form of SRT to fifty people (RPE ratees)

Step four—Select final fifteen sentences and correlate scores with RPE rating
- Select final fifteen sentences from preliminary form of SRT by examining the discrimination index and difficulty level for each sentence
- Extract scores of subjects for each of the final fifteen-sentences
- Tape-record the final form test tape (fifteen sentences)
- Calibrate final fifteen-sentence score with RPE rating, calculating coefficient of correlation and margin of error (SEE)

Step five—Train the test administrators
- Prepare the training materials
- Train the administrators
  - Familiarization
  - Practice scoring
- Maintain interadministrator reliability

Step six—Use in the field in bilingualism surveys

4
Survey of the Literature

4.1 Investigations into sentence imitation

The use of sentence repetition—often called elicited imitation—in the assessment of language proficiency spans almost three decades. A 1963 study by Fraser, Bellugi, and Brown used this technique in what has been called "a landmark beginning attempt at controlled study of comprehension" (Slobin 1973:464). Another seminal study, reported by Slobin and Welsh in 1968, offers convincing arguments and supporting data that repetition of sentences involves linguistic processing and challenges linguistic competence. The authors conclude, "We believe that elicited imitation is a useful probe for revealing linguistic competence" (1968:18). Oller cites that study and others such as Menyuk's 1969 work (including her 1964 studies) and the 1971 (and 1975) Natalicio and Williams report. All of these "argued that if the material to be repeated pushed the limits of the short-term memory of the examinees, it was in fact a valid test of both comprehension and production skills" (Oller 1979:65).

Slobin cites studies of elicited imitation published prior to his 1973 review which "make it quite clear that imitation DOES work through comprehension" (1973:464, emphasis his). Oller (1979:78) notes that "at least since 1969, it has been known that school children who speak different varieties of English perform about equally badly in tests that require the repetition of sentences in the other group's variety", citing Baratz' 1969 study among others.

With the early studies dealing with young children as catalyst, researchers in the field of psycholinguistics, specifically child language development and disorders, developed standardized tests (for example, Lee 1970 and Carrow 1974). These, in turn, have spawned a host of other studies investigating the different aspects of various types of sentence repetition tests. Controversy reflected in the literature in recent years has mainly centered on the use of sentence repetition tests for diagnostic purposes rather than the general screening purposes for which they appear to be better suited (e.g., Connell and Myles-Zitzer 1982; Dailey and Boxx 1979; McDade, Simpson, and Lamb 1982; Prutting, Gallagher, and Mulac 1975). Screening, in this sense, refers to identifying a delayed child in a population of normal children, while diagnosis refers to the more complicated task of identifying the specific areas of disability of a given language-delayed child. It can be further understood that when researchers (such as Prutting and Connolly 1976; or McDade, Simpson, and Lamb 1982) state that they are not certain exactly what a sentence repetition test is measuring, they are viewing the method in terms of this diagnostic versus screening controversy and the extent to which results of such a tests can be analyzed in detail. None of these researchers would dispute the fact that sentence repetition tests assess a child's general ability to control the grammar, vocabulary, and phonology of his or her mother tongue, that being in all these cases, English.

But sentence repetition testing has not been limited to research in language development. The use of elicited imitation in testing has been vast and varied. Gallimore and Tharp (1981) review the literature and cite the successful use of elicited imitation by researchers investigating second-language acquisition, nonstandard dialects, acculturation, and deviant speech.

A study by Miller (1973) contributed much to the understanding of the phenomenon of repetition, especially in the support he found for the model of sentence imitation proposed by Slobin and Welsh (1968). He found that "sentence length is a factor in sentence imitation in children and was predictive of the difficulties experienced by children in recalling sentences" (1973:11). He suggested that lack of control of sentence length could have contributed to the equivocal results obtained by earlier studies. While the purpose of his study was not to determine whether imitated sentences are processed or not, he concludes that "it is evident that imitative responses containing alterations such as contractions and word order changes are an indication that some processing is taking place" (1973:10). Slobin and Welsh are more decisive: "This very preliminary analysis has convinced us that sentence recognition and imitation are filtered through the individual's productive linguistic system" (1968:17).

Support for the linguistic processes underlying sentence repetition has come through the analysis of the type of errors made by subjects. Miller (1973) analyzed the errors made by subjects on his repetition task and in that found support for the Slobin and Welsh sentence imitation model. For example, the substitution errors were "all of the same form class as the original word in the model sentence. This indicated that appropriate syntactic marking of the lexical items of the model sentence was accomplished even though the original word did not remain available in short-term memory" (Miller 1973:10). In the Slobin and Welsh study they examined elicited imitation in a young child, but they add that "data from sentence imitation by adults... suggests a similar model in adult sentence recognition: retrieval of a syntactic structure, lexical items appropriately marked as to the syntactic and semantic function, and an attempt to fill in the syntactic structure with whatever of the lexical items from the model sentence are available in short-term memory" (Slobin and Welsh 1968:10). They cite evidence from a study by Robin Chapman that adults, especially drowsy ones, "frequently make the same sort of assimilatory deformations as the child when presented with longer, more complex, even anomalous sentences" (1968:18).

Miller found a significant interaction between the mean count on a measure of surface structure complexity and transformational sentence type. Results show that there was a significant difference ($p < .01$) in the recall of high and low counts of surface structure complexity for passive and wh-question sentences, but no significant difference for active and negative sentence types. These results agree with four other studies that Miller cites which used adults. On the basis of his own findings and their correlation with the adult studies, he concludes, "It appears that children perform like adults on sentence recall tasks in which [surface structure complexity] and transformational sentence type are controlled. The similarity of performance of children and adults would indicate that children make use of the same cues in sentence recall as those used by adults" (1973:7).

A second-language French study by Swain, Dumas, and Naiman (1974), which compared elicited imitation with translation tasks, is discussed at some length by Oller (1979). "If the sentences children were to repeat exceeded immediate memory span, then elicited imitation ought to be a test both of comprehension and production skills" (1979:66). Swain, et al. compared imitation with translation into the second language and from the second language into the first, as tests of productive ability and comprehension ability, respectively, in the target language. They found no differences in the strategies with which the children in the study approached the two tasks, imitation and translation. Indeed, similar error patterns were found in the imitation and production tasks (sixty-nine to seventy-five percent), lending weight to the proposition that these two tasks tap into the same underlying competence factor. Similar error patterns between imitation and productive translation were also observed in a separate study by Naiman (1974), also discussed by Oller: "Children were observed to make many of the same errors in spontaneous speech as they made in elicited translation from the native language to the target language" (Oller 1979:66).

The repetition test described by Gallimore and Tharp (1981), used with children, included many different aspects of English grammar, but not plurality. They compared performance on that test with another measure specifically designed to test plurality, and found high agreement. They also found high agreement between the repetition test and percentage of correct use of plurals observed in a natural play setting. These findings led them to suggest the repetition test "reflects some general language ability, because it is related to a non-included feature (plurality), both as plurality is measured in a test of its own, and by its appearance in natural speech" (1981:382).

The same authors compared the performance on a repetition test of children who were native speakers of standard English with children who were native speakers of nonstandard dialects or codes. As was to be expected, the standard English group performed significantly better ($p. < 002$) than the nonstandard group. As a reliability test for sentence repetition, they monitored children's performance on the repetition test over a four-year period. They found considerable stability in relative scores and concluded, "elicited imitation in a standardized format yields highly stable, test-retest correlations over a period of years" (Gallimore and Tharp 1981:378).

Hamayan, Markman, Pelletier, and Tucker (1978) examined the differences in performance on a repetition task between French monolingual and English-speaking bilingual children. They note, "The validity of the [repetition] technique rests on the assumption that the child, or the second-language learner, when presented with a sentence longer than his immediate memory span, will pass it through a type of filter—his interim grammar—before repeating it. If a specific syntactic feature is not part of an individual's grammar, that element will be distorted during production" (1978:331). They found the performance of the second-language children to be inferior to the monolingual children's performance in all respects; nevertheless, typical and consistent patterns of errors for a few of the linguistic features were observed. They conclude: "It may be said that by using a sentence repetition task, with groups of native speakers and second-language learners, insights may be gained about the production system that a language learner is using at a given time in his learning" (1978:337).

Oller contends that "elicited imitation is similar to dictation and partial dictation except that the response is oral instead of written. Therefore, it can be conveniently used with preliterate children or non-literate adults" (1979:300). He sets language tests like dictation and elicited imitation in the framework of a pragmatic theory of language use and language learning. He states that they meet "three stringent construct validity criteria: (a) they satisfy the requirements of a theory; (b) they typically show strong positive correlations with tasks that meet the same theoretical requirements; (c) the errors that are generated by dictation procedures correspond closely to the kinds of errors learners make in real-life language uses" (1979:299). Gallimore and Tharp (1981) and Swain et al. (1974) also observed this, as was noted above.

4.2 Second-language proficiency assessment in adults

Second-language proficiency assessment is a common application of elicited imitation studies with adults. It has been a standard methodology in second-language teaching classrooms. In her textbook on language testing, Valette (1977) includes sentence repetiton testing as a type used in bilingual programs. Repetition presumes the ability to retain in memory a given stimulus; retention is closely linked to students' ability to assign meaning to that stimulus.

> Native speakers of a language are able to listen to lengthy questions in that language and answer with ease. When learning a second language, however, these same people can retain only a part of what they have just heard. ... Experiments evaluating student ability to remember lists of nonsense words or syllables have shown that those students who impose a certain pattern on the words or syllables increase their retention span. In other words, once students have given a certain meaning to the words, they can remember them more easily. Thus, in the target language, once students find themselves at ease in the language and understand it with little difficulty, they can retain longer sentences. Retention is a serious problem for beginners but presents less of an obstacle for the intermediate and advanced student. (Valette 1977:75–76)

Sentence imitation is one of the PRAGMATIC techniques espoused by Oller and others as a replacement for the more traditional type of second-language testing referred to as DISCRETE POINT tests. Discrete point testing utilizes focused test items in order to assess whether a language learner has acquired the ability to correctly apply particular grammatical rules (e.g., plural formation) or to recognize specific phonological distinctions. In contrast, Oller proposes tests which evaluate proficiency skills from a more integrative perspective. He defines these pragmatic language tests as those which meet two naturalness criteria: "first, they must require the learner to utilize normal contextual constraints on sequences in the language; and, second, they must require comprehension (and possibly production also) of meaningful sequences of elements in the language in relation to extralinguistic contexts" (Oller 1979:70). He goes on to give examples of pragmatic tests such as dictation, cloze procedure, combinations of cloze and dictation (partial dictation), oral cloze tasks, dictation with interfering noise, paraphrase recognition, question-answering, oral interview, essay writing, narration, translation, and closely related techniques to dictation such as dictation/composition, and elicited imitation. The reason that a pragmatic task like dictation or imitation works well is that "the whole family of auditory tasks that it comprises faithfully reflect crucial aspects of the very activities that one must normally perform in processing discourse auditorily" (1979:266).

Many studies have investigated the relationship of sentence repetition or imitation with other measures of proficiency. Henning (1983) compared the oral interview, imitation, and completion methods of second-language proficiency testing on adult ESL students. Extensive statistical studies on the convergent, discriminant, and predictive validity of the three measures "support the use of imitation methods above completion and traditional interview methods" (1983:327). Perkins, Brutten, and Angelis (1986) also used sentence repetition with adult ESL students. "The correlational analysis indicates that the sentence repetition test assesses short-term memory capacity and derivational complexity: as the sentences become longer, the item difficulty increases; as the number of transformations necessary to derive the surface structure increases, the item difficulty increases" (1986:136). Showalter (1989) conducted a brief pilot study in a field situation with adults where he found a correlation between a sentence repetition task and an FSI-type oral interview of $r = .69$. The correlation between the sentence repetition task and an oral cloze procedure was $r = .92$. Henning (1983) reported a correlation of $r = .72$ between an FSI-type interview and an imitation test. Carrow (1974) obtained a correlation of $r = .79$ for children between a repetition task focusing on grammatical items and their measurement in a standardized method for sampling spontaneous speech. Hendricks, Scholz, Spurling, Johnson, and Vandenbury (1980) administered a battery of tests to second-language students of English. They found that of all the pragmatic oral proficiency tests used, sentence repetition correlated most highly ($r = .70$) with the overall score of an FSI-type oral proficiency interview. They had subjects repeat the sentences of connected paragraphs taken from standard English readers.

The sentence repetition test as described in this manual is specifically designed as a SCREENING instrument to give a general assessment of an

Survey of the Literature

individual's proficiency necessary for the purposes of a bilingualism survey. On the other hand, other types of sentence repetition tests are widely used in other applications, especially educational settings, both for adults and children. For example, Gallimore and Tharp (1981) used results from a standardized repetition test for children to chart progress in English as a second language or acquisition of standard English as an alternate code for children from different language or cultural backgrounds.

A study by Natalicio and Williams (1971:1) examined the "degree to which sentence imitation of Black and Mexican-American children (grades K–2) could be used as a basis for language evaluation" and subsequent placement in an educational program. Rather than being scored as such, the taped responses were evaluated by panels of specialists on a questionnaire utilizing semantic differentials and open-ended questions. One goal of the study was to determine if a language sample obtained through tape-recording a child's imitation of sentences was sufficient to allow the specialists to evaluate that child's language. A high degree of consistency was found between all the raters for all the different aspects of each child's language performance rated by the specialists. Thus the recorded performances of children's repetitions of sentences "do permit independent evaluations with a high degree of reliability" (1971:31).[27]

Spolsky, Murphy, Holm, and Ferrel also used a repetition task in a placement test. Their oral placement test for adults contained a section of sentences to repeat. The repetitions required the Spanish-speaking adult English learner to overcome certain critical language problems of phonology and syntax. "The assumption is that the person who can repeat these items with such underlying structural differences is better able to function in English than one who cannot repeat them" (1975:85).

It can be seen, then, that the repetition of sentences is a technique often used in research with adult as well as child subjects. It has been shown to correlate highly with a number of other proficiency-assessment techniques.

---

[27]Even though the sentence repetition test scoring methodology described in this manual is different from that of Natalicio and Williams, this finding could serve to help support the premise of the current SRT study that a corpus of repeated sentences may be sufficient to make a general evaluation appropriate to the purposes of a bilingualism survey. Additionally, the one caution given by Natalicio and Williams is against using such imitation data as a basis for broad prescriptive interpretation, direction for therapeutic interventions or educational strategies. Rather, they should assist in making decisons for over-all program placement (Natalicio and Williams 1971:85). This, too, is in keeping with the premises of the current SRT study—that an SRT, as described in this manual, is best used as a screening test in a community-wide study rather than as a diagnostic tool for directing one individual's program of study.

It has also been used to chart progress in language acquisition and for placement in educational programs.

4.3 Different aspects of the test methodology

The methodology for test development recommended in chapter 3 is designed to allow development of the SRT in a research project where the members of the research team do not necessarily have fluency in the test language. This is why, for example, the sample of sentences for the test are taken from spontaneous texts by mother-tongue speakers, whether oral or written, and why the selection of sentences for the test is based on their ability to discriminate among the performances of second-language speakers of varying proficiency levels. On the other hand, sentences used for other types of sentence repetition tests are often selected by the researchers themselves, according to strict internal criteria, as the following shows.[28]

A common goal is to have the sentences selected for the tests reflect various grammatical constructs. For example, the test described by Spolsky, et al. (1975) uses the repetition of English sentences by Spanish-speaking adults chosen to contain such constructions as verbal complementation. Gallimore and Tharp (1981:374) report research with a test using standard English features that had been observed to show variation in the speech of Hawaiian Islands Creole English-speaking children who were in the process of learning standard English. Perkins, Brutten, and Angelis (1986) examined the derivational complexity of sentences, counting the number of transformations necessary to derive the surface structure.

Other studies, primarily those concerned with identifying children with delayed language acquisition, attempt to include grammatical structures which increase in difficulty similar to the normal developmental sequence. Two prominent instances of this type of sentence selection are the standardized sentence imitation tests designed by Lee (1970) and Carrow (1974). Both tests underwent extensive validation and reliability studies. For example, Carrow reports significant differences ($p < .001$) between age groups ($n = 475$), indicating that "the test reflects the changes in grammaticality in children as age increases" (1974:440). She also found test-retest reliability of .98 and a correlation between the test and a sampling technique of spontaneous speech of .79.

---

[28]Although the researchers use different, defensible reasons for sentence choice, they are generally selecting sentences in their own mother tongue, in all these reported cases, English.

Different aspects of the current SRT methodology are similar to those employed by other researchers. Gallimore and Tharp (1981) summarize a six-year program of research on a standardized sentence repetition test used for standard English as a second language and second code assessment. They also reported high test-retest reliability of r = .89. The final form of their test was obtained by reducing a pool of sentences to fifteen through item-total correlations, item difficulty, and redundancy. This is similar to the discrimination index and difficulty level measures recommended for sentence selection for SRT (see chapter 3).

Spolsky, et al. (1975) used a block of fourteen sentences for imitation in their placement test for adults. Baratz (1969) used fifteen sentences in standard English and fifteen in Black nonstandard English. Perkins, Brutten, and Angelis (1986) used twenty-six sentences for repetition in their study with adult second-language English students. The use in an SRT of fifteen sentences is in line with these studies, although no mention was noted in the research reports which argued any optimal number of sentences for a test.

Finally, some research is presented which supports the claim that an SRT, once developed, can be used in all areas where that test language is spoken, regardless of the mother tongue of the test subjects. This is especially true since the emphasis in scoring an SRT is on grammatical and semantic content; 'foreign accent' is taken into account only when it intrudes to the extent of garbling a word.

Drawing upon research conducted over the last two decades on the acquisition of second languages, Dulay, Burt, and Krashen (1982) focus on the kinds of speech language learners produce at each level of acquisition.

> Researchers have learned that the first language has a far smaller effect on second-language syntax than previously thought. Studies show, for example, that only 5 percent of the GRAMMATICAL errors children make and at most 20 percent of the ones adults make can be traced to crossover from the first language. Learners' first languages are no longer believed to interfere with their attempts to acquire second-language grammar. (1982:5, emphasis theirs)

In investigations of cultural and social-group influences on standard English performance, Gallimore and Tharp (1981) cite research that compared the performance of ten American culture/language groups on a standard English repetition test (SERT). Relative performance by the ten groups on twenty-nine grammatical features tested by the repetition measure was examined. It was found that for each group the relative order of difficulty of the grammatical features was the same and the rank-order correlations were uniformly positive and statistically significant. Included in the ten groups were second-language English speakers, native speakers of standard English, and nonstandard-English speakers of various groups. The conclusion drawn was that, "What is difficult for a Hawaiian child is also difficult, in relative terms, for a Pima, and an Asian, and the native speaking Anglo child. The invariant order of item difficulty suggests that whatever the SERT [repetition test] measures about Standard English, it is the same thing for all children, regardless of the cultural/language community in which English is being learned" (1981:385).[29]

4.4 Studies using sentence repetition in dialect testing

In the context of "interdialectal learning", a comment by Sarah Gudschinsky (quoted in Casad 1974:88) focuses on other sociolinguistic purposes for examining sentence repetition, namely, dialect intelligibility testing. She points out that research in psycholinguistics has shown that ability to mimic sentences of a different dialect is dependent upon one's knowledge of both the grammatical structure and the phonological structure of that dialect. One may conjecture, then, that for related dialects the inherent knowledge of these structures would produce the same results as this learned knowledge of unrelated dialects. Indeed, Crawford (cited in Casad 1974:61), in studying Mixe dialects in Mexico, discovered that for highly intelligible dialects, the "sentence repeat" test became so easy that a subject's response seemed more like mimicry than a test of intelligibility. Crawford's response was to drop this test from his battery. Simons (1983:30), however, suggests that this may not be such a liability; rather, it simply indicates that the test is not sensitive enough to distinguish among different degrees of high intelligibility which, he continues, is usually not required anyway. Such statements are reminiscent of the diagnostic versus screening controversy in psycholinguistics, but in this case the 'diagnosis' would be the fine degree of similarity between closely related (intelligible) dialects of the same language. Both Simons and Casad conclude their discussions on this matter with recommendations to investigate sentence

---

[29]Given these views of the language learning process, it can be argued that one SRT developed and calibrated for a given test language can be used without further modification in all the different vernacular areas where that language is spoken. An individual's mother tongue should not make any qualitative difference in his or her performance on an SRT, since performance is related to the amount of the test language the individual has learned. It may be that having a mother tongue similar to the language of wider communication allows one to learn that language more quickly, but this would be a quantitative advantage, not changing the relationship between SRT score and second-language proficiency.

repetition as a method for testing "interdialectal learning" (bilingualism) and "inherent interdialectal intelligibility."

Other studies have used sentence repetition techniques in what could be termed 'dialect' testing. The classic study is that by Baratz (1969) in which she showed that white, standard English-speaking children perform as badly on a sentence repetition test in black nonstandard English as black children perform on a repetition test in standard English. Analysis of error patterns for both groups showed intrusion of the dominant dialect into repetitions of sentences in the nondominant dialect. While the intent of the study was not to assess inherent comprehension between dialects of English nor was the focus directly on assessing the extent of learning of the other dialect, it demonstrates the plausibility of using the sentence repetition technique in assessing proficiency in closely related language varieties.

Politzer, Hoover and Brown reports the results from a repetition test "designed to test ability in both standard and nonstandard Black English as well as the balance between the two" (1975:93). Their results confirmed those of Baratz (1969) in that "speakers of Black nonstandard English will often transform standard to nonstandard in a repetition task." Their methodology was to pause at certain points in a short story for children to repeat key sentences containing the grammatical items in focus.

Additionally, many of the studies reported by Gallimore and Tharp (1981) and indeed even the study by Natalicio and Williams (1971) could be considered to have aspects that deal more with using sentence repetition tests in studying dialect differences than strictly second-language applications.

Although the cited research has employed the sentence repetition technique in dialect-oriented studies, the application of this technique in the current study is limited to questions of second-language proficiency. To utilize SRT as outlined in this manual for dialect intelligibility testing would require significant adaptation and further research. [30]

---

[30]The use of sentence repetition tests for dialect-intelligibility studies (such as described by Casad 1974 or Simons 1983) would be feasible, of course. However, the goals of a dialect-intelligibility study are significantly different than those addressed in this manual. Therefore, the methodology employed in the construction of an intelligibility test and the rationale underlying the scoring of subjects' responses would have to be greatly altered. An additional departure from the methodology as outlined in this manual is that some of the members of the research team, particularly the test scorers, would have to be speakers of the dialects under investigation.

4.5 Summary

This review of the literature on the use of sentence repetition must be seen as only a brief overview; much more has been written. Since the technique has been around and used for so long, it has almost ceased to be the central focus of much research and has become instead a means by which to pursue other questions. Whether dialect dominance or second-language proficiency, whether screening for language disorders or assisting in adult ESL placement or investigating aspects of grammatical acquisition, the phenomenon of sentence repetition as a measure of productive and receptive language skills has been proven and is widely embraced for its practicality, reliability, and validity. The primary aim of this present review has been to establish the fact that sentence repetition is a time-honored technique. The present application to the field study of community-wide bilingualism may not be typical, but it is well supported historically and methodologically.

5
Studies in Reliability and Validity

From its inception, the investigation of the sentence repetition test (SRT) as a tool for bilingualism surveys has been based on several assumptions regarding test content. One assumption was that for each language tested, a fresh set of sentences would have to be elicited. Theoretically, a standard set of sentences could be constructed where each sentence would reflect an increasing level of difficulty of vocabulary used, complexity of grammar, and overall length (keeping within the range of average adult capabilities). This set could then be translated into each language to be tested, thus facilitating standardization across languages and ease of test construction. However, since languages reflect differing world views and thought processes, it is not feasible to construct such a basic set of sentences that could be adequately and consistently translated into each language desired to be tested. Nor could one be sure that a sentence that is more difficult or complex in one language is necessarily more difficult or complex in another. Therefore, the assumption was made that for each language tested, a fresh set of sentences would have to be elicited.

It was further assumed that in order to insure clarity and naturalness in the sentences, they should be extracted from spontaneous texts. This would include those given in response to a specific question or prompt, as well as those selected from such published sources as newspapers or textbooks.

A third assumption was that the person constructing the test most probably would not be a speaker of the test language; therefore, the methods used to elicit sample sentences would have to be designed to prompt the use of a range of complexity and difficulty in the sentences.

The fourth assumption was that an educated mother-tongue speaker of the test language would give the most coherent texts and also be able subsequently to break up that text into sentences. If that mother-tongue speaker also shared a common language with the researcher, he would further be able to give the translation of the sentences, which facilitates selection and subsequent test administration.

Based on these assumptions, a pilot study on the feasibility of repeating sentences as a measure of second-language proficiency was begun and carried out during the first half of 1986 (see Radloff and Marshall). Different techniques were explored for eliciting and selecting sentences for the test. Different avenues were explored for obtaining the necessary external calibrating measure. The final recommendations formed the basis for the field study of SRT, which began in the fall of 1986 and concluded two years later. The conclusions of that initial pilot study presented a step-by-step methodology for test development. The premises of that methodology are three-fold: using actual performance of second-language speakers as the basis for final sentence selection, using a simple mathematical formula to further help in sentence selection, and using the opinions of educated mother-tongue (MT) speakers of the test language as the basis for calibrating an SRT (presented in this report as the Reported Proficiency Evaluation or RPE). Many additional points were tested, refined, kept, or discarded in the field study process reported below.

The first SRT to be developed in the field study was in the Urdu language, the national language of Pakistan and medium of instruction in government schools. The Urdu SRT was the best 'first effort' in carrying out the recommendations from the pilot study.

The second SRT was developed in the Pashto language, which is the *lingua franca* of the Northwest Frontier Province of Pakistan and surrounding tribal territories. The Pashto SRT improved on the Urdu SRT through a more critical discrimination index as a statistical measure for helping in sentence selection. Calibration of the Pashto SRT also showed that a higher correlation between test scores and RPE proficiency ratings was possible.

The third phase of the field study was the revision and recalibration of the Pashto SRT, to the end of making it a more difficult and discriminating test. This revision answered many questions raised through the development of the first two SRTs. The main question was whether or not a more difficult SRT could indeed discriminate between the higher RPE proficiency levels. The answer suggests the affirmative; the revised Pashto SRT appears to clearly distinguish between RPE levels 3+ and 4.

The remainder of the first part of this chapter details the processes that the team of researchers went through to develop each SRT in the field study to its final, calibrated form. Rationale and support for important decisions made during each test which affected the development of the subsequent tests are also given. The latter part of this chapter covers the results of several subsidiary investigations carried out in conjunction with the development of these tests.

5.1 Development of the Urdu SRT

The sample of sentences for the preliminary form of the Urdu SRT (USRT) was taken from a text given by an educated Urdu speaker and from an intermediate textbook in Urdu. This preliminary form, consisting of thirty sentences, was administered to thirty-two second-language speakers of Urdu. They were primarily mother-tongue Pashto speakers, but also included Dari, Chitrali, Baluchi, Hindko, and English speakers. Ages ranged from thirteen to approximately forty-five years. Urdu is primarily learned through education, and nineteen subjects were educated through Urdu medium to at least the third class. Thirteen subjects were included who had not been educated through Urdu; five of them had received no education at all.

The performances of these subjects on the preliminary form of the test were analyzed according to the mathematical formula recommended in the SRT pilot study mentioned above.[31] The fifteen most discriminating sentences were selected on this basis and tape-recorded by an educated mother-tongue Urdu speaker. Preceded by three short, simple practice sentences, the sentences were recorded in increasing order of difficulty. This tape, then, served as test tape for the final form of the Urdu SRT. These eighteen sentences are presented in (61), appendix C.

5.1.1 Urdu calibration—first attempt. In order to calibrate the Urdu SRT, two attempts were made. The first was later not used, for reasons outlined below, but it gave positive direction to subsequent calibrations. In that first calibration attempt, thirty subjects were rated on their Urdu proficiency by high-level proficiency Urdu speakers. They used the proficiency criteria of the reported proficiency evaluation (RPE) as the standard by which to rate their acquaintances (see chapter 6 for the complete methodology). The criteria had been translated into Urdu. In the

---

[31]This mathematical formula subtracts the total of scores on each sentence for the twenty-seven percent of subjects scoring the lowest on the test overall from the total, on that sentence, from the twenty-seven percent scoring the highest. This difference is then divided by the total number of points possible on that sentence for all subjects. The resulting figure is reported to be an index of the ability of that particular sentence to separate higher from lower proficiency level performance. The use of this formula was replaced by the discrimination index as discussed below in §5.2.2. A step-by-step description of how to apply that new discrimination index is provided in §3.4.1.

area of the country where this first calibration attempt was carried out, there were few mother-tongue Urdu speakers; indeed, only one rater was a mother-tongue Urdu speaker. The others were mother-tongue Panjabi and Pashto speakers who had been educated in Urdu medium through college level. The thirty subjects rated by these non-mother-tongue raters were given the final form (fifteen sentences) of the Urdu SRT. The mother tongues of these subjects was primarily either Pashto or Dari.

The results of this calibration were equivocal, for several reasons, and therefore not used. One main reason was that the proficiency ratings made by the non-Urdu mother-tongue raters were probably not as accurate as ratings by actual mother-tongue Urdu speakers would have been. This is probably true especially for subjects with intermediate- and higher-level Urdu proficiency. Another important reason was that the Urdu translation of the proficiency criteria used by these first raters in their evaluations was found to be inaccurate in many places. A third contributing reason could have been that the fieldworker conducting the interviews with the mother-tongue raters was not sufficiently trained, since the methodology was still being developed.

Three major lessons were learned, then, from this first attempt. First, it is worth the effort to conduct the calibration process in an area where mother-tongue speakers of the test language are available. Second, translation of the proficiency criteria to be used by the mother-tongue raters in their evaluations of their second-language acquaintances must be done with care and carefully checked (§5.1.3). And third, training for the fieldworker(s) responsible for interviewing the mother-tongue raters is important (see also §5.3.3 and chapter 6).

5.1.2 Natural conversation-style speed. Another area of concern about this first attempt at calibrating the Urdu SRT was that the mother-tongue Urdu speaker who made the tape recording of the final-form test sentences used a slow, dictation-style manner. It was felt that this unnatural speed might distract from or even interfere with repetition of the sentences. A new recording of the test sentences was made, in which the mother-tongue Urdu speaker used normal conversation speed and natural intonation appropriate to each sentence.

Most of the thirty original subjects were found and administered this re-recorded, conversation-speed Urdu SRT. This was done approximately three months after the initial testing. The scores from this retesting were then compared with the original scores on the dictation-speed test. The scores are displayed in appendix A, (55) and show that for these twenty-seven subjects, the speed of the stimulus sentence made essentially no difference. The correlation between scores on the two different forms of this test is r = .94, signifying that speed of stimulus presentation has almost no effect on test performance.[32]

The concerns that the dictation-speed stimuli would be distracting or interfering were not supported. However, it was felt that presenting test sentences at a normal, conversational rate with natural intonation was more acceptable to test participants, especially educated ones or those with greater fluency in the test language. It is also interesting to note that fluent speakers of Urdu would repeat back the dictation-speed sentences at a normal, or faster than normal rate of speed. They would also introduce normal intonation patterns into their repetition that were not present in the stimuli. Therefore, for reasons of acceptability, normal conversational speed with natural intonation was set as the standard for tape-recording test sentences.

5.1.3 Translation of the RPE proficiency criteria. Before attempting to calibrate the Urdu SRT the second time, the RPE proficiency criteria, used by the mother-tongue raters in their evaluations, were retranslated into Urdu from English (see §5.1.1). This was accomplished by a committee consisting of the fieldworkers responsible for conducting the interviews with the RPE mother-tongue raters and two of the researchers. The resulting translation was of good quality. The back translation of this Urdu translation is presented as the expansion of the more telegraphic original criteria in §6.5.

An important side effect of this translation effort was that the field workers emerged with an excellent understanding of the gradations between the different proficiency descriptions and so better understood the task. It was determined to include translating the proficiency criteria into the language of the mother-tongue raters as an integral step in the training of those responsible for conducting RPE interviews in the future. See §6.3.1, regarding training the field workers.

5.1.4 Urdu calibration—second attempt. The second attempt to calibrate the Urdu SRT was carried out in an area where more mother-tongue speakers of the test language actually live. This allowed the trained fieldworker to contact a much wider sample for the calibration process. The fieldworker guided fifteen mother-tongue Urdu raters as they assigned RPE proficiency ratings to seventy-two of their acquaintances, who were primarily mother-tongue Panjabi speakers. These seventy-two subjects were then administered the final fifteen-sentence form of the Urdu SRT.

---

[32]This comparison can also be viewed as test-retest RELIABILITY. In this light, the test shows high reliability with r = .94. See §5.3.7 and discussion in chapter 4.

The scattergram showing the correlation between the RPE ratings and Urdu SRT scores for the seventy-two subjects is presented in (32). Examination shows that while there is a wide scatter at the top of the chart, overall a pattern emerges whereby subjects given a lower proficiency rating by the mother-tongue raters also scored lower on the Urdu SRT, and those given a medium-proficiency rating scored in the medium range on the Urdu SRT. The same trend is true for the upper range, though the wide scatter masks it somewhat and creates a somewhat sizable margin of error as well (standard error of estimate or SEE = 14.09). Still, the correlation coefficient of $r = .71$ was satisfactory for this first attempt at developing and calibrating an SRT, and this Urdu SRT is currently used in bilingualism surveys.

The ranges of Urdu SRT scores corresponding to the different RPE levels were figured following the procedure outlined in §3.4.7. They are presented below in (33). In the RPE, the mother-tongue raters assign proficiency ratings which are then converted into proficiency levels ranging from 0+ to 4+ (see §6.1.1 for more discussion on the RPE levels). For this calibration of the Urdu SRT, over ten subjects were rated at each of the highest levels of Urdu proficiency, that is, RPE levels 3+, 4, and 4+. However, these subjects all appeared to perform at about the same level on the Urdu SRT. It was therefore determined that this test does not discriminate between these three highest proficiency levels. Accordingly, the highest equivalent RPE level assignable from performance on the Urdu SRT is '3+ & up'[33] (see (33)).

The question naturally arose at this point if ANY SRT could discriminate between these highest RPE levels. As mentioned above, this question was ultimately answered in the affirmative in the third phase of the field study. Meanwhile, different reasons were proffered as to why the performance curve on the Urdu SRT 'flattened out' at the highest levels, and different suggestions made for avoiding it in future s. The primary solution offered was to make the test more difficult, but other suggestions like increasing the scope of behaviors counted during the test, such as keeping track of

---

[33]Bilingualism survey field projects using the present Urdu SRT to investigate community levels of proficiency in that language, report proficiency in half levels up through RPE level 3, then report 'level 3+ and above' for those sections of the population scoring above 36 points, the cut-off level on the Urdu SRT. See Rensch (1988), for a case study, and chapter 6 for descriptions of RPE levels.

Studies in Reliability and Validity

(32) RPE ratings with scores on the final form Urdu SRT, used for calibration of the Urdu SRT

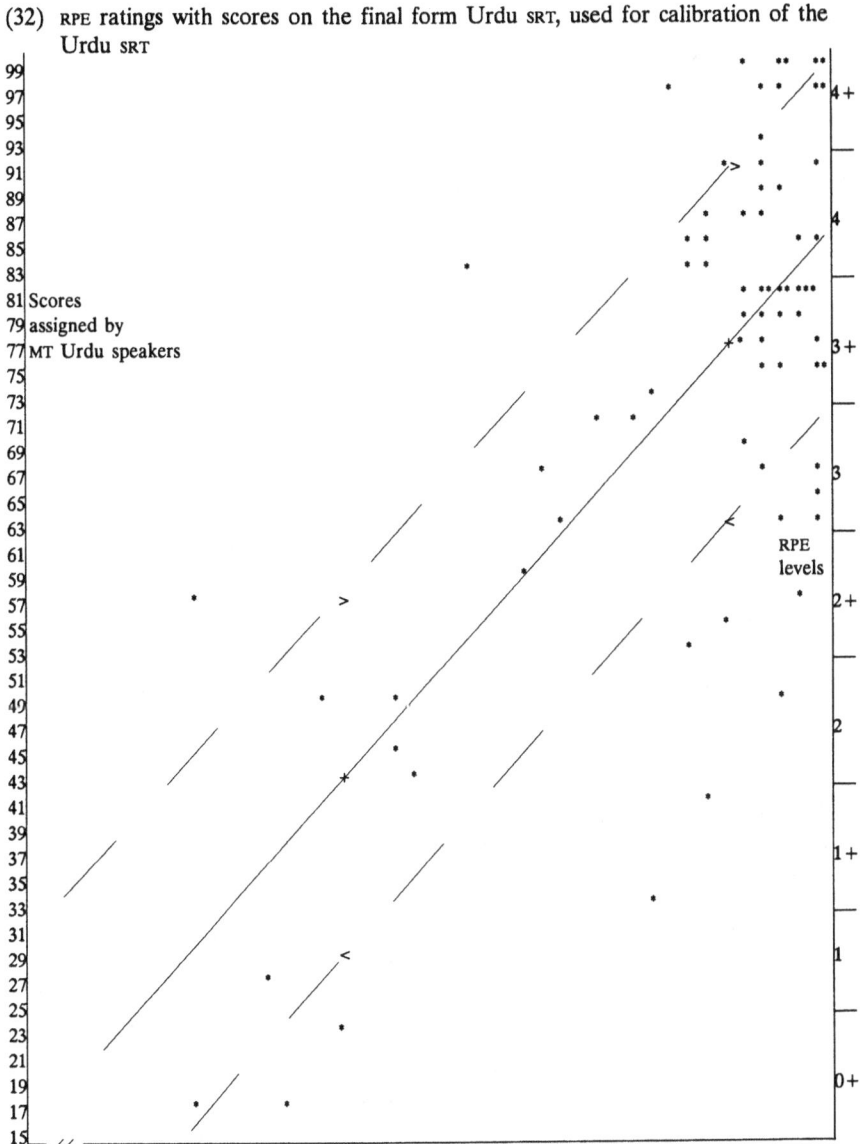

+ = Connect points for regression line   > = Connect points for top SEE line
< = Connect points for bottom SEE line
Correlation coefficient r = .71417019   SEE $S_{y,x}$ = 14.087391   n = 72
Line of regression for RPE score/level (Y) = 12.162616 + 1.618528 * SRT score (X)

'fluency of reponse', were also made.[34] Since the development of the Pashto SRT was almost parallel with that of the Urdu SRT, investigation of possible remedies was left for the revision of the Pashto SRT, phase three of the field study.

(33)   Score ranges on Urdu SRT corresponding to RPE levels

USRT	=	RPE
37 & up	=	3+ & up
31–36	=	3
25–30	=	2+
19–24	=	2
13–18	=	1+
9–12	=	1
2–8	=	0+

5.2 Development of the Pashto SRT

Sentences for the preliminary form of the Pashto SRT were obtained from oral texts elicited from both educated and uneducated mother-tongue Pashto speakers of the Yusufzai dialect. Yusufzai is recognized as the standard dialect of Pashto in Pakistan and is taught as a subject in many parts of the Northwest Frontier Province.

5.2.1 An early form. Initially, the preliminary form of the Pashto SRT (PSRT) was given to a group of twenty-six people. Eleven sentences were selected on the basis of their performances for inclusion in the test.

---

[34]During the revision of the Pashto SRT (see §5.3, below), an attempt was made to score for 'fluency of response' in addition to scoring for verbatim repetition as a possible means for further discriminating different levels of proficiency. This attempt was made because it had been observed that higher-level proficiency speakers of the test language repeated the test sentences at the same rate that they were presented or even faster. Speakers at lower proficiency levels tended to repeat the sentences more slowly than the recorded stimulus and hesitated more. The fieldworker responsible for administering the preliminary form revised Pashto s found that he could not score each reponse for fluency and still pay adequate attention to the accuracy of the repetition. He did, however, assign an overall 'fluency' rating to each subject according to his or her observed fluency while taking the test and in the general conversation which preceded and followed it. While these 'fluency' ratings did correspond quite nicely to the subject's performance on the revised Pashto SRT, they were eventually not used. This was because increased sentence difficulty alone was sufficient to separate out the different proficiency levels. See the discussion in §5.3.6 and also the fluency ratings in (60), appendix A.

The mathematical formula from the pilot study (see §5.1) was used in the selection process. When subsequent use of this early test showed that it was quite 'easy', suspicions were confirmed that this early group contained mainly subjects with lower proficiency levels in Pashto. In other words, since the sample did not include higher level speakers, the more difficult sentences were eliminated as being 'nondiscriminatory', and only those sentences challenging the ability level of the lower level speakers were retained.

This, of course, necessitated making a different form of the test, but it also taught a good lesson: it is necessary to have subjects from the full spectrum of proficiency levels in the group taking the preliminary form of an SRT. An additional lesson learned in phase three of the field study but applicable here, is to first obtain the proficiency ratings on a group of subjects and then administer the preliminary form of an SRT to them. This way the researcher knows the proficiency levels present among the group of subjects and sentences selected for the final form of the test should discriminate between them.

5.2.2 A new discrimination index. Another source of dissatisfaction with this early form of the Pashto SRT was that the performances of the subjects on the preliminary form sentences were analyzed according to the mathematical formula carried over from the pilot study of SRT and described above in the discussion of the Urdu SRT (§5.1.1). It was felt that this formula could too easily render skewed results if too many subjects with very high or very low proficiency were included. It also did not include the performance of subjects with intermediate proficiency in the calculations. Therefore, a new discrimination index was developed.

The new discrimination index was developed specifically for the purpose of selecting sentences for an SRT. It was inspired by analogy to the Kendall W correlation coefficient described by Casad (1974:177). By using a formula similar to that, the new discrimination index compares the subjects' overall performances (on all preliminary form sentences) with their performances on each individual sentence, and selects the sentences which are the most consistent with the overall performances. The discussion in §3.4.1 gives step-by-step instructions in how to use this discrimination index.

5.2.3 The final form. Nine sentences from the original texts elicited from mother-tongue Pashto speakers were added to the eleven sentences of the early form of the Pashto SRT. The performances of seventy-nine second-language speakers of Pashto[35] on these twenty sentences were analyzed according to the new discrimination index. Fifteen sentences were selected on this basis as being the most discriminating and thus chosen for the final form of the Pashto SRT. Preceded by three simple practice sentences, these sentences were placed in increasing order of difficulty according to the difficulty level (see §3.4.2) and tape-recorded by a mother-tongue speaker of Yusufzai Pashto. This tape, then, comprised the test tape for the final form of the Pashto SRT. These eighteen sentences are listed in (62), appendix C.

5.2.4 Calibration. For the calibration of the Pashto SRT, the RPE technique was again used. Each of five mother-tongue Pashto raters evaluated second-language speakers of Pashto with whom they were well acquainted. Guided in these evaluations by the trained fieldworker, the mother-tongue raters used the retranslated proficiency criteria in their evaluations (see §5.1.3). Thirty-seven of the people rated were contacted in order to give the Pashto SRT to them. These subjects were primarily Hindko and Chitrali speakers, with a few speakers of Dari and Uzbeki. These thirty-seven subjects were each administered the final form of the Pashto SRT by the same trained fieldworker who had guided the mother-tongue raters in the RPE.

In the RPE methodology the mother-tongue raters initially assign letter ratings to the subjects in each of five skill areas. These letter ratings are subsequently converted into RPE proficiency level equivalents (see chapter 6 for a detailed description of the RPE methodology). While the fieldworker wrote down each rating as the mother-tongue rater gave it, the total RPE score for each subject was generally added up and the RPE proficiency level equivalent was determined by the researcher. Also, the fieldworker administered and scored the Pashto SRTs, but the researcher added up the total Pashto SRT score for each subject. This is not necessarily part of the recommended design of calibrating an SRT, but it does help show that any potential bias of the fieldworker was minimized.

A scattergram showing the correlation between the RPE ratings and the Pashto SRT scores for the thirty-seven subjects is presented in (34). Examination shows a much narrower scatter than for the Urdu SRT, which leads to a higher correlation coefficient, $r = .90$ and a lower margin of error (SEE) of 8.69 points on the scale of RPE raw scores.

Several reasons were suggested for this tighter correlation, one being the fact that the sentences selected for the Pashto SRT were done so on the

---

[35]These seventy-nine subjects had a wide variety of mother tongues, including Hindko, Chitrali, Dari, Uzbeki, English, Bateri, and Duberi Kohistani.

(34) RPE ratings with scores on the final form original Pashto SRT, used for calibration of the original Pashto SRT

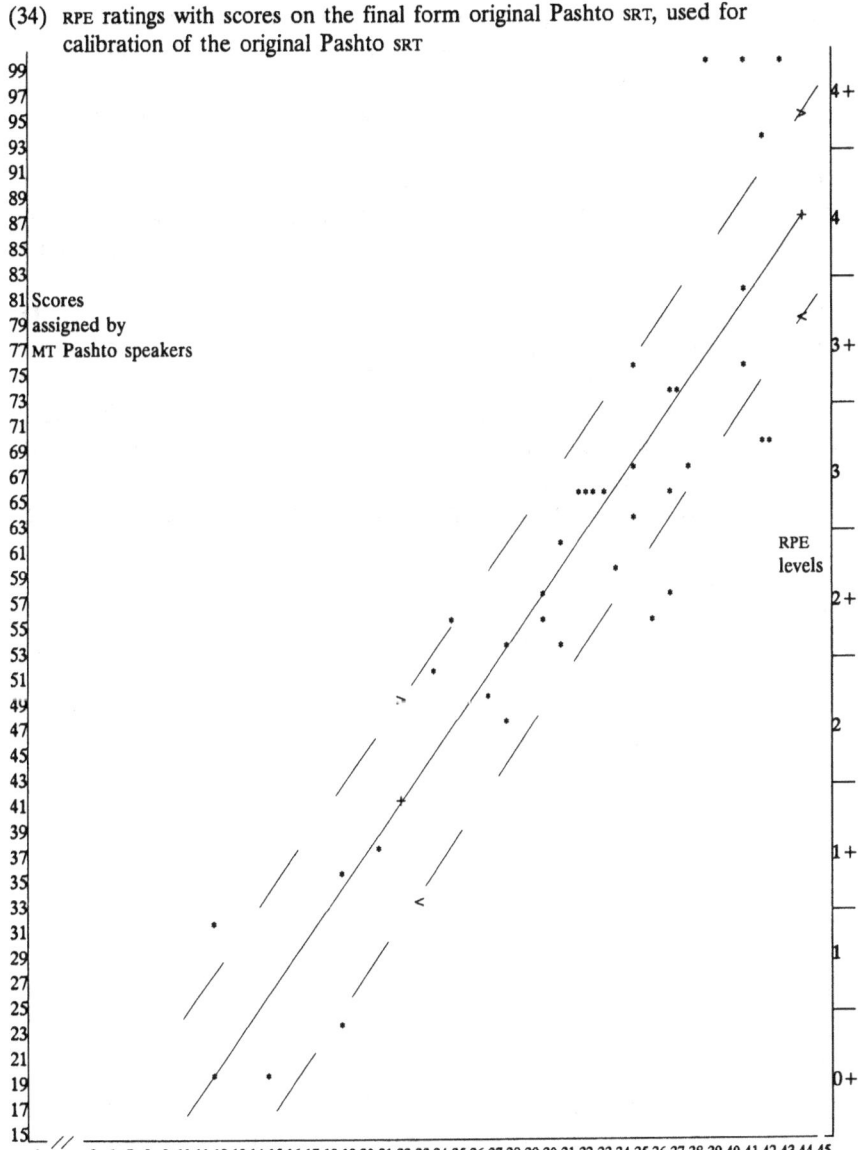

+ = Connect points for regression line   > = Connect points for top SEE line
< = Connect points for bottom SEE line
Correlation coefficient r = .8967272   SEE $S_{y,x}$ = 8.69318   n = 37
Line of regression for RPE score/level (Y) = -5.0325 + 2.08957 * SRT score (X)

basis of the new discrimination index. This should have resulted in a more discriminating test. Another important reason may be that the fieldworker responsible for conducting the RPE interviews with the mother-tongue Pashto raters was more careful to follow standard procedures for that technique than was the fieldworker who did the RPE interviews with the mother-tongue Urdu raters. While this is conjecture in the case of the Urdu SRT, a documented case of the importance of adhering to the standard procedures of the RPE is shown in the revision of the Pashto SRT, presented in §5.3.3 below.

Examination of (34) also shows the same 'flattening out' of the scatter of scores at the highest levels of proficiency, a similar phenomenon to that observed in the Urdu SRT. However, it can be seen that the flattening out is less than on the Urdu SRT; this may be due to the new discrimination index for sentence selection or better RPE procedures. Still, second-language Pashto-speaking subjects rated at RPE proficiency levels 3+, 4, and 4+ all appeared to score similarly on the Pashto SRT. Therefore, it was determined that this test does not discriminate between these three highest proficiency levels. As in the Urdu SRT, the highest equivalent RPE level assignable from performance on the Pashto SRT is '3+ & up'. Table (35) lists the ranges of Pashto SRT scores corresponding to the different RPE levels.

(35) Score ranges on original Pashto SRT corresponding to RPE levels

PSRT	=	RPE
37 & up	=	3+ & up
33–36	=	3
28–32	=	2+
23–27	=	2
18–22	=	1+
14–17	=	1
10–13	=	0+

As with the Urdu SRT, it was hypothesized that the Pashto SRT was not difficult enough to discriminate between the highest RPE levels. The sentences were selected on the basis of the performance of a group of subjects whose RPE proficiency levels were not known. Perhaps these subjects were only at the intermediate and lower levels of proficiency in Pashto. If that were the case, it would stand to reason that the sentences would not be difficult enough to separate out the performances of the higher-level speakers included in the calibrating group. Accordingly, it was decided to revise the Pashto SRT, to introduce new, more complex and longer sentences into the test and to administer this new preliminary form to subjects whose proficiency in Pashto had been previously rated according to the RPE technique. The process and results of this revision are described later in §5.3.

5.2.5 Mother-tongue Pashto performance. As a check on different factors that might influence performance on an SRT, this Pashto SRT, hereafter referred to as the 'original Pashto SRT', was administered to thirty-three mother-tongue Pashto speakers of the Yusufzai dialect with whom good personal contact had been established. The range of ages for these subjects was from fourteen to fifty-seven years of age, and years of education ranged from none to fourteen. The highest possible score on the Pashto SRT is forty-five points. The scores of these mother-tongue Pashto subjects ranged from thirty-eight to forty-five, or eighty-four to one hundred percent correct, with a mean score of forty-two points or ninety-three percent correct. As would be expected, these mother-tongue speakers did not all score perfectly, demonstrating that the Pashto SRT discriminates a range of proficiency. But they all scored very well, above the cut-off level for second-language speakers with RPE proficiency level 3+ and above. This adds to the validity of the SRT and demonstrates that the Pashto SRT is indeed a challenging test. Second-language speakers who score above the level indicated can be said to have a 'good' level of proficiency in that language. This data is included in the discussion on a screening test for the SRT presented below in §5.5, which presents a more elaborated discussion of factors affecting SRT performance. See also §3.4.11 for further discussion on control testing an SRT.

5.3 Development of the revised Pashto SRT

As referred to several times above, the revision of the Pashto SRT was undertaken in an effort to answer questions raised during the development of the Urdu and Pashto SRTs. The primary question was, Can an SRT discriminate between the higher RPE proficiency levels?

Pursuit of the answer to this question followed two main avenues. One was in the selection of more difficult sentences for the test, including those whose complexity and length would challenge the ability of an educated mother-tongue speaker of the test language. The second was to select the sentences on the basis of performance of second-language speakers whose RPE proficiency level in Pashto was known.

5.3.1 Using educated mother-tongue speakers. A secondary reason for revising the Pashto SRT was to replace certain sentences in the test. Some of the sentences elicited for use in the original Pashto SRT came from a text by an uneducated barber, who talked about his work. Four sentences describing different aspects of barbering were chosen to be included in the final fifteen sentences on the basis of their discrimination index. The educated mother-tongue speakers who helped screen sentences for the preliminary form evidently found nothing wrong with these sentences. However, as the test was used in the field situation, these four sentences were found to be a source of ridicule from people taking the test, particulary educated subjects. It seems that barbering is a low social status profession, and talk about shaving and haircuts is inappropriate for such an 'important' thing as research. Therefore, since the Pashto SRT was to be revised, replacing these four sentences became a secondary goal.

The lesson learned from this is to make sure to use educated mother-tongue speakers in the initial stages of collecting the sample of sentences for the preliminary form of an SRT, as well as checking the acceptability of sentences. This helps to ensure that the prestige form of the language is used in the test sentences and that the sentences have wide acceptability.

5.3.2 The preliminary form. A number of long sentences with a greater perceived complexity of structure were selected from Pashto newspapers and elicited from educated mother-tongue speakers of Pashto. Some of these were eliminated on the advice of other educated mother-tongue speakers. The rest were tape-recorded and played for a few other educated mother-tongue speakers. Those sentences were eliminated which, because of length, were totally beyond their ability to repeat. The fifteen sentences of the original Pashto SRT and these new sentences were tape-recorded and played for six mother-tongue Pashto speakers. On the basis of their performance some of the longer sentences were eliminated and several 'easy' and 'medium' sentences (also elicited from educated mother-tongue speakers) were added. The resultant twelve new sentences and the original fifteen sentences, with three new short practice sentences, were again tape-recorded and presented, along with their transcription, to a Pashto scholar. This gentleman corrected some of the Pashto script spelling and eliminated one sentence as unsuitable.

A new tape recording was then made by a mother-tongue speaker of Yusufzai Pashto to be used as the preliminary form of the revised Pashto SRT (RPSRT) for calibration purposes. This preliminary form revised Pashto SRT test tape consisted of the three new short practice sentences, then the fifteen original Pashto SRT sentences, and then the eleven new sentences ordered by length and perceived complexity, giving a total of twenty-nine sentences. These twenty-nine sentences are presented in (62) and (63) of appendix C.

5.3.3 Revised Pashto SRT calibration—first attempt. The RPE technique (see chapter 6) was used for the calibration of the revised Pashto SRT. Eighteen mother-tongue Yusufzai Pashto speakers rated their second-language Pashto acquaintances' proficiency. The trained fieldworker guided these mother-tongue raters in their evaluation, but the final scores and level equivalents were figured by the researcher in an attempt to minimize any bias on the fieldworker's part. This same fieldworker was able to contact forty-nine of the mother-tongue raters' acquaintances and administer the preliminary form of the revised Pashto SRT to them.

As the data for this new preliminary test were plotted, a much wider scatter for the scores was observed than had been seen for the original Pashto SRT. A scattergram showing the RPE ratings plotted against scores on the preliminary form of the revised Pashto SRT is presented in (36). The correlation coefficient for this data was $r = .65$ and the standard error of estimate was 12.16, both quite different from the original Pashto SRT. Scores for the preliminary form of the revised Pashto SRT and, what turned out to be, the INCOMPLETE PROCEDURE RPE ratings are listed in table (58) of appendix A.

In an effort to ascertain a possible cause for these differences, the fieldworker responsible for collecting the data was interviewed in depth about the procedures he was following. It was discovered that he was following all the standard procedures for administering the SRT and also for the RPE—except one. The training he had been given for collecting the data for this new study had not emphasized enough the need for the mother-tongue rater, in the RPE process, to RANK the ratees for each skill area before assigning the rating for that area, so this step was not being done (see §6.3.2). The mother-tongue raters were assigning proficiency levels in each skill area just as they came up, without any framework to work in. The result was that the ratings thus assigned through this INCOMPLETE RPE procedure were more arbitrary than had been the case for the original Pashto SRT. And this arbitrariness resulted in the wider scatter of results shown in (36).

The decision was made to start over and find new mother-tongue raters and ask them to rate their second-language Pashto acquaintances according to the correct RPE procedure. The correct RPE procedure is to first familiarize the mother-tongue rater with the proficiency criteria for the skill area, then have him RANK his acquaintances according to their perceived proficiency in that area, then have him RATE each of them on the criteria for that skill area (see also §6.3.2).

5.3.4 Revised Pashto SRT calibration—second attempt. The fieldworker, using this complete RPE procedure, guided twenty-three educated mother-tongue

(36) Scores on the preliminary form revised Pashto SRT (twenty-nine sentences), with INCOMPLETE PROCEDURE RPE ratings

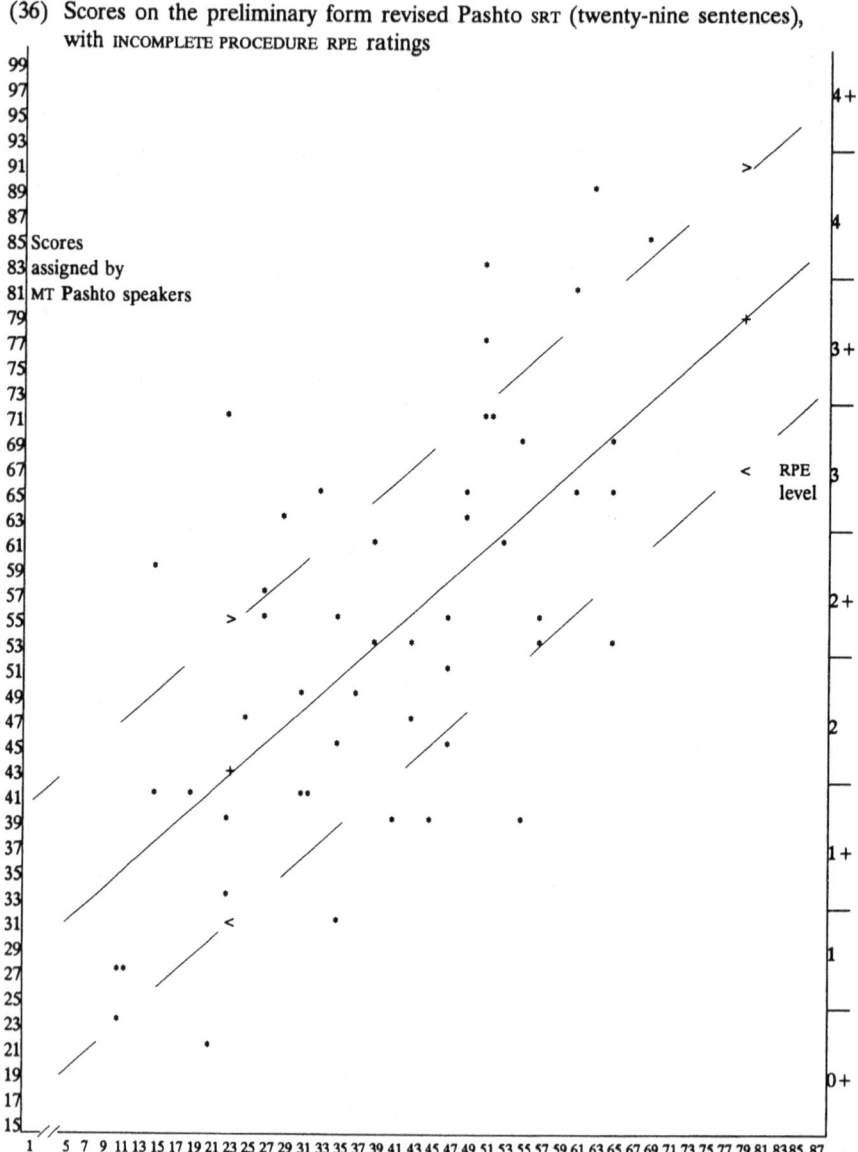

+ = Connect points for regression line   > = Connect points for top SEE line
< = Connect points for bottom SEE line
Correlation coefficient r = .6506638   SEE $S_{y,x}$ = 12.1638   n = 49
Line of regression for RPE score/level (Y) = 28.2255 + .641523 * SRT score (X)

Studies in Reliability and Validity

(37) Scores on the preliminary form revised Pashto SRT (twenty-nine sentences), with CORRECT PROCEDURE RPE ratings

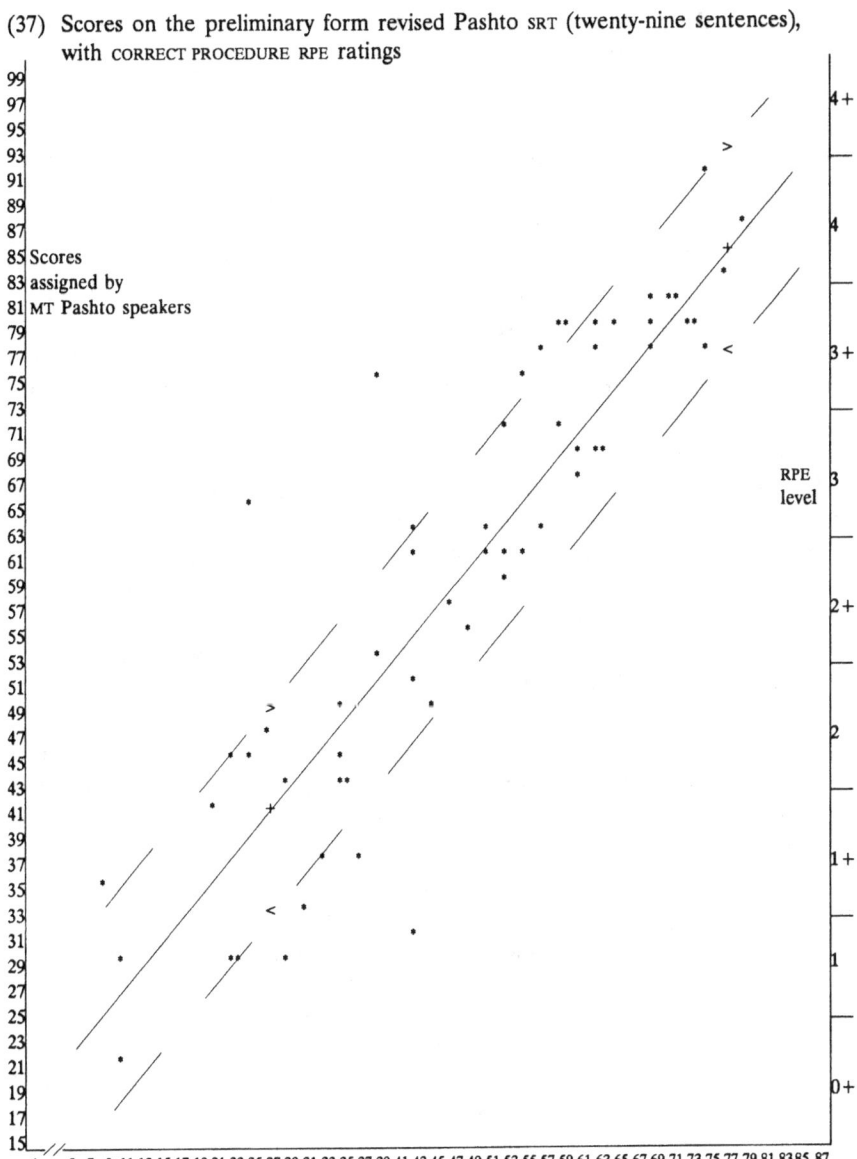

+ = Connect points for regression line   > = Connect points for top SEE line
< = Connect points for bottom SEE line
Correlation coefficient r = .901914   SEE $S_{y,x}$ = 7.852499   n = 58
Line of regression for RPE score/level (Y) = 17.4953 + .878015 * SRT score (X)

speakers of the standard dialect of Pashto in the evaluation of their second-language Pashto-speaking acquaintances, each mother-tongue rater usually rating three people. Fifty-eight subjects evaluated by these new mother-tongue Pashto raters, according to the correct RPE procedure, were contacted and given the preliminary (twenty-nine-sentence) form of the revised Pashto SRT. These subjects were primarily mother-tongue speakers of Hindko, Panjabi, and Gujari.

The relationship between these correct procedure RPE ratings and the scores on the preliminary form of the revised Pashto SRT for these 58 subjects is shown in the scattergram in (37). The correlation between these scores is $r = .90$ and $SEE = 7.85$, a striking difference from the correlation for the incomplete procedure RPE shown in (36). Scores on the preliminary form revised Pashto SRT and CORRECT PROCEDURE RPE ratings are listed in (59), appendix A.

It appears that ranking their acquaintances before rating them gives the mother-tongue rater a framework within which he can more accurately assign a proficiency rating. By keeping in mind that one acquaintance is more proficient than another and a third is somewhere in between, a more accurate placement of all three on the scale of proficiency can be made. This is an important finding and confirms the methodology for the RPE which is described in detail in §6.3.2 and supported by the literature, §6.2.1.

5.3.5 Selection of sentences for the final form. The test results for these fifty-eight subjects were analyzed to obtain the difficulty level (DL) and discrimination index (DI) for each of the twenty-nine sentences on the preliminary form of the revised Pashto SRT (see §3.4). Based on these two calculations, fifteen sentences were selected for the final form of the revised Pashto SRT, and three easy sentences were selected for practice sentences. Added consideration was given to sentence content, and the four sentences concerning barber topics, mentioned above, were eliminated. Quality of the tape recording and other factors also resulted in the elimination of some sentences. Table (38) presents the difficulty levels and discrimination indexes for the twenty-nine sentences of the preliminary form, along with the final test form numbers for sentences selected and the reasons for not selecting certain other sentences.

Extracted test scores (see §3.4.4 for description) were obtained for each of the fifty-eight subjects by adding up the points correct for the fifteen sentences chosen for the final form. These extracted test scores were correlated with the total points scores of the RPE rating according to the statistical formulas described in §3.4. Results show a very high correlation between the final form revised Pashto SRT scores and the RPE ratings of $r = .91$, signifying a very dependable relationship between the two measures.

Studies in Reliability and Validity

(38) Rationale for selection of sentences, final-form revised Pashto SRT

Prelim. number *	(DI)	(DL)	Final number	Reason for rejecting sentence
1	8	.06	P2	
P1	14	.09	P1	
16	20	.18	P3	
2	26	.21	1	
3	20	.22	2	
P3	26	.28	x	tricky vocabulary
4	30	.28	3	
5	26	.29	X	"barber"
6	24	.29	x	"barber"
P2	28	.32	4	
7	30	.32	x	hesitation in recording
10	30	.33	5	
19	44	.41	x	high DI
9	36	.44	6	
18	36	.44	7	
8	36	.47	8	
12	30	.47	x	"barber"
11	24	.53	x	"barber"
13	26	.56	9	
21	37	.56	10	high DI
14	28	.58	11	
20	24	.59	12	
24	30	.65	13	
17	34	.66	14	
23	22	.70	15	
25	40	.71	x	high DI
15	30	.75	x	potentially offensive
26	26	.78	x	too difficult
22	20	.83	x	too difficult

* Preliminary form sentence numbers 1–15 are the original Pashto SRT sentences.

The square of this figure, or its coefficient of determination (Oller 1979:70; Woods, et al. 1986:168), means that observed variation in RPE ratings accounts for eighty-three percent of the observed variation in revised Pashto SRT scores, an encouraging result. In other words, it can be

(39) RPE ratings with extracted scores on the revised Pashto SRT, used for calibration of the final form revised Pashto SRT

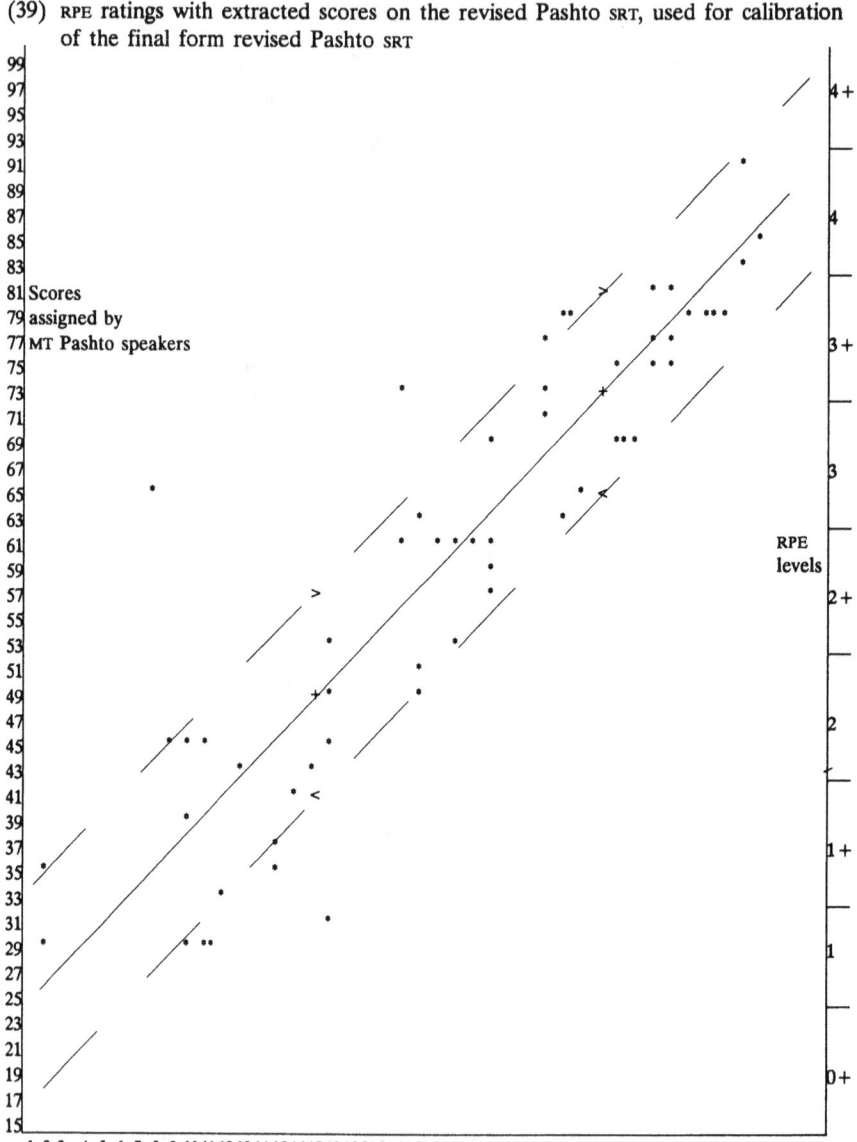

+ = Connect points for regression line   > = Connect points for top SEE line
< = Connect points for bottom SEE line
Correlation coefficient r = .90635   SEE $S_{y,x}$ = 7.681819   n = 58
Line of regression for RPE score/level (Y) = 23.6723 + 1.49929 * SRT score (X)

Studies in Reliability and Validity

said on this basis that eighty-three percent of the variance in Pashto SRT scores is explained by the variance in the RPE scores.[36] The margin of error (SEE) for predicting an RPE score from performance on the revised Pashto SRT is 7.68 points on the RPE rating scale.

A scattergram of each subject's extracted final form revised Pashto SRT score plotted against his or her RPE rating is presented in (39). The line of regression has been plotted, as have the lines for the margin of error. Results of the statistical procedures, as given above, are listed at the bottom of the figure. The extracted revised Pashto SRT scores and the RPE ratings are presented in (60), appendix A.

The range of scores on the revised Pashto SRT that correspond to each of the RPE proficiency levels is presented in (40). These ranges were determined according to the procedures described in §3.4.7. As the revised Pashto SRT is used in actual field application, the scores of the members of the community being studied can be compared to these ranges and the equivalent RPE level for each individual can be determined. The composite of these scores would give a profile of the second-language proficiencies of that community. Case studies illustrating such use of RPE level equivalents are presented in chapter 2.

(40)   Score ranges on revised Pashto SRT corresponding to RPE levels

SRT	=	RPE
40–45	=	4
33–39	=	3+
26–32	=	3
20–25	=	2+
13–19	=	2
6–12	=	1+
2–5	=	1
0–1	=	0+

5.3.6 Discriminating between RPE levels 3+ and 4. Examination of (39) clearly suggests that this revised Pashto SRT can discriminate between performances of RPE level 3+ proficiency and those of RPE level 4 proficiency, as rated by educated mother-tongue speakers of Pashto. Considerable effort was devoted to finding subjects who would be rated at RPE

---

[36]The square of the simple correlation between two tests is an unbiased estimate of their variance overlap. It is an index of the amount of variance that they have in common. The technical term for the square of the correlation is the coefficient of determination. Correlations are not compared linearly, but rather by their squares. (Oller 1979:56, 70)

level 4 or 4+, but only the three shown were found. The consequence of these many attempts is revealed in the presence of a greater proportion of people rated at RPE level 3+ than at the other levels (twenty-eight percent of total). The fact that this 'loading' at level 3+ did not skew the results is evident in the configuration of the scattergram. As can be seen, the data presents a rather narrow scatter, with only a few cases where people were either rated higher or lower than their revised Pashto SRT performance indicated,[37] a fact which leads to the high coefficient of correlation and the low margin of error. The most probable reason for the difficulty in finding second-language speakers of Pashto who function at RPE level 4 and 4+ is that Pashto proficiency is acquired casually by people. Pashto is actually taught as a subject in the government schools only in the lower grades, if at all, so an educated standard of grammar or vocabulary is difficult to acquire. Subjects who were rated at RPE level 4 either had relatives who were Pashto speakers, and thus spent much time talking Pashto with them, or had a prolonged, intense exposure to the language by living in a Pashto-speaking neighborhood, even though they spoke another language in their homes.

The important factor, underlined in this study, is not so much how many people cluster at each proficiency level, but rather the fact that each proficiency level is represented in the calibration, especially those at the two extremes. Since the application of an SRT is statistically determined, it is necessary that the full range of proficiency levels be present in the calculations so that the results can be fully applied. In other words, had there been no subjects rated at RPE level 4, no statement could have been made about the ability of an SRT to discriminate between RPE levels 3+ and 4.

Examination of the configuration of the scattergram for this revision, (39), gives insights into the configuration of the scattergram for the calibration of the original Pashto SRT, shown in (34). Even though the correlation

---

[37]Those subjects whose performance fell outside the lines of the standard error of estimate in (39) may have either been rated too high or too low by the mother-tongue raters or may not have performed at their ability level on the revised Pashto SRT. Results discussed in §5.4, show that performance of uneducated subjects may be adversely affected by suspicion if they are not properly introduced to test administrators. Additionally, observation has suggested that expatriates actively studying the test language do not generally perform well on an SRT, presumably due to test-taking anxiety. People who learn the test language casually, which is the norm in many multilingual cultures, do not appear to manifest any such anxiety. Also, the fact that an SRT is a brief test presents the possibility that sudden interruptions could affect performance. The few cases of these 'outliers', however, show that such factors evidently have minimal effect.

coefficients for the two calibrations are almost identical (original PSRT r = .90, RPSRT r = .91) and the margin of error for the two is similar (original PSRT SEE = 8.69, RPSRT SEE = 7.68), only the revised Pashto SRT is able to discriminate between RPE levels 3+ and 4. The configuration of the scattergrams shows that the original Pashto SRT was not difficult enough, and thus people rated at RPE level 3+ were able to repeat the sentences with basically the same accuracy as people rated at RPE level 4+. The leveling off of the angle of increase of the data at the upper end illustrates this.[38] Merely by ensuring that more difficult sentences were part of the test, however, resulted in a configuration of data that continued to rise without flattening out as seen in (39).

The conclusion to be drawn from this is that the configuration of the scattergram of the final fifteen sentences in any calibration should be considered along with the difficulty level and discrimination index in selecting the sentences for the final form of an SRT. In other words, the difficulty level and the discrimination index are the initial means by which sentences are selected. But if the configuration of the scattergram shows a flattening out of scores, some more difficult sentences should be included in the final fifteen test sentences.

Another important factor was that for the original Pashto SRT, the discrimination index and difficulty level were done on the basis of performance by one group of subjects and the calibration with the RPE ratings on another. In the revised Pashto SRT all aspects were done with the same subjects. This is the preferred procedure. The difficulty with doing the difficulty level and discrimination index based on the responses of subjects for whom there is no RPE proficiency rating is that the researcher does not know what their performance means. Evidently the subjects for the original Pashto SRT were generally of a lower and intermediate proficiency level, because the sentences selected (by difficulty level and discrimination index) based on their performances were too easy to discriminate between RPE levels 3+ and 4. The fact that subjects rated at RPE level 4+ were included in the calibration with the RPE could not raise the discrimination, since the sentences had already been selected. This resulted in the 'flattening out' in the upper ranges of the original Pashto SRT seen in (34). Therefore, the recommended methodology for test development in §3.3, specifying that all aspects of the calibration and sentence selection be done with the same subjects, is confirmed.

---

[38]It is proposed that a flattening out of the data at the lower end would signify a similar interpretation—there are too many easy sentences in the test, and people with a lower proficiency are able to repeat too many of the sentences with the same accuracy as people with higher proficiency.

One additional observation on the comparison between the original Pashto SRT and the revised Pashto SRT would be the evidence it gives for REPLICABILITY. The fieldworker who collected the data for the original Pashto SRT calibration was different from the fieldworker who was responsible for the revised Pashto SRT calibration data collection. Yet, both tests show a similar, very high correlation between test scores and calibrating proficiency ratings ($r = .90$ and $r = .91$) and a low SEE (8.69 and 7.68 RPE raw points). It will be interesting to see the extent of this replicability as new SRTs are developed and calibrated with RPE in other language groups and countries.

5.3.7 Checking reliability. The purpose of the calibration of an SRT is to allow the prediction of proficiency levels from the SRT scores. This procedure had already been completed successfully ($r = .90$) for the original Pashto SRT as reported in §5.2, above. A good reliability check on those predicted proficiency levels would be to compare them with actual proficiency levels as assigned by other mother-tongue raters. The calibration of the revised Pashto SRT provided the opportunity for this type of check.

As was previously described in §5.3.2, the fifteen sentences of the original Pashto SRT were part of the twenty-nine sentences for the preliminary form of the revised Pashto SRT. Fifty-eight subjects participating in the calibration of the revised Pashto SRT were given this preliminary form of the test and were also assigned actual RPE proficiency levels by mother-tongue raters. The score for each subject on just the fifteen sentences of the original test was calculated (forty-five possible points). This score for each subject was then compared to the chart of range of scores on the original Pashto SRT, as shown in (35) above, to obtain the PREDICTED RPE proficiency level for each subject. This predicted level was then compared with the ACTUAL RPE proficiency level assigned by the mother-tongue rater. The results of this comparison are presented in (41).

As can been seen in (41), for eighty-one percent of the fifty-eight subjects the predicted RPE level was within one-half level of the actual RPE level assigned to them by the mother-tongue raters.[39] Forty-seven percent had the same predicted and actual RPE level. The correlation coefficient for the relationship between the predicted and actual RPE levels is $r = .85$.

A figure as great as eighty-one percent within one half RPE level says much about the reliability of the SRT and its companion measure, the RPE.

---

[39]Since RPEs predicted from scores on the original Pashto SRT could only go as high as level 3+, assigned RPEs of level 4 (from the revised Pashto SRT calibration) were considered as 3+.

(41) Comparison of predicted and actual RPE levels, showing number of subjects for each category of difference

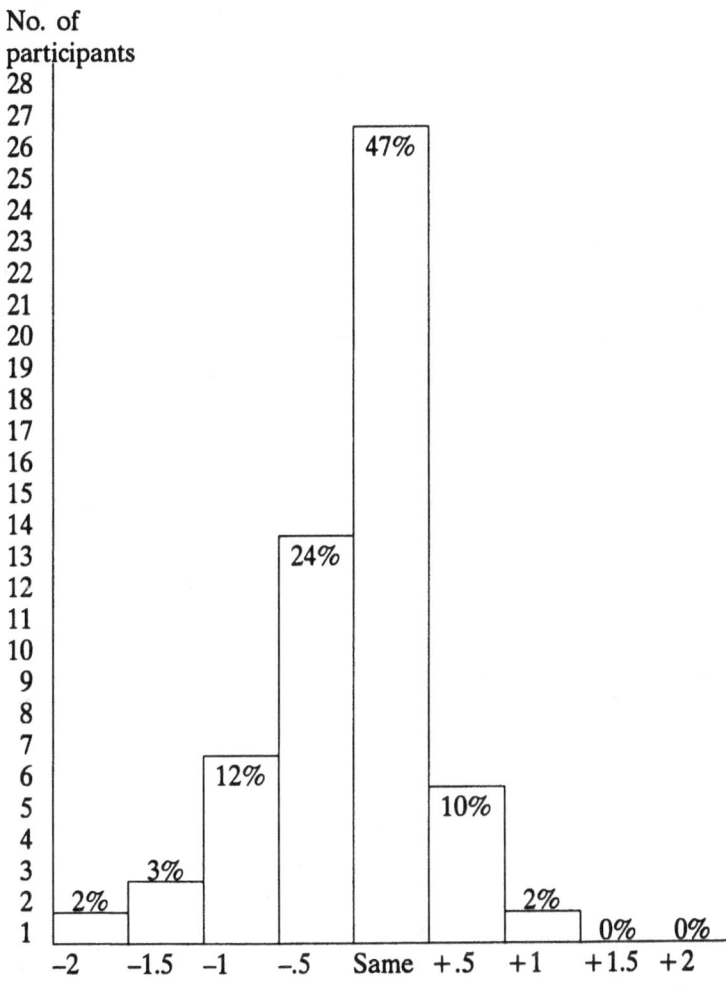

n = 58, correlation coefficient r = .85, standard error of estimate = .55

Other studies have measured the reliability between evaluations by different people doing FSI-type oral interviews and have obtained correlation coefficients between .70 and .90 (see, for example, Hendricks, et al. 1980 and other articles in that volume). The correlation coefficient of r = .85 between the predicted and actual RPEs compares favorably to these. The fact that the predicted and actual RPEs were the same for forty-seven percent of the total bolsters the argument that SRT is a reliable proficiency indicator.

5.4-5.7 Other issues

The following four sections describe the investigation of issues adjunct to the development of the Urdu and original Pashto SRTs. All of the research reported in these sections occurred in the first two phases of the SRT field study, that is, prior to the development of the revised Pashto SRT.

5.4 A screening test versus control testing

In the early stages of the SRT field study, the question arose about the need for a 'screening' test in the subject's first language. The primary concern for suggesting such a test was to be able to identify and remove from testing those individuals whose performance on the SRT would be distorted because of depressed memory capability and therefore not reflect their second-language proficiency.

A second question brought to the attention of the team of researchers was whether or not such factors as education or age would have an effect on a subject's overall performance on an SRT and thus influence the interpretation of results. The exposure to test-taking situations and training in concentration concomitant with education might tend to raise scores, for example. An increase in age, on the other hand, might tend to lower scores as the ability to concentrate and hearing acuity decrease. Performance on screening tests in the subjects' own first languages could conceivably shed light on this question, since, if these hesitancies were well-founded, subjects with lesser education or greater age should perform less well on such a screening test.

5.4.1 Design of the vernacular screening tests. Accordingly, screening tests were constructed for five separate vernacular languages and administered to each subject prior to the language of wider communication SRTs. Each screening test consisted of six sentences in the vernacular: three practice and three test sentences. An attempt was made to extract sentences from an elicited text, but that was discarded in favor of translating a set of six sentences into each vernacular. Test administrators attempted to become familiar with the sentences of the screening test in order to be able to score them.

After giving these vernacular screening tests in the five language areas to over 100 people, the decision was made to stop administering screening tests and reassess the need for them and the questions about the population they were supposed to answer. The main reasons for this were the

Studies in Reliability and Validity 115

difficulties encountered in constructing a different screening test for each vernacular and then training test administrators to score them.

5.4.2 Difficulties with the vernacular screening tests. In the first place, it was difficult to obtain a reliable translation of the sentences in each vernacular or subsequently to have it checked. A second difficulty arose in obtaining sentences of the necessary length, since the goal was to have them reflect the length of the longest sentences in the test language SRT. The primary difficulty, though, was in training test administrators to score these vernacular screening tests, since the fieldworkers did not necessarily speak any of these vernaculars. To be confident in scoring, the entire procedure for establishing scoring standards for an SRT (see §3.3.4) would need to be repeated in each vernacular—a demand far beyond the time and personnel available at each test site and, indeed, beyond the projected scope of usefulness for these screening tests.

The fact that the results obtained from these screening tests were inconsistent further precipitated the decision to stop and reconsider. Some subjects who performed well on the test language SRT did poorly on the screening test in their own language while the converse was true for others. Other inconsistencies probably related to the fact that subjects sometimes spoke different dialects of the vernacular from the one the screening test had been prepared in; this resulted in its being more of a dialect intelligibility test than a test to screen out people with deficient repetition ability.

5.4.3 Control testing the SRT. A reexamination of the questions about a population that a screening test was designed to answer brought two issues into focus: the need to know the effect of different factors on SRT test performance, specifically age and education, and the importance of identifying potential subjects who would skew the results because of having less than normal memory span. It was determined that giving the original Pashto SRT to mother-tongue speakers of the Pashto language as a control test would give needed insight into these issues.

The ability of mother-tongue speakers to perform on an SRT in their own language should be relatively uniform, since the variable of proficiency in the language is held constant. Any pattern of variation in scores should provide the insight needed into the effect on performance of different factors. Additionally, since one would expect all the members of one subgroup to perform relatively consistently, subjects scoring significantly differently from other subgroup members could be suspected of having interference from other, yet unidentified factors. It was thought that a control test could give an idea of what percentage of a population is likely to be affected by these other, more personal factors.

Accordingly, the original Pashto SRT was administered to forty-one mother-tongue speakers of Yusufzai Pashto, the dialect of the test. The Urdu SRT was also given to twenty-five of the subjects[40] as a check for the kind of inconsistencies found in the vernacular screening tests, where an individual would do less well on his own language's screening test than on the test language SRT. The results of this testing are presented in (42).

An examination of the results in (42) shows clearly that the inconsistencies noted in the vernacular screening tests were not evident here, that is, subjects did better on the SRT in their own mother tongue than on the Urdu SRT. The four subjects who scored higher on the Urdu SRT than on the Pashto did so by an average of only 1.5 points and their scores on the Pashto were all within three points of a perfect score. Thus the difference is negligible and in any case would not amount to a lower proficiency level equivalent in their mother-tongue than in Urdu. Probably the most salient contributing factor in the consistency of scores is the fact that test administrators were well trained in the administration of the Pashto and Urdu tests and could be confident in the scores they gave. This is coupled with the fact that all the subjects were from the same dialect of Pashto, so the problem of dialect variations between villages found with the vernacular screening tests was not encountered.

In the analysis of the results, age was found to make no significant difference. Scores from three age groups were examined: those forty-five years or above (average score = 41.25, standard deviation = 1.67, n = 8), those twenty-five years or younger (average = 38.73, standard deviation = 4.78, n = 11), and those whose age was in between (average = 41.36, standard deviation = 4.84, n = 22). A one-way analysis of variance test showed no significant difference between these three groups ($p < .01$).[41] The educated subjects, on the other hand, did score significantly higher than the uneducated ($p < .01$). Closer analysis, however, revealed that it was not education per se, but rather a combination of education and quality of personal contact with the test administrators that produced a significant difference between performances. This divided the test group into three subgroups: educated subjects, uneducated subjects with good personal contact with the test administrator prior to the test, and uneducated

---

[40]Since Urdu is principly the language of education in the area where the testing was located, rather than the actual language of wider communication (the function Pashto fulfills), many of the uneducated subjects were not given the Urdu SRT.

[41]All tests of significance reported in this section were one-way analysis of variance tests.

Studies in Reliability and Validity

(42) Scores from control testing the original Pashto SRT

Subject ID no.	Age	Years educ	PSRT total	PSRT statistics	USRT total	USRT statistics
10	30	14	44		44	
9	45	14	43	Educated group	43	
6	26	12	42		44	
11	35	11	42	n = 21	40	n = 19
4	38	10	43	Standard	44	Standard
7	30	10	43	deviation = 1.5368	44	deviation = 11.223
2	27	10	43	Average = 42.476	38	Average = 34.789
5	40	10	42		44	
8	35	9	41		41	
3	30	8	43		41	
1	57	7	41		26	
15	40	6	45		41	
17	38	5	45		37	
13	39	5	44		35	
19	35	5	43		32	
21	38	4	40		22	
18	52	3	44		23	
14	55	3	41		18	
25	22	2	43			
31	55	Q*	40			
12	50	Q*	40		4	
36	32	0	45			
27	25	0	44	Uneducated group-A	3	
26	14	0	44	(good contacts)	3	
38	38	0	43	n = 12		n = 6
39	29	0	43	Standard		Standard
16	50	0	42	deviation = 1.8990	18	deviation = 7.8486
28	32	0	42	Average = 42.167	16	Average = 7
34	25	0	42			
29	17	0	42		0	
37	29	0	41			
30	19	0	40		2	
35	30	0	38			
40	45	0	39			
24	19	0	37	Uneducated group-B		
41	35	0	36	(no contacts)		
20	16	0	36	n = 8		
33	18	0	34	Standard		
23	18	0	34	deviation = 5.3452		
22	17	0	30	Average = 33.5		
32	40	0	22			

Uneducated—A&B Standard deviation = 5.62
Average = 38.70
n = 20

*Q = Quranic education

subjects with no personal contact with the administrator before the test. The subgroups and the significance of the differences between them are summarized in (43).

(43) Scores for mother-tongue Pashto speakers

Group	vs.	Group	vs. Group	Significant Difference?
Older		Middle	Younger	No (p<.01)
Educated			Uneducated—A&B	Yes (p<.01)
Educated			Uneducated—A (good contacts)	No (p<.01)
Uneducated-A (good contacts)			Uneducated—B (no contacts)	Yes (p<.01)

It was found that for uneducated subjects the fact of whether they were introduced to the test administrators through an acquaintance or relative or were merely recruited off the street made a significant difference in their scores. Their culture places very high value on social networks of relatives and friends; operating within that network allays the suspicions and resistance to cooperation that are otherwise commonplace.[42] When the test administrators approached a potential subject without following the usual procedures of being introduced by an acquaintance or relative before initiating testing, they noticed an attitude of suspicion and a general unwillingness to cooperate, even though the person ultimately agreed to take the test. This is in contrast to the situation where an introduction by an acquaintance or relative created an atmosphere of trust and cooperation. Among these uneducated subjects, those introduced by good contacts scored an average of nine points higher on the Pashto SRT than those without such introductions. This difference is statistically significant (p<.01).[43]

In the educated group, however, the scores were uniformly high. There was no apparent difference between the performance of those who were approached through a contact as opposed to those approached without a

---

[42] It should be noted that the current political situation in that area also contributes to suspicion of the motives of strangers.

[43] The negative effects of approaching uneducated subjects 'cold' would most probably not be realized in an actual bilingualism survey. This is because time spent in the community by the survey research team determining the need for testing, collecting the data for the community profile to direct sampling, and accomplishing other aspects of the survey such as filling out questionnaires, will doubtlessly introduce the team into networks of contacts that can be utilized for obtaining participants for the testing.

personal contact. It is suggested that because of the resources open to an educated person and the broadness of his background, he would not feel vulnerable or defenseless in encountering the suspicious situation of a researcher and his questions. Thus the educated person would be able to overcome the adverse effects of suspicion on his test performance.

Finally, there were only two subjects who scored more than two standard deviations below the average for their own subgroup. One was in the uneducated group with good contacts, the other in the uneducated group without good contacts. It could be suggested that such a large difference is not related to any identified factor affecting test performance of the subgroup as a whole; rather it is due to unidentified factor(s) operating on an individual basis. These unidentified factors affecting the subject's ability to perform on the SRT could include a below normal memory span, some distraction that occurred during the test, or some personal concern that affected their ability to perform on the SRT. These two individuals represent only five percent of the total group. While five percent may have some effect on the profile of a certain subgrouping based on social factors, such a small percentage of low functioning subjects would not alter the profile of a population. This is especially true in bilingualism testing where a greater number of people are tested. Thus, from this study, it appears that no special accounting need be made for the miscellaneous personal factors that could affect test performance.

In conclusion, the results of testing mother-tongue Pashto speakers on the original Pashto SRT suggest that for a group taking an SRT in their own first language, the effects of age and education are not significant. Thus, the scores can be interpreted at face value without any need for extrapolation or adjustment on account of these two factors. On the other hand, the importance of having good personal contacts with test subjects has been underscored. While this particular test population probably represents an extreme on the continuum of culturally-based need for good contacts, the importance of approaching a community from the inside, spending the time necessary to make good personal contacts, is obvious. The advantage brought by an SRT to a bilingualism field study, then, is that it minimizes the time needed for actual testing, freeing researchers and test administrators to spend more time making networks of personal contacts, the key to any good field study.

5.5 Effect of two presentations on test score

In the pilot study of the SRT and in the initial stage of the field study each sentence was presented twice. This gave the subject a second chance at repeating each sentence correctly. It was the impression of test administrators that this second presentation of the sentence made little difference in the overall score of the individual and therefore could be eliminated, effectively cutting administration time in half, as well as simplifying the scoring procedure.

In order to determine whether this impression were true, the scores for forty-two subjects on both the original Pashto and the Urdu SRT were examined, twenty-six subjects scored by one administrator and sixteen by another. Two total scores were figured for each subject for each test: one was the total score taking only the response to the first presentation into account, and the second took both presentations into account. The scoring conventions listed in (44) were used.

(44) 3 points—perfect first time
2 points—1 error first time or perfect second time
1 point —2 errors first time or 1 error second time
0 points—3 or more errors first time or 2 or more second time

The score for any sentence based on the second presentation was used only if it was better than the score based on the first presentation of that sentence. The two-presentation score could improve a person's score, but could not lower it. A test of significance (one-tailed t-test) was run to see if the two-presentation scores were significantly higher than the one-presentation scores.

Keeping the results of these tests separate as to language and administrator allowed four separate comparisons to determine whether either of those factors influenced the effect of the second presentation on the total score. Table (45) lists the average score (avg), the standard deviation (sd), and the number of subjects (n) for each total.

(45) Comparison of one presentation of test sentences with two; scores for four test groups.

Test	Administrator	One presentation	Two presentations	Difference significant?
Pashto SRT	A1	avg = 31.308 sd = 2.1683 n = 26	31.423 1.9426 26	no (p<.01)
Pashto SRT	A2	avg = 30.5 sd = 1.8974 n = 16	30.75 1.6125 16	no (p<.01)
Urdu SRT	A1	avg = 19.308 sd = 16.514 n = 26	19.577 17.238 26	no (p<.01)
Urdu SRT	A2	avg = 26.375 sd = 12.904 n = 16	27.875 12.606 16	no (p<.01)

In each case the differences between the scores on the first presentation only and the combined scores of both presentations were found to be not significant (p<.01). The fact that the tests were given by different administrators and tested different languages did not change the results. There was no difference between the scores. Thus, the impressions and decisions by the administrators to eliminate the second presentation of each test sentence were upheld.

5.6 Interadministrator reliability

It is natural that as the development of the SRT as a technique was fine-tuned through the construction of the Urdu and original Pashto SRTs, the training procedures for test administrators would also be undergoing change and fine-tuning. Final recommendations for training test administrators are given in §3.5. As one part of the development of these procedures, a measure was taken of the reliability among administrators in scoring both the Urdu and the original Pashto SRTs. This was done as a check of the efficacy of the training procedures developed to that point. Only this pretest data is available; the follow-up data was not obtained which would show the result of further training efforts. This single set of data is presented, however, to show the encouraging kind of consistency that was obtained with training procedures as they were developed to that point.

In order to assess the consistency among administrators in scoring tests, an interadministrator-reliability checking tape was prepared. This tape had both the SRT test stimulus and the subject's response for each sentence, for seventeen subjects on the Urdu SRT and sixteen subjects on the original Pashto SRT. The responses on the tape were scored by four different administrators for the Urdu and three administrators for the Pashto SRT. The results of this scoring were compared in order to get an idea of interadministrator consistency.

Table (46) has three sections. The first section displays the mean score and standard deviation for the test scores assigned by each administrator.[44] In the second section the administrators are grouped in a two-by-two comparison and the results of a paired t-test are given to indicate whether the scores given by one administrator were significantly different ($p < .01$) from those given by the other. The language of the test tape and the number of subjects scored for each language are also presented.

(46) Interadministrator reliability testing results

Mean and standard deviation for scores given by test administrators

Administrator	SRT scored	No. of subj.	Mean score	Standard deviation
A1	Urdu	17	25.53	13.05
A2	Urdu	17	28.59	14.10
A3	Urdu	17	29.12	12.24
A4	Urdu	17	28.35	12.94
A1	Pashto	16	28.88	6.08
A2	Pashto	16	34.25	5.42
A3	Pashto	16	33.88	5.52

---

[44]The large standard deviations are due to the fact that subjects evidencing a wide range of proficiency levels were included in the test sample. That is, subjects with lower proficiency scored fewer points on the SRT while subjects with greater proficiency scored higher. The wide range of variability in the subjects' proficiency levels and, consequently, the SRT scores more closely approximates what would be expected in any second-language proficiency testing in a community.

Studies in Reliability and Validity

Significant differences between test administrators

Administrators compared	SRT scored	Number of subjects	Difference significant? (p < .01)
A4 vs. A2	Urdu	17	no
A4 vs. A3	Urdu	17	no
A2 vs. A3	Urdu	17	no
A4 vs. A1	Urdu	17	yes
A2 vs. A1	Urdu	17	yes
A3 vs. A1	Urdu	17	yes
A2 vs. A3	Pashto	16	no
A2 vs. A1	Pashto	16	yes
A3 vs. A1	Pashto	16	yes

Correlations between test administrators (r =)

Urdu

	A1			
A2	.98	A2		
A3	.97	.98	A3	
A4	.99	.98	.98	

Pashto

	A1	
A2	.85	A2
A3	.72	.84

As can be seen in (46), the test administrators were applying the scoring criteria quite consistently. Among the four administrators of the Urdu SRT and the three administrators of the original Pashto SRT, no significant difference was found between the scores assigned, except for one administrator. The scores given by administrator A1 were consistently significantly different from those of the other administrators. He evidently was applying the scoring criteria differently from the others, yielding the lower scores. The next logical step in a situation like this is to investigate why the differences are occuring and reinstitute training procedures.

The correlations between the scores assigned by the different administrators for the Urdu SRT are very high. Those for the Pashto test are somewhat lower; nevertheless, they are to be considered high correlations (see §3.4.9).

These results are encouraging, especially since the training procedures for administrators had not been as fully developed as they are in the final recommended procedures (chapter 3). In other words, with the training they had received, the test administrators for the Urdu and Pashto s achieved this high agreement, suggesting that it is not difficult to obtain good interadministrator reliability with the SRT technique. Presumably, with the complete, more rigorous training procedure as outlined in §3.5, an even higher agreement will be reached among administrators on future SRT's.

5.7 Comparison with recorded text test

The standard method for dialect intelligibility testing described by Casad (1974) utilizes narrative texts. This technique was introduced in §1.3. That introductory discussion presents some of the difficulties which researchers encounter when extending the use of this recorded text test (RTT) technique beyond intelligibility testing, for which it was originally designed, into bilingualism testing. While there are situations in different bilingualism studies where there has been no choice but to use an RTT as the test instrument, it is argued that wherever possible, an SRT should be developed in a language and used for testing. This is because an SRT, once developed, can be used without subsequent modification, it discriminates a wide range of proficiency levels, and its methodology is easy for people to understand.

To compare results of the SRT technique with the RTT technique in bilingualism testing, an RTT in Yusufzai Pashto was given to all the subjects participating in the calibration of the original Pashto SRT. This meant that three measures were available for each subject: the Pashto SRT score, the RPE rating given by an educated mother-tongue Pashto speaker, and the Pashto RTT score. Chart (47) shows the scattergram of the relationship between the Pashto RTT score and the Pashto SRT score for each of the thirty-seven subjects involved in this testing.

This comparison shows that the Pashto SRT is a more sensitive test than the Pashto RTT, a fact not surprising since the two techniques were designed for different purposes. From a cutoff of eighty percent or more correct on the Pashto RTT, a broad spread of SRT scores is observed. This helps to demonstrate the greater potential for an SRT to discriminate a wider range of proficiency levels. It must be noted that a different RTT with a different text or different questions would probably evidence a somewhat different scatter. But due to the nature of texts, the basic configuration would probably show a similar spread since RTT testing is based on one text and ten questions. As Grimes (1986) points out, one text is generally at one particular level of complexity. If a cutoff level of ninety percent correct is set, this particular narrative text test appears to discriminate between subjects with a medium level of proficiency and those with lower proficiency, judged from its correspondence with the Pashto SRT. This supports the claim by Grimes (1986) and Kamp (1987).

(47) Comparison of scores on the Pashto RTT and original Pashto SRT

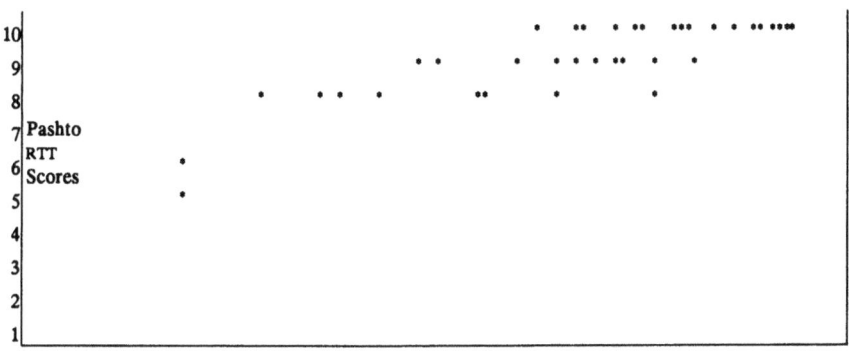

Correlation coefficient r = .825 n = 37

6
The Reported Proficiency Evaluation

6.1 Introduction

The stated goal for the development of sentence repetition testing was to provide a practical means for assessing bilingual proficiency in the field. In keeping with this, the reported proficiency evaluation (RPE) technique was developed concurrently as a practical method for obtaining the descriptive evaluation of a person's second-language proficiency necessary for calibrating scores on an SRT. The RPE technique utilizes naive or untrained educated mother-tongue speakers of the test language to evaluate the proficiencies of their second-language acquaintances according to standard proficiency criteria. They are guided in their evaluations by a trained fieldworker. Thus, the RPE is a reported evaluation, rather than a direct one. This technique is based on the premise that an educated or 'language aware' native speaker is able to provide a reliable general assessment on the second-language proficiency of a person he speaks with regularly, provided he is given a proper framework within which to make his judgments.

6.1.1 Mother-tongue raters use standard proficiency criteria in their evaluations. For the RPE, the educated mother-tongue speaker who is serving as the mother-tongue rater is asked to consider the proficiency of three to five second-language speakers with whom he communicates regularly in his own language. He is given a set of second-language proficiency criteria describing different levels of attainment for the language-skill areas of accent, comprehension, fluency, grammar, and vocabulary. After the fieldworker has ensured that the mother-tongue rater is familiar with the criteria, the mother-tongue rater is asked to place his acquaintances in ranked order and rate each one according to his level of attainment in each of those five language-skill areas. The mother-tongue rater assigns a letter score to each ratee corresponding to that level. These letter scores are then converted to number equivalents and summed. The resulting total score conforms to a certain 'RPE level' of proficiency.[45] The mother-tongue rater receives no training beyond the explanations given by the fieldworker.

Proficiency criteria for the different language skill areas that are used in the RPE are the original Foreign Service Institute skill area descriptions, taken from the *Manual for Peace Corps Language Testers* prepared by the Educational Testing Service (1970; reproduced in Hendricks et al. 1980). These criteria describe a range of proficiency from level 0+ (very minimal proficiency) to level 4+ (approaching the proficiency of a native speaker). It is important to note that since proficiency levels obtained through the RPE have not been correlated with any direct FSI-type oral-proficiency evaluations, the resultant scores are referred to as 'RPE levels' as opposed to the more familiar 'FSI levels'.[46] It should also be noted that the FSI currently uses a much revised set of criteria in its evaluations: the Interagency Language Roundtable 'Language Proficiency Skill Level Descriptions'. The orientation of the present FSI oral-proficiency interview has also been revised (see Bruhn 1990).

The proficiency criteria should be translated into the language most read by the mother-tongue raters. For example, for mother-tongue Pashto raters in Pakistan, a translation of the criteria into Urdu was preferred over their own Pashto. Urdu is the medium of instruction in government schools, so educated people of the area are most comfortable reading Urdu regardless of their mother tongue. The proficiency criteria are reproduced at the end of this chapter (§6.5). The criteria are described in 'telegraphic' English;

---

[45]In the typical FSI-type interview, the trained interviewers compare the ratings they gave the subject in the different skill areas with the overall description of that proficiency level before assigning that subject to a specific level of proficiency (see, for example, Educational Testing Service 1970 or Jones 1975). This is not done in the RPE; rather, the total rating is the sum of the rating in the individual skill areas. That this methodology yields consistent results with these mother-tongue raters is confirmed by the high correlations ($r = .71$, $r = .90$, and $r = .91$) shown with the SRTs developed (see chapter 5 and §6.1.3, below).

[46]In the RPE pilot study (Radloff and Marshall 1986), five second-language speakers of Nepali were evaluated by both an mother-tongue rater and a Peace Corps-trained interviewer. One participant was too shy for that interviewer to be able to rate. Of the remaining four, the mother-tongue rater's evaluation resulted in the same level as that assigned by the trained interviewer for two of the ratees, a half-level higher for the third ratee and a half-level lower for the fourth. On the strength of this agreement, the RPE method was field tested and further developed as a calibrating instrument for the field study of the SRT.

The Reported Proficiency Evaluation 129

back translations of the translation of the criteria into Urdu are presented as 'expansions', which can facilitate future translations into other languages. The tables for converting the numerical ratings for each skill area into the overall proficiency levels are also presented (§6.3.3). The weighting and conversion tables for transforming the evaluations by the mother-tongue raters into proficiency levels are also taken from the *Manual for Peace Corps Language Testers* (Educational Testing Service 1970). At the end of this chapter, composite descriptions of each RPE proficiency level are also given (§6.6). These composite level descriptions are not taken from the ETS Peace Corp manual, nor are they used in the standard RPE evaluation process; rather they are presented to assist in the interpretation and reporting of the results of the evaluation.

6.1.2 Trained fieldworkers conduct RPE interviews. The interviews with the mother-tongue raters are conducted by trained fieldworkers, who are members of the research team. It is appropriate for the fieldworkers to be local persons, ideally mother-tongue speakers of, or at least very fluent in, the test language, trained by the ones overseeing the research. The best training for such workers, besides practicing rating their own second-language acquaintances, is to take part in the translation of the proficiency criteria into the language most read by the mother-tongue raters. In this way the fieldworkers will be familiar not only with the overall content and idea but also with the fine gradations between the levels of proficiency within each language factor.

The advantage of having more than one such fieldworker is that the data can be collected more quickly. Trained fieldworkers can work by themselves, developing networks of contacts and interviewing the mother-tongue raters. The interview procedure of ranking and then rating within each language skill area is not complex but must be followed rigorously to obtain the best results. Revision of the Pashto SRT showed a dramatic increase in the correlation coefficient (from $r = .66$ to $r = .90$) between preliminary form SRT scores and RPE levels when the procedure of ranking and then rating within each language skill area was followed rigorously. (See §5.3.3 for details and §6.3.2, for further discussion.) The fieldworkers must report regularly to the research team, and the calculation of the numerical equivalent of the ratings and the assignment of the RPE level (see §6.3.3) can be done by the research team or together with the fieldworker(s). When the RPE ratings are being used to calibrate an SRT, results of interviews must be monitored to ensure that the broadest range of proficiency levels is represented in the ratings. Each mother-tongue rater should put the fieldworker into contact with his ratees. If the fieldworker is also trained in administration of the SRT, he can then proceed directly to test the RPE ratees on the preliminary form of the SRT (described in §3.3).

6.1.3 RPE technique advantages. The primary advantage of the RPE technique is that the evaluations come from within the very language community that the second-language speakers have to relate to and be received by—the mother-tongue speakers of the test language.[47] "Language use by bilinguals (like language use generally) needs to be understood in terms of COMMUNITY norms rather than some idealized notion of a perfect bilingual speaker" (Milroy 1987:211, emphasis hers). The RPE subjects are evaluated on the basis of real-life relationships that tell the true impact of their proficiency. The evaluations depend not on performances in highly structured interview situations, but rather on the strength of extended personal relationships.[48]

Another advantage is that the RPE is a cost-effective instrument. Only one research team member, the trained fieldworker, is involved in data collection. Any number of mother-tongue raters are involved, but each only on a short-term basis: the time it takes to evaluate their second-language acquaintances. The translation of the proficiency criteria and the training of the fieldworker, of course, require the involvement of more people, but the actual process of interviewing the mother-tongue raters is accomplished independently by the trained fieldworker.

A third distinct advantage which the RPE has over other interview techniques is the time involved for the actual interview and interpretation of results. The fieldworker for the field study of this methodology reported that he usually spent two hours with each mother-tongue rater. But when this interview is finished, a valid and reliable assessment of three to five second-language speakers is the result. No further time is required for interpretation of the results other than converting the ratings into their numerical and RPE level equivalents.

---

[47]"There are no single-style speakers and no single-style speech communities. That is to say, no one speaks in the same way all of the time, and no community is composed of speakers who all have identical verbal resources at their command" (Fishman and Cooper 1978:31). The authors make this statement in the context of arguing for the "sociolinguistic contextualization of language assessment procedures." Certainly the methodology of the RPE is a step in this direction; a person who interacts with second-language speakers in different (sociolinguistic) situations over time has the best access to information which, with proper guidance, can result in an accurate evaluation of their proficiency levels.

[48]Using the RPE technique, then, as the external calibrating standard for an SRT means that the proficiency-level equivalents obtained through SRT testing should relate to this real-life use of the test language.

But the highest recommendation for the RPE technique comes from the high correlations obtained between results of SRT testing and the RPE ratings. The ability of RPE to provide reliable assessments of the full range of second-language proficency levels has been demonstrated and verified in the field study of this technique and the SRT. An examination of the results of the calibration of SRTs in the Urdu and Pashto languages reveals that the mother-tongue raters' evaluations of the subjects' second-language proficiencies correlated highly with the subjects' scores on the respective SRTs, showing a marked relationship between the two measures. This is graphically illustrated in (32), (34), and (39) in chapter 5. The correlation coefficient for the Urdu SRT and RPE, the earliest developed test, was $r = .71$. With improved sentence selection, among other things, the correlation increased to $r = .90$ for the original Pashto SRT and the RPE. And the correlation rose to $r = .91$ for the revised Pashto SRT and the RPE as a measure of the full application of recommended procedures (see chapter 3). This lends support to the proposal that RPE is a valid measure of second-language proficiency. Chapter 5 reports the history of the development of the SRT and RPE techniques and the results of the statistical analyses of the data.

6.2 Support from the literature

6.2.1 Untrained evaluators in second-language proficiency research.

The idea of using untrained or naive mother-tongue evaluators is not new in the field of second-language proficiency evaluation. Numerous studies have shown the different aspects of proficiency that native speakers have been able to evaluate. Others concentrate on correlating such evaluations with other measures of speaking skills. Still others compare the evaluations of naive versus experienced judges. The studies cited below should be understood to be only a sampling of what has been written on this subject.

The ability of classroom teachers to assess the proficiencies of their students has been the focus of a number of studies. Indeed, Ingram (1978:11) states that the judgment of experienced teachers is a good external criterion against which to correlate a new test. Teachers are usually not trained evaluators in the sense of being trained FSI oral-proficiency interviewers (e.g., Educational Testing Service 1970). However, their knowledge of the test language and their extended relationship with their students gives them valuable insights into their students' proficiencies much the same as RPE mother-tongue raters understand how well their second-language acquaintances speak the raters' own mother tongue.

Callaway compared teachers of English as a second-language and naive native speakers of English as judges of oral proficiency. He termed them "naive judges" since they had no linguistic or teaching background. Results indicated that "both groups can distinguish degrees of proficiency with substantial reliability" (1980:102). He summarizes, "from these analyses, it can be concluded that there is very substantial agreement among the Rs [raters], regardless of whether they are naive or experienced" (1980:107). Cartier (1980:11) also found "fairly high inter-rater reliability" among Vietnamese instructors' ratings of taped oral-proficiency test batteries. Spolsky, Murphy, Holm, and Ferrel (1975) designed their oral placement test for adults as a functional approach based on the observation that a trained and experienced teacher can decide the level of competence of a student after a certain amount of time.

Teacher-ratings were used as the control measure in an experiment reported by Oskarsson (1981). Adult second-language learners rated themselves on a 0–5 level rating scale in four skill areas. Their teachers also rated them on the same scale. No special training was given to either group before the rating. A correlation of $r = .77$ was found between the self- and teacher-ratings.

Another study examined how accurate the subjective judgments of classroom teachers are concerning the language skills of their students. Streiff found that "the subjective judgments by [classroom] teachers and aides of the Hopi [Native American] students' language dominance and fluency were statistically significant predictors, separately, of the students' cloze test performance" (1978:93).

Many studies have used untrained native speakers to evaluate different aspects of second-language learners' speech. The following point out the reliability of naive raters in assessing different areas. Richards (1970) found that naive native speakers are fairly reliable ($r = .775$) judges of word familiarity (see also Oller 1979:48). Fayer and Krasinski (1987), in their study of native and nonnative judgments, found that all their naive raters were able to separate out the three categories of proficiency presented on the test tapes. Albrechtsen, Henriksen, and Faerch (1980) found that adult and sixteen- to seventeen-year-old naive informants were able to differentiate between the texts of recorded speech produced by different learners. The adults gave more reliable evaluations than the teenagers. These naive informants were able to give evaluations of code, message, personality, and learner comprehensibility. The authors note that their results confirm preliminary results of Palmer (1973). In his study, Palmer questioned whether the "linguistically unsophisticated judges" could rate the speech samples reliably. He discovered that they were "quite consistent in their judgments," achieving correlations of r = .74-.83 in judging reading, retelling, and narration tasks by second-language learners (1973:46, 47).

Many other studies have also examined native speaker reaction to nonnative speech. Stressing the importance of how native speakers interpret nonnative speech, Gass and Varonis (1984) investigated the effects of different types of familiarity on comprehension of nonnative speaker speech. Smith and Bisazza (1982) studied the comprehensibility of nonnative speakers based on the judgment of native speakers of that language. By the very nature of their research, the studies mentioned here and many others have acknowledged the importance of native speaker opinion in the evaluation of second-language learners' proficiency. It is interesting also that almost all of them make use of rating scales to quantify the judgments of the native speakers, whether a simple five-point scale, or a more elaborate semantic differential. The RPE use of the proficiency criteria, with their scaled descriptions of the five skill areas, expands upon this, allowing the mother-tongue raters to make finer, more comprehensive ratings.

Another finding from the Fayer and Krasinski (1987) study points out the need for a framework within which the naive raters can evaluate the second-language speakers. The raters in their study listened to tape recordings of second-language speakers' performances. The researchers found that the ratings seemed to be influenced by the intelligibility of the previous speakers. In Palmer's 1973 study, the naive judges listened to groups of four taped test responses. Presumably, this gave the judges a framework within which to make their ratings. A study cited by Ingram (1978:11) concludes that "ranking lists produced by teachers who know their classes well probably constitute the most valid criterion [against which to validate other tests] available... provided the ranking includes only one group or class at a time." In the RPE procedure, that type of framework is provided by having the mother-tongue raters rank the subjects and then use standard skill area descriptions against which to make their ratings (see §6.3.2).

Countering critics of the use of such subjective techniques as rating scales, Oller states, "There is no escape from subjective judgment in the interpretation of normal expression in a natural language... the crucial question in any appeal to such judgments is whether or not they are reliable" (1979:392).[49] Carroll and Hall speak to the issue of 'subjective assessment' which some testers have dismissed as inferior to 'objective assessment'. They state, "The more complex types of communication, such as an extended oral interaction... cannot be decimated and counted" in the way spelling or vocabulary could be (1985:76). They defend the use of

---

[49] See §5.3.6 for a measure of the reliability of the RPE.

rating scales as a framework for subjective judgments and cite the FSI language scale for assessing the language skills of foreign service staff as a classic example of their wide-spread use and time-honored status. As mentioned above, the proficiency criteria used in the RPE (see §6.5) are taken from the original FSI scale (Educational Testing Service 1970).

6.2.2 Calls for a new type of assessment technique. Calls in the literature for an assessment instrument such as the RPE have been made more than once. Cartier points out the fact that several alternative methods of oral-proficiency assessment are needed because 1) there are several reasons for wanting to assess oral proficiency, and 2) the circumstances and environments of test administration differ and do not always permit the use of what many people consider to be the standard, face-to-face interview (1980:7). He commends simplicity in test design in the search for new techniques of measuring oral proficiency, which would allow even untrained participants such as students to complete administration and scoring or rating (1980:11).

Clark (1980:19, 20) discusses the practical impossibilities of reconstructing a genuine communicative setting in an oral interview, and he suggests further examination of two possible approaches for sufficiently accurate or extensive criterion measures of real-life communicative performance against which other tests could be validated: self-report data and independent or second-party evaluation of speaking performance in 'on-the-job' situations. He suggests that the second-party evaluations should be done by persons who are in a position to observe the examinee's performance in an extensive and detailed way.

In their investigation of different methods of second-language proficiency assessment, Carroll and Hall echo Clark in their description of what they term "non-invasive assessments." Such are methodologies which would aim essentially "to observe as unobtrusively as possible how the participant performs under authentic communication conditions" (1985:67). In this light they discuss using "agreed criteria of effectiveness supplemented by the judgments of the person himself and of those who have to communicate or work with him" (1985:68, 71). They mention that this approach has been widely used in the industrial field. They also note that the main use they have made of noninvasive assessment techniques has been in validating other tests.

These calls and recommendations certainly support the methodology underlying the RPE. The judgments of the subjects' proficiencies are made by those whose personal relationships encompass communicating with them in the test language—the mother tongue of those doing the rating. The judgments of the mother-tongue raters are elicited in terms of such 'criteria of effectiveness'—the proficiency criteria with their scaled descriptions. Also, the motive behind the development of the RPE technique has been to provide a validating or calibrating instrument which is representative of the skills desired and yet practical in its administration, able to be easily used under the demanding circumstances of fieldwork.

6.3 Methodology

6.3.1 Personnel and preparation. Various factors need to be taken into consideration when selecting personnal and preparing them for the task.

The trained fieldworker. The fieldworkers who guide the mother-tongue raters in their evaluations are members of the research team. They are ideally local persons, who are also mother-tongue speakers of the test language. Local people will more easily be able to develop the necessary network of contacts to meet the mother-tongue raters. The fieldworkers should be mother-tongue speakers of the test language, or at least very fluent in it, so that they will not be limited in the recruiting or interviewing of the mother-tongue raters. Non-mother-tongue fieldworkers must have sufficient control of the test language to be able to discuss the abstract concepts of language proficiency with the mother-tongue raters. Also, using trained fieldworkers who speak the language of the raters to guide them in the evaluations makes it possible to use mother-tongue raters who do not share a common language with other members of the research team.

The best method for training fieldworkers is to have them assist in the process of translating the descriptions into the test language. This provides them with a good exposure to what is desired in evaluating a person according to the descriptions as well as an understanding and familiarity with the descriptions themselves and the fine gradations between them. They should also practice rating people they know who speak their own mother tongue as a second language, as well as conducting practice sessions with some of their friends or relatives serving as mother-tongue raters. They must be well versed in the procedures of the RPE technique; although the procedures are not complicated, it is important that they be followed rigorously (see §6.3.2).

Translating the proficiency descriptions. The proficiency criteria are listed at the end of this chapter (§6.5). Each description is first presented in the original 'telegraphic' style employed in the original FSI skill-area descriptions (Educational Testing Service 1970). This is immediately followed by a suggested expanded form, which is based on a back translation from an

Urdu version of the criteria. These descriptions must be translated into the test language or the preferred language for reading to make them directly accessible to the mother-tongue raters. As related in chapter 5, the mother-tongue Pashto raters preferred a translation of the proficiency descriptions into Urdu, rather than Pashto, the language of those RPE evaluations.

The translation of the proficiency criteria should be a team effort. The researcher should be involved to ensure that the fine gradations between the proficiency descriptions is communicated. As mentioned above, an integral part of the training of the fieldworker is to be involved in this translation process. If the fieldworker is not a mother-tongue speaker of the language into which the criteria are being translated, an educated mother-tongue speaker of that language should be also involved. The language of the translated descriptions must also be checked by another educated mother-tongue speaker for faithfulness to the original, naturalness, clarity, etc. The final result should be produced neatly so that the mother-tongue raters will be able to read it easily.

Selecting the mother-tongue raters. If the RPE technique is being used to calibrate an SRT, it is best to interview approximately fifteen mother-tongue raters. Each rater will rate three to five second-language speakers. There is some safety in numbers with the RPE; a greater number of ratees allows the pattern of relationship between the RPE and SRT to emerge more clearly. It is also necessary to have ratees from the low-, mid-, and high-levels of proficiency represented in the calibration process. A greater number of ratees helps to ensure this.[50]

Only mother-tongue speakers of the language being investigated should be selected as mother-tongue raters. Second-language speakers, no matter how proficient, will not be able to make appropriate judgments for all the different skill areas—accent and fluency in particular. People selected to be mother-tongue raters should be educated, so they can read and understand the abstract concepts of language proficiency more easily, or at least be people who are considered to be informed and capable or 'language aware'. Mother-tongue speakers selected as raters should know three to five second-language speakers well enough to rate them. They should be

---

[50]If, after interviewing fifteen or so mother-tongue raters, there are too few or no subjects identified at a given proficiency level, the fieldworker should specifically look for mother-tongue raters who know someone who 'has very good ability' in the test language, or someone who 'hardly knows how to speak' the test language. Mother-tongue raters in general should think of a broad range of second-language acquaintances before they begin their ratings.

encouraged to consider their acquaintances who manifest a broad range of proficiencies. They should also be willing to spend the time that it will take to do the ratings and, as necessary, assist the fieldworker in finding those ratees for purposes of administering the SRT.

The mother-tongue rater should be an adult. The impression of the researchers in the field study of the RPE was that adults make more reliable raters; however, this was not formally investigated. A study by Albrechtsen, et al. (1980) found that adult naive informants gave more reliable evaluations than did sixteen- to seventeen-year-old informants.

Questions to ask about the mother-tongue rater. The following is suggested as useful information to gather concerning the rater, primarily to verify that he or she is indeed a first-language speaker of the test language. Having other pertinent information could be beneficial for a number of reasons, including possible future investigation into the profile of an ideal mother-tongue rater. Practically speaking, it will probably occur that the mother-tongue rater will need to be contacted again in order to locate ratees, etc., so having much of the information listed in (48) is necessary.

(48) Name
Address or contacting information
Age
Education
Sex
Occupation
Language spoken in the home
Language of father? of mother?
Other languages known, length of time known
Major places lived and how long lived in each place, e.g., birthplace, present home, other places lived

Selecting the ratees. For RPE ratings, the mother-tongue raters should select second-language speakers with whom they communicate regularly in their own language and are well acquainted. They should have known the subjects over a long period of time or have had intense interaction over a shorter period. The mother-tongue raters must have had experience with the individuals to be rated in a number of different types of situations where the individuals were speaking the test language—both formal and informal, emotionally charged and peaceful, quality-demanding as well as conversational. The mother-tongue raters should honestly feel that they have communicated with the concerned individuals in enough situations and over sufficient time that they know their language proficiencies well enough to rate them. A casual acquaintance is not sufficient. And, again, the mother-tongue raters should be encouraged to select acquaintances who function at the extremes of proficiency as well as those who communicate fairly well.

Relationship between the mother-tongue rater and ratee. The mother-tongue rater should be asked questions such as those in (49) to establish the quality of communication relationship the rater has with each subject. There is no fixed requirement for deciding if the mother-tongue rater has enough contact with the subject in the test language to qualify for rating. Rather, the questions help the fieldworker and the mother-tongue rater himself decide if there is sufficient communication in the test language with the subject to enable an accurate rating to be made.

(49) Ratee's name
Address or contacting information and other personal information
How long has the mother-tongue rater known that ratee?
What is the nature of the relationship? (employer-employee, neighbor, co-worker, school fellow, etc.)
What language does he/she usually speak with the ratee? (give the percentage of time they speak together in the test language)
How many times in the last two months have they spoken in the test language?
What do they generally talk about? what kinds of subjects?

In the RPE field study it was observed that a low figure given in response to the question of the percentage of time they speak in the test language does not necessarily disqualify that subject as a ratee. If a potential subject's proficiency in the test language is very low, the mother-tongue rater will probably have to resort to other languages in order to communicate. The fieldworker should ask follow-up questions to determine if this is the case. Such subjects should be retained in the rating process, since subjects with lesser proficiency are also required in a bilingualism study.

Example (50) presents a sample interview rating form for the field workers to use while guiding the mother-tongue raters in their evaluations. Space is provided on the form for the fieldworker to write in an abbreviated answer to many of the suggested questions. A separate form should be used for each mother-tongue rater.

6.3.2 Conducting the interview. In conducting the interview, the following aspects should be covered.

The Reported Proficiency Evaluation

(50) Sample form for RPE interview, to be filled out by fieldworker

RPE—MT Pashto rater on second-language Pashto-speaking friends

Location of interview: Date of interview:

MT rater's Name	Address or Ident.	Occup.	Age	Educ.	Sex	MT	In home Lang.	Places lived & Time Birthpl.	Current	Other pl

OT ratee's Name	Address or Ident.	Occup.	Age	Educ.	Sex	MT	In home Lang.	Places lived & Time Birthpl.	Current	Other pl
1										
2										
3										
4										
5										

No	Time known	Relation w/rater	Lang. speak	Freq. Pash in 2 mo.	Normal topics of conversation	RPE Acc	Com	Flu	Grm	Voc	Tot RPE
1											
2											
3											
4											
5											

Introducing the mother-tongue rater to the procedures. The introduction to the procedure of the interview should include the fact that this is an opportunity for the mother-tongue rater to help the researchers understand about the mother-tongue rater's own language and how different people have learned to speak it. The mother-tongue rater should be assured that his or her ratings will be held confidential and will not be shared with the ratees. The fieldworker should inform the mother-tongue rater at the beginning that he or she will be contacting the ratees to ask them to repeat some sentences in the rater's language from a tape. The worker will need the mother-tongue rater's help in contacting them.

The fieldworker should show the mother-tongue rater a copy of the proficiency criteria translated into his own language or language that he is most familiar with reading. If the mother-tongue rater would like to have the proficiency descriptions overnight, for example, in order to read through them at leisure and become acquainted with them, this is acceptable. However, the actual rating should be done in the presence of the trained fieldworker, and the fieldworker should make the notations of the ratings on the interview form.

The mother-tongue rater must rate all the three to five subjects chosen in one session.[51]

When the rating interview actually begins, the fieldworker should go over the proficiency criteria (again) with the mother-tongue rater. For example, they should begin by reading over the (translated) proficiency descriptions for the skill area of accent. The trained fieldworker should explain any concept the mother-tongue rater may not understand, giving examples, etc. This underscores the benefits of having the fieldworker assist with the translation of the criteria.

Ranking the subjects. The mother-tongue rater should rank the subjects according to perceived proficiency and then rate them for each skill area in turn. For example, he or she should rank and then rate them for accent, then rank and rate them for comprehension, then for grammar, and so on until this procedure has been repeated for all the five skill areas. The actual order that the skill areas are evaluated is not necessarily fixed.

For each skill area, then, the mother-tongue rater should rank the three to five subjects by perceived proficiency. For example, he or she should decide who has the best accent, the next best, the next, the poorest, etc. The rater should hold this ranking in mind as he evaluates the subjects. It may be helpful for the rater to tell the fieldworker the ranking.[52]

---

[51]The study cited by Ingram (1978:11), mentioned in §6.2.1, concluded that ranking lists produced by teachers who know their classes well are a valid criterion for validating other tests PROVIDING the ranking includes only one group or class at a time. This supports the RPE methodology of ranking the subjects and rating them all in one session.

[52]As was mentioned in §6.1.2, the field study proved ranking to be an important aspect of the RPE procedures through the dramatic increase in correlation found when the procedures of ranking then rating within each skill area were followed rigorously. The ranking provides a framework within which the mother-tongue rater can more accurately evaluate the proficiencies of his or her acquaintances. See also the discussion in §6.2.1.

Rating the subjects. Once the mother-tongue rater has the ranking of his or her acquaintances in mind, he or she should think of the person with the best ability in the skill area under examination. Then he or she should rate that best person according to the descriptions. The mother-tongue rater should assign that subject the letter rating that best fits his or her proficiency in that skill area, for example, in accent. If a subject falls between two descriptions, the rater may assign a half-level rating. Thus, the mother-tongue rater may assign any one of the following letter ratings, according to the perceived proficiency of that subject (in ascending order): A, A+, B, B+, C, C+, D, D+, E, E+, or F.

The mother-tongue rater next should think about the person with the poorest ability in the skill area under examination. For example, he or she should assign the ratee the letter rating that best describes his or her accent.

Then the mother-tongue rater should rate the remaining people, one at a time. It should be stressed that the mother-tongue rater rate the people accurately, even if he or she assigns two or more to the same rating letter.

This process should then be repeated for the next skill area, for example, comprehension. First the fieldworker should familiarize the rater with the criteria. Then the mother-tongue rater should rank the subjects according to their perceived ability to comprehend the test language as described by the proficiency criteria. Then he or she should rate the subject who has the best comprehension, assigning the appropriate letter rating. Then the subject with the poorest comprehension is assigned a letter rating, then the remaining subjects in between, each according to the proficiency perceived by the mother-tongue rater in his or her communication with them.

This process continues for the factors of fluency, grammar, and vocabulary. When it has been completed for all the ratees, the interview is finished. (There is no set order for the different factors like accent, grammar, etc.; this may be changed as the research team or mother-tongue raters show preference.) The mother-tongue rater should be thanked for helping and reminded that he or she will be contacted later to help locate the people he or she rated. The calculation of the overall score for each subject is done apart from the presence of the mother-tongue rater.

Example (51) presents a protocol of the procedures for an RPE interview that could be given to the fieldworker(s) as a reminder of the steps he or she must follow in guiding the mother-tongue raters in their evaluations.

(51) Protocol for an RPE interview (for fieldworkers)

Reported Proficiency Evaluation—Rating methodology for Pashto

Step 1—Find mother-tongue speakers of Pashto who can rate how well others speak Pashto. Photocopy an interview form for each mother-tongue rater.

Step 2—Fill in the form with the following information about the mother-tongue rater:

Location of interview
Date of interview
Name
Address or other identification
Occupation
Age
Education (in years)
Language usually spoken in the home, and for how long
Other languages spoken, and for how long
Major places lived and how long lived in each place: birthplace, current residence, other places lived

Step 3—Ask the mother-tongue rater this information about EACH person he will rate:

Name
Address or contacting information
How long he has known the person
What relationship is the person to the rater (employee, co-worker, brother-in-law, neighbor, etc.)
What language does he USUALLY speak with the person
In the last two months how many times have he and the person spoken in Pashto:
  1) daily
  2) several (3–4) times a week
  3) once a week
  4) once in two weeks
  5) once a month
  6) once in two months
  7) not at all (never)
What do he and the person usually talk about when speaking Pashto? (Summarize his answer.)

The Reported Proficiency Evaluation

Step 4—Let the mother-tongue rater read over the accent sheet and explain to him anything he doesn't understand, and give examples if necessary. Next, have the rater rank the people he is rating in order of accent ability and ask him the following:

a) Which person has the best Pashto accent? How would you rate him? (Choose the appropriate letter for the description or in between: A, A+, B, B+, C, C+, D, D+, E, E+, F)

b) Which person has the poorest Pashto accent? How would you rate him?

c) How would you rate the others?

Then do the same for the comprehension sheet, repeating substeps a), b), and c). Do the same, then, for each of the sheets of proficiency descriptions, fluency, grammar, vocabulary.

Step 5—Then contact the ratees. Collect the same information for each one as you did for the rater in Step 2. Administer the preliminary form of the Pashto SRT) to each one.

6.3.3 Calculating the weighted score and equivalent RPE level. These calculations are done as outlined in the following sections.

The weighted scores. The weighted scores are then calculated for each subject rated. This may be done by the primary researcher alone or together with the fieldworker.[53] The letter ratings assigned to the subject by the mother-tongue rater are converted into numbers utilizing the weighting table in (52). This conversion simply requires the researcher to find the number corresponding to the letter score assigned to each subject for each of the five skill areas. For example, a letter rating of C for accent corresponds to a number score of two. A letter rating of D+ for vocabulary corresponds to a number score of 18. This weighting table is taken from the *Manual for Peace Corps Language Testers* (Educational Testing Service 1970, reproduced in Hendricks, et al. 1980).

---

[53]The main reason the fieldworker might not be involved in this conversion process is to minimize the possible effect of bias on the part of the fieldworker. This is primarily true if the same fieldworker will be also administering the preliminary form of the SRT to the subjects rated, as part of the validation or calibration process for the SRT.

(52) Weighting table for converting letter ratings to number equivalents (Educational Testing Service 1970)

Proficiency description	A	B	C	D	E	F	
Accent	0	1	2	2	3	4	———
Grammar	6	12	18	24	30	36	———
Vocabulary	4	8	12	16	20	24	———
Fluency	2	4	6	8	10	12	———
Comprehension	4	8	12	15	19	23	———
Total points score (use in conversion table)							———

The sum of the numbers for each of the five skill areas is the subject's 'RPE total points score'; it is used to find the RPE proficiency level for that subject. This is also the figure to use in the calculations for calibrating the SRT, §§3.4.6–9.

Converting the weighted scores to RPE proficiency levels. The last step is to convert the total points score to the RPE proficiency level. This is done by finding the range containing the subject's total points score on the table in (53). The corresponding proficiency level is listed immediately below the range. For example, a total points score of 23 is equivalent to RPE proficiency level 0+. A total points score of 92 corresponds to RPE proficiency level 4. This conversion table is taken from the *Manual for Peace Corps Language Testers* (Educational Testing Service 1970).

(53) Conversion table for converting number scores to RPE proficiency levels (Educational Testing Service 1970)

Total	16–25	26–32	33–42	43–52	53–62	63–72	73–82	83–92	93–99
Level	0+	1	1+	2	2+	3	3+	4	4+

As mentioned above, a composite description for each RPE level is presented at the end of this chapter in §6.6. These descriptions are presented to assist in the interpretation and reporting of the results of the RPE evaluations, but are not part of the evaluation process. They are not taken from the ETS training manual; rather, they are a composite of the proficiency criteria descriptions for each level corresponding to performance by subjects evaluated through the RPE process.

6.4 RPE as an independent measure of second-language proficiency

The motivation for the development and the primary use of the RPE technique has been limited to the calibration of sentence repetition tests. Providing the criterion standard for such indirect tests is also probably the best use. It is conceivable, however, that the RPE technique could be used as an independent measure of second- language proficiency, not specifically for calibrating another test. This would probably be best thought of as a preliminary measure for obtaining an estimation of the ranges of second-language proficiency evidenced in the community being studied which would help determine the need for further assessment. Mother-tongue speakers of the test language (mother-tongue raters) who live in the target community could be guided in their evaluations of their second-language acquaintances by a trained fieldworker. The more mother-tongue raters interviewed in that community, the greater the understanding of the range of proficiency exhibited by second-language speakers of that test language.

The information gained from the evaluations could be used to help determine if community-wide testing is called for or to speed the process of subject selection during the calibration of an SRT. Suppose, for example, the goals of a community bilingualism study were to determine whether members of this community were sufficiently bilingual in the test language that it could be used for educational purposes. If, perhaps after guiding ten mother-tongue raters in their evaluations, no ratees above RPE level 2 were identified, the researchers might reconsider the need for wide-spread testing since the RPE results indicate that people may not be sufficiently proficient in the test language. Or, as another example, if an FSI-type oral interview were to be used to calibrate an SRT, the RPE technique might be used as a quick way to identify some potential subjects at the different levels of proficiency. Since the oral interview method requires a significant amount of time to evaluate each subject's proficiency, using the RPE in this way might help in preventing too many subjects at the same level from being tested unnecessarily and thus help ensure the best use of interview time.

It is not recommended that the RPE be the only measure used in developing a community's second-language proficiency profile, since such a picture is dependent on many factors, both quantitative and qualitative. Since it is impossible to control the social, educational, or age factors of the people rated by the mother-tongue raters, it could be difficult to end up with enough people in each category necessary to complete a profile of the community (see chapter 2 for additional factors to be considered). But the RPE used as an independent measure could be of help in an initial stage in the overall process.

The primary disadvantage of using RPE as an independent measure of second-language proficiency, beyond not being able to dictate variables, is that it cannot be used efficiently in all field situations. It is dependent on the availability of educated mother-tongue speakers of the test language to act as mother-tongue raters. At times the test language is used as the language of wider communication in an area where no mother-tongue speakers of that language live, or at least no mother-tongue speakers of the standard dialect of that language. This is often the case for Urdu, the national language of Pakistan. It is the medium of instruction in government schools and, therefore, people all over the country learn to speak and read it as a second language. Mother-tongue speakers of Urdu, however, are generally concentrated in the southern areas and cities of the country, so would not be readily available to act as mother-tongue raters in other areas of the country.

A similar situation arises in the Swat Valley of northern Pakistan. There the language of wider communication is Pashto, and many of the minority-language speakers of northern Swat display high levels of proficiency in Pashto. Mother-tongue speakers of Pashto who live among these people, however, speak a nonstandard dialect of Pashto (Rensch 1987), so could not be used as mother-tongue raters for evaluating proficiency in the standard dialect. Furthermore, these Pashto speakers are for the most part uneducated, which further disqualifies them as mother-tongue raters. (There are, however, a small number of educated mother-tongue speakers of the standard dialect of Pashto living in the area as government servants who could serve as mother-tongue raters.)[54]

Thus, use of the RPE technique, independent of the validation of other tests, is an option. But both its potential contributions to and limitations in providing a community-wide profile of second-language proficiencies should be carefully considered.

6.5 Proficiency descriptions

The proficiency descriptions reproduced in this section are the original FSI skill area descriptions presented in the *Manual for Peace Corps Language Testers* (Educational Testing Service 1970; reproduced in Hendricks,

---

[54]If it were desired to use RPE to evaluate second-language proficiency in a language where there was no educated standard, uneducated but 'language aware' mother-tongue speakers could be used as mother-tongue raters. It would be more difficult because the entire process of presenting and explaining and ranking and rating would have to be done orally, but it would be possible.

et al. 1980). They are in TELEGRAPHIC English. The expansions given immediately after each of the telegraphic descriptions are from the back translation of an Urdu version of these criteria, done during the course of the field study. They are given as possible helps for future translations into other languages (see §6.3.1). In the translation of these criteria, the actual name of the test language should be used instead of 'test language' and the subject's vernacular should be named instead of 'vernacular'. These proficiency criteria are the basis for the evaluation by the mother-tongue raters. They are the standard against which the mother-tongue raters measure their judgments of their acquaintances' second-language proficiencies. Therefore, it is self-evident that any translation of them should be done with the utmost care and attention to quality.

6.5.1 Accent proficiency descriptions

(a) Pronunciation frequently unintelligible: Because his pronunciation is very bad, people often cannot even understand his speech.

(b) Frequent gross errors and a very heavy accent make understanding difficult, require frequent repetition: Because of frequent big errors in pronunciation and a very heavy accent, it is difficult for people to understand him. People time and again ask him to repeat himself.

(c) 'Foreign accent' requires concentrated listening and mispronunciations lead to occasional misunderstanding and apparent errors in grammar or vocabulary: People must listen carefully to understand him because he speaks the test language with a vernacular accent. Sometimes his mispronunciation makes people not understand or think he used the wrong word or bad grammar, but really it was only his poor pronunciation.

(d) Marked 'foreign accent' and occasional mispronunciations which do not interfere with understanding: People can easily understand his speaking, even with his pronunciation errors. People can easily tell from his accent that the test language is not his mother tongue.

(e) No conspicuous mispronunciations, but would not be taken for a native speaker: Even though there is no obvious error in his pronunciation, people still do not consider him a mother-tongue speaker of the test language because of his slight accent.

(f) Native pronunciation, with no trace of 'foreign accent': His pronunciation and accent are so good that you would think that the test language is his mother tongue.

6.5.2 Grammar proficiency descriptions

(a) Grammar almost entirely inaccurate except in stock phrases: He makes many grammatical mistakes in almost every sentence, except sentences he has memorized or uses very frequently.

(b) Constant errors showing control of very few major patterns and frequently preventing communication: People often cannot understand what he is saying because of his grammatical mistakes. People can tell that he understands only a few grammatical rules.

(c) Frequent errors showing some major patterns uncontrolled and causing occasional irritation and misunderstanding: Because he cannot use some important grammatical rules, he makes errors frequently. These mistakes occasionally irritate other people and sometimes make them misunderstand.

(d) Occasional errors showing imperfect control of some patterns but no weakness that causes misunderstanding: There are a few mistakes that he makes occasionally because he forgets those grammatical rules. People always understand him, even with these grammatical errors.

(e) Few errors, with no patterns of failure: He makes very few grammatical errors and almost never makes the same error twice.

(f) No more than two errors during the interview: Even in a long conversation, he will make only one or two grammatical errors, if any.

6.5.3 Vocabulary proficiency descriptions

(a) Vocabulary inadequate for even the simplest conversation: Even in the most simple conversation, this person has difficulty because there are so many words he doesn't know.

(b) Vocabulary limited to basic personal and survival areas (time, food, transportation, family, etc.): He knows only enough words to talk about simple personal and survival topics such as his family, time, travel and food.

The Reported Proficiency Evaluation

(c) Choice of words sometimes inaccurate; limitations of vocabulary prevent discussion of some common professional and social topics: He knows enough words to talk about most everyday topics like chit-chat and work. Sometimes he chooses the wrong word because he doesn't know the exact word. Because he doesn't know enough words, he cannot discuss a few everyday topics or topics related to his job.

(d) Professional vocabulary adequate to discuss special interests; general vocabulary permits discussion of any nontechnical subject with some circumlocutions: Because he knows all the special words, he can discuss his own work and his own special interests easily. Also, he knows enough words to talk about all general topics. Sometimes, though, he has to explain his meaning because he doesn't know the exact word.

(e) Professional vocabulary broad and precise; general vocabulary adequate to cope with complex practical problems and varied social situations: He knows all the words in his work and special interests so that he can always choose the exact word he needs. He knows enough words to discuss even complicated and unexpected things that happen in general life.

(f) Vocabulary apparently as accurate and extensive as that of an educated native speaker: He knows as many test-language words as a mother-tongue speaker of the test language, and always uses the exact word, so that no one realizes that the test language is not his mother tongue.

6.5.4 Fluency proficiency descriptions

(a) Speech is so halting and fragmentary that conversation is virtually impossible: Test-language conversation with this person is almost impossible because his talk is so halting and he has to stop every few words.

(b) Speech is very slow and uneven except for short or routine sentences: He always speaks slowly and full of stopping and starting, except for short or routine sentences.

(c) Speech is frequently hesitant and jerky; sentences may be left uncompleted: He hesitates when he speaks. He often slows down and speeds back up and sometimes he cannot finish his sentence.

(d) Speech is occasionally hesitant, with some unevenness caused by rephrasing and groping for words: He occasionally hesitates while talking. His speech is sometimes uneven because he is trying to remember a word or decides to begin again to say something.

(e) Speech is effortless and smooth, but perceptibly nonnative in speed and evenness: He speaks smoothly and without difficulty, but because of slight unevenness in speed, people can tell he is not a native speaker.

(f) Speech on all professional and general topics as effortless and smooth as a native speaker's: No matter what topic is discussed—general or special interest—his speech in the test language is as smooth and effortless as a mother-tongue speaker.

6.5.5 Comprehension proficiency descriptions

(a) Understands too little for the simplest type of conversation: When people speak to him in the test language, he understands so little that it is impossible to have even the simplest conversation with him.

(b) Understands only slow, very simple speech on common social and touristic topics; requires constant repetition and rephrasing: He understands only very slow and simple talk and things used in common chit-chat, in travel, and in buying and selling. For him to understand, people must always repeat themselves and try to say things in simpler words.

(c) Understands careful, somewhat simplified speech directed to him, with considerable repetition and rephrasing: He can understand the test language if people speak carefully, but they have to repeat things a lot and many times say things in a simpler way for him to understand.

(d) Understands normal educated speech directed to him quite well, but requires occasional repetition or rephrasing: He understands people even when they don't take extra care or don't speak extra slowly, but occasionally he doesn't understand so they have to repeat themselves or say it in a different way.

(e) Understands everything in normal educated conversation except for very colloquial or low-frequency items or exceptionally rapid or slurred speech: When he is talking with test-language-speaking people, he understands everything very well except for very uncommon words, slang or very fast or slurred speaking.

(f) Understands everything in both formal and colloquial speech that an educated native speaker understands: He understands everything very well, whether general or special topics, formal or informal conversation, just as well as a mother-tongue speaker of the test language.

6.6 RPE level descriptions

As mentioned above, the following composite RPE level descriptions are presented to assist in the interpretation and reporting of the results of the RPE evaluations, but are not used as part of the evaluation process. They are not the original FSI proficiency-level descriptions; rather, they are a composite of the proficiency-criteria descriptions for each level corresponding to ratings of subjects evaluated through the RPE process. The researcher is encouraged to read through the actual FSI skill-area descriptions to obtain an idea of the wide range of proficiency represented in each area.

These composite level descriptions were obtained in the following manner: The RPE scores for subjects who were evaluated as part of the calibration of the revised Pashto SRT were combined to produce an average letter score for each of the five skill areas at each RPE proficiency level. The equivalent description for that average letter score for each skill area was then used in the composite level description. RPE scores of subjects which fell within the bounds of the standard error of estimate lines (see (39)) were used to compose these descriptions. The average letter score for the discrete levels (i.e., no half-levels) used as the basis for the level descriptions are given in (54).[55]

---

[55]As has been stated, it is not claimed that these RPE level descriptions are FSI level descriptions. They have not been taken from the Educational Testing Service manual (1970), and it is not claimed that they are FSI level descriptions. However, it is encouraging that these RPE level descriptions, which were obtained as composites from subject performance and arrived at independently from the FSI criteria, turn out to be parallel and very similar to the FSI level descriptions (reproduced in Educational Testing Service 1970 and Hendricks, et al. 1980). It will be interesting to see if this can be replicated in other studies.

(54) RPE levels

	Level 1	Level 2	Level 3	Level 4
Accent	B	B+	D	E+
Grammar	A	C	D	E+
Vocabulary	B	C	D+	E
Fluency	B	C	D+	E+
Comprehension	B+	C	D	E

To conclude this chapter, then, the composite RPE level descriptions are listed. Included are brief, two- to three-word descriptors for the intermediate, 'half' levels.

RPE level 0+. Very minimal proficiency.

RPE level 1. Minimal, limited proficiency.

A person at this level has a very heavy accent which makes understanding difficult and forces people to ask for repetition. There seem to be more mistakes in grammar than correct usage, except for stock phrases. Vocabulary is limited to basic personal and survival areas. Speech is slow and halting except for short or routine sentences. Understanding is limited to slow, very simple speech, with very frequent repetition and rephrasing.

RPE level 1+. Limited, basic proficiency.

RPE level 2. Adequate, basic proficiency.

A person at this level has a heavy accent that forces people to concentrate when listening and sometimes causes misunderstanding and gives the appearance of errors. Some important grammatical rules are not controlled which occasionally causes misunderstanding and even irritation. Vocabulary is broad enough for daily topics, but limited in some common domains and sometimes inaccurate. Hesitations and jerkiness are frequent. Sometimes sentences cannot be completed. Understanding is possible if people speak carefully and simplify their speech somewhat, but they must repeat and/or rephrase frequently.

The Reported Proficiency Evaluation

RPE level 2+. Good, basic proficiency.

RPE level 3. Good, general proficiency.

A person at this stage has a marked 'foreign' accent, with occasional mispronunciations, but these do not interfere with understanding. Imperfect control of some grammatical patterns causes occasional errors, but understanding is not affected. Vocabulary is adequate to cope with varied social situations and special interests in professional domains with some circumlocutions. Speech is occasionally hesitant and perceptibly nonnative in speed and evenness. Normal educated speech is understood quite well, with only occasional need for repetition or rephrasing.

RPE level 3+. Very good, general proficiency.

RPE level 4. Excellent proficiency.

A person at this level still has a very slight accent but no longer mispronounces words. No patterns of grammatical error remain and only rarely are errors made. Vocabulary is broad and precise, adequate for all technical, social, and practical situations. Only a slight difference in the speed and evenness of speech separates this speaker from a native speaker. Comprehension is complete except for very slurred or rapid speech or perhaps uncommon words or idioms.

RPE level 4+. Approaching native speaker proficiency.

7
Conclusion and Call for Research

This manual and field study report has been devoted to the description of the use, construction, and developmental history of the sentence repetition test (SRT) technique. While there are undoubtedly many different ways in which an SRT could be constructed, the methodology that is prescribed in this manual is based on the premise that a test must be developed separately for each language. That is, unique sentences are selected for each test and these sentences are calibrated with a more direct method of assessment for maximum interpretability of test results.

The SRT prescribed in this manual is first and foremost a methodology fitted for the conditions of field research, specifically, investigation into patterns of community-wide bilingualism. It is a screening test, designed to facilitate testing the large number of people required for drawing conclusions about an entire community. Its administration time is brief and it can be scored on the spot; a fifteen-sentence SRT with three practice sentences requires approximately five minutes. It has been shown to discriminate a broad range of second-language proficiency levels, and has proven to give consistent, reliable results in actual field use.

That the SRT is a valid, general test of second-language proficiency has been demonstrated in other studies and confirmed in the present one. High correlations have been found between the performance of second-language speakers on SRTs and a descriptive estimation of second-language proficiency, called the reported proficiency evaluation (RPE).

The RPE has been developed as a calibrating instrument for the SRT. It is designed to provide a practical means for obtaining the descriptive assessment of second-language proficiency needed to calibrate an SRT under field conditions. It is based on the premise that an untrained native speaker of a language can provide reliable judgments regarding the bilingual proficiency of close acquaintances when provided the proper framework and guidance in making those judgments.

Both of these practical, field-oriented techniques have been described in detail, and step-by-step methodologies for their application have been provided in this manual. It is hoped that the presentation has been such that other research teams who deal with different languages set in different cultures will be encouraged to develop and calibrate SRTs for their own investigations into community bilingualism.

Many aspects of using SRTs in studies of community bilingualism remain to be investigated. Additionally, aspects of the test methodology itself should be confirmed or refuted through replicative studies. Researchers are encouraged to share their results and questions with the South Asia survey team as they develop and use SRTs in other languages.

One primary question for further research is the replicability of the results obtained in the current study. Can the same high correlations between SRT and RPE be found by other research teams? Can other SRTs be developed that will discriminate between RPE levels 3+ and 4, as the revised Pashto SRT appears to do?

Other aspects of reliability need to be investigated, for example, how consistent are test-retest scores for subjects? One type of test-retest was done (see §5.1) with results of $r = .94$; can this be replicated? Also, will the extracted scores for subjects match actual performance on the final-form test (see §3.4.4)? How easily will other research teams be able to achieve high consistency between SRT test administrators?

Although the SRTs developed and calibrated in the field study were in two totally different languages, they obtained similar results. What will an SRT look like when developed in a language from a different language family? Although the phenomena underlying the ability of sentence repetition to tap into language proficiency remains the same, what will be the surface form of an SRT in, say, an agglutinative language? It is proposed that subject performance will enable researchers to select discriminating sentences in that type of language even though an easy sentence, for example, might consist of only one long 'word'. Will these claims hold up?

What will future attempts to validate SRTs uncover? The SRTs developed in this field study of the technique have shown high correlations ($r = .71$, .90, .91) with the RPE. What will other studies find? Will mother-tongue raters for the RPE process in other cultures be as consistent and confident in their judgments of their close acquaintances' language proficiency as these mother-tongue raters apparently were? What will be the correlation if oral-interview scores are used to calibrate an SRT? The process gone through to obtain the skill area averages for making the composite RPE level descriptions (see §6.6) could be carried out by other researchers who

Conclusion and Call for Research 157

have themselves developed an SRT and calibrated it with the RPE procedure. Would they find similar agreement with the Foreign Service Institute level descriptions? And, finally, RPE levels themselves need to be compared with Foreign Service Institute levels obtained through the oral interview methodology. How close will that correlation be?

There are many more questions to be asked than time or research projects to answer them. However, it is still hoped that many questions will be able to be answered in the course of developing and calibrating new SRTs for use in new field projects studying community bilingualism. The catalyst for the development of the SRT technique was the need for a practical instrument for assessing second-language proficiency in bilingualism surveys. It is hoped that these further questions can be answered in equally practical ways.

Appendix A
Figures and Statistics

(55) Data for the comparison of scores on the Urdu SRT, dictation speed versus conversation speed (see §5.1.2), RPE point total not used (non-MT raters)

Subject	RPE point total	Dictation speed USRT(Y)	Y^2	YX	X^2	Conversation speed USRT(X)
1	75	41	1681	1517	1369	37
2	81	39	1521	1638	1764	42
3	94	41	1681	1681	1681	41
4	77	36	1296	1332	1369	37
5	24	13	169	104	64	8
6	49	28	784	896	1024	32
7	51	34	1156	1054	961	31
8	50	43	1849	1634	1444	38
9	73	31	961	1116	1296	36
10	69	34	1156	1190	1225	35
11	38	33	1089	891	729	27
12	49	38	1444	1596	1764	42
13	77	35	1225	1330	1444	38
14	79	31	961	1302	1764	42
15	75	40	1600	1680	1764	42
16	27	14	196	154	121	11
18	75	36	1296	1404	1521	39
20	79	37	1369	1295	1225	35
22	77	41	1681	1681	1681	41
23	79	41	1681	1681	1681	41

(55), continued

Subject	RPE point total	Dictation speed USRT(Y)	Y^2	YX	X^2	Conversation speed USRT(X)
24	79	38	1444	1558	1681	41
25	77	35	1225	1155	1089	33
26	29	10	100	60	36	6
27	27	20	400	300	225	15
28	31	14	196	154	121	11
29	79	39	1521	1443	1369	37
30	80	38	1444	1368	1296	36
		880	31126	31214	31708	874
		sum Y	sum Y^2	sum YX	sum X^2	sum X

$a_0 = 6.7433$ $a_1 = .7985$ $n = 27$
$s_{y,x} = 3.13889$ $r = .94402$

(56) Data for the calibration of the Urdu SRT (USRT), USRT extracted final form scores and RPE ratings (see (32))

Subject ID No.	RPE total (Y)	Y^2	XY	X^2	(Extracted) USRT(X)
7.5	99	9801	4455	2025	4
10.1	99	9801	4257	1849	43
11.3	99	9801	4257	1849	43
2.4	99	9801	4455	2025	45
14.1	99	9801	4059	1681	41
15.5	98	9604	4410	2025	45
15.1	98	9604	4410	2025	45
13.1	97	9409	4171	1849	43
9.5	97	9409	4074	1764	42
14.2	96.5	9312.25	3763.5	1521	39
4.4	93	8649	3906	1764	42
11.4	92	8464	3588	1521	39
10.5	91	8281	3822	1764	42
12.4	91	8281	4095	2025	45
10.3	90	8100	3780	1764	42
6.5	89	7921	3827	1849	43
15.2	87	7569	3654	1764	42
5.4	87	7569	3567	1681	41

Appendix A

(56), continued

Subject ID No.	RPE total (Y)	Y^2	XY	X^2	(Extracted) USRT(X)
7.1	87	7569	3393	1521	39
13.4	86	7396	3354	1521	39
15.4	86	7396	3870	2025	45
3.5	85	7225	3230	1444	38
8.3	85	7225	3825	2025	45
6.2	84	7056	3192	1444	38
6.6	83.5	6972.25	3089.5	1369	37
13.3	83	6889	2158	676	26
13.2	82	6724	3444	1764	42
2.1	82	6724	3608	1936	44
9.3	81.5	6642.25	3504.5	1849	43
10.4	81	6561	3564	1936	44
11.2	81	6561	3564	1936	44
14.5	81	6561	3402	1764	42
8.1	81	6561	3483	1849	43
7.3	81	6561	3321	1681	41
14.4	80	6400	3280	1681	41
6.3	80	6400	3200	1600	40
9.4	79	6241	3397	1849	43
5.5	79	6241	3476	1936	44
4.1	78	6084	3120	1600	40
8.5	78	6084	3510	2025	45
4.5	76	5776	3192	1764	42
9.1	75.5	5700.25	3397.5	2025	45
9.6	75.5	5700.25	3171	1764	42
2.5	75	5625	3225	1849	43
9.2	74.5	5550.25	3352.5	2025	45
3.4	73	5329	2628	1296	36
8.2	71	5041	2343	1089	33
8.4	71	5041	2485	1225	35
6.4	70	4900	2800	1600	40
11.1	68	4624	3060	2025	45
12.2	67	4489	2747	1681	41
5.3	67	4489	2010	900	30
4.2	65	4225	2925	2025	45
2.2	63	3969	2835	2025	45
15.3	63	3969	1953	961	31

(56), continued

Subject ID No.	RPE total (Y)	Y^2	XY	X^2	(Extracted) USRT(X)
12.1	62.5	3906.25	2687.5	1849	43
7.2	60	3600	1680	784	28
12.3	58	3364	2552	1936	44
3.3	57	3249	627	121	11
12.5	56	3136	2240	1600	40
14.3	54	2916	2052	1444	38
13.5	50	2500	2100	1764	42
6.1	49.5	2450.25	1089	484	22
3.2	49	2401	882	324	18
4.3	46	2116	966	441	21
5.2	43	1849	989	529	23
2.3	42	1764	1722	1681	41
7.4	33	1089	1188	1296	36
11.5	28	784	420	225	15
5.1	24	576	456	361	19
10.2	16	256	256	256	16
3.1	16	256	176	121	11
Sums	5304	419891	210742	109646	2736

$a_0 = 12.162616$ $n = 72$ $a_1 = 1.618528$
$r = .7141702$ $s_{y,x}$ (SEE) $= 14.08739$
$Y_{est} = a_0 + a_1 x = 12.163 + 1.6185x$

(57) Data for the calibration of the original Pashto SRT (PSRT), original PSRT extracted final form scores and RPE ratings (see (34) and (47))

Subject	RPE total (Y)	Y^2	XY	X^2	PSRT(X)	RTT
49	69	4761	2898	1764	42	10
50	69	4761	2898	1764	42	10
51	82	6724	3362	1681	41	10
52	58	3364	2088	1296	36	8
53	73	5329	2701	1369	37	10
54	93	8649	3906	1764	42	10
56	55.5	3080.25	1998	1296	36	9
57	99	9801	4257	1849	43	10
67	55.5	3080.25	1665	900	30	9

Appendix A

(57), continued

Subject	RPE total (Y)	Y^2	XY	X^2	PSRT(X)	RTT
68	53.5	2862.25	1658.5	961	31	8
69	54	2916	1458	729	27	8
70	66	4356	2112	1024	32	10
71	57	3249	1710	900	30	10
74	76	5776	3116	1681	41	10
75	24	576	456	361	19	8
76	51	2601	1224	576	24	9
79	67	4489	2345	1225	35	10
80	65	4225	2145	1089	33	9
82	47	2209	1316	784	28	9
83	48.5	2352.25	1309.5	729	27	8
84	36	1296	648	324	18	8
86	20	400	240	144	12	5
87	32	1024	384	144	12	6
89	65	4225	2080	1024	32	10
90	99	9801	3861	1521	39	10
91	63	3969	2205	1225	35	10
92	99	9801	3960	1600	40	10
93	59	3481	2006	1156	34	9
94	65.5	4290.25	2423.5	1369	37	10
96	37	1369	777	441	21	8
100	75.5	5700.25	2642.5	1225	35	10
101	56	3136	1400	625	25	9
102	73.5	5402.25	2719.5	1369	37	10
103	65	4225	2080	1024	32	9
104	67	4489	2546	1444	38	9
105	61	3721	1891	961	31	9
106	20	400	300	225	15	8
Sums	2256.5	151891	76786.5	39563	1169	

$n = 37$ $a_0 = -5.0325$ $a_1 = 2.08957$
$r = .8967272$ $s_{y,x}$ (SEE) $= 8.69318$
$Y_{est} = a_0 + a_1 * x = -5.0325 + 2.08957 * x$

(58) Data not used for the calibration of the revised Pashto SRT (RPSRT), RPSRT preliminary form scores, INCOMPLETE PROCEDURE RPE ratings (see (36))

Subject	RPE total (Y)	Y^2	YX	X^2	Preliminary RPSRT(X)
1.1	77	5929	3927	2601	51
1.2	89	7921	5607	3969	63
1.3	71	5041	1562	484	22
2.1	65	4225	2145	1089	33
2.3	61	3721	3233	2809	53
3.2	60	3600	840	196	14
3.3	48	2304	1488	961	31
4.1	41	1681	574	196	14
4.2	40	1600	960	576	24
5.2	61	3721	2379	1521	39
5.3	71	5041	3621	2601	51
6.1	56	3136	2016	1296	36
6.2	22	484	242	121	11
6.3	52	2704	2236	1849	43
7.1	62	3844	3038	2401	49
8.1	66	4356	4224	4096	64
8.2	45	2025	1575	1225	35
8.3	40	1600	1680	1764	42
9.1	56	3136	1568	784	28
9.2	69	4761	3795	3025	55
9.3	46	2116	1978	1849	43
9.4	22	484	440	400	20
10.1	81	6561	4941	3721	61
10.2	64	4096	3136	2401	49
10.3	48	2304	1872	1521	39
10.4	54	2916	2538	2209	47
11.1	62	3844	1798	841	29
11.4	27	729	297	121	11
12.1	41	1681	1189	841	29
12.2	51	2601	2397	2209	47
13.1	47	2209	1128	576	24
13.2	42	1764	1260	900	30
13.3	32	1024	1152	1296	36
14.1	68	4624	4420	4225	65
14.2	84	7056	4368	2704	52

Appendix A

(58), continued

Subject	RPE total (Y)	Y^2	YX	X^2	Preliminary RPSRT(X)
14.5	54	2916	2160	1600	40
15.1	40	1600	1840	2116	46
15.2	71	5041	3550	2500	50
15.3	85	7225	5865	4761	69
16.1	27	729	297	121	11
16.2	58	3364	1508	676	26
16.3	42	1764	756	324	18
17.1	53	2809	3498	4356	66
17.2	56	3136	3248	3364	58
17.3	45	2025	2115	2209	47
17.4	52	2704	2964	3249	57
17.5	40	1600	2160	2916	54
18.4	34	1156	748	484	22
18.5	65	4225	3900	3600	60
	2643	155133	114233	91654	1964
	sum Y	sum Y^2	sum YX	sum X^2	sum X

$a_0 = 28.2255 \quad\quad a_1 = .6415 \quad\quad n = 49$

$s_{y,x} = 12.1638 \quad\quad r = .6507$

(59) Data for the preliminary form of the revised Pashto SRT (RPSRT), CORRECT PROCEDURE RPE ratings, (see (37) and (39)). Calculations for preliminary form RPSRT (29 sentences) statistics

Subject	RPE total (Y)	Y^2	YX	X^2	Preliminary RPSRT(X)
19 1	78	6084	4602	3481	59
19 2	64	4096	3584	3136	56
19 3	49	2401	1715	1225	35
20 1	80	6400	5520	4761	69
20 2	65	4225	1625	625	25
20 3	35	1225	245	49	8
21 1	83	6889	6391	5929	77
21 2	70	4900	4340	3844	62
21 3	29	841	812	784	29
22 1	74	5476	4070	3025	55
22 3	53	2809	2067	1521	39

(59), continued

Subject	RPE Total (Y)	Y^2	YX	X^2	Preliminary RPSRT(X)
23 1	78	6084	4992	4096	64
23 2	57	3249	2622	2116	46
23 3	46	2116	1104	576	24
24 1	79	6241	4977	3969	63
24 2	63	3969	2709	1849	43
24 3	43	1849	1505	1225	35
25 1	78	6084	5772	5476	74
25 2	61	3721	3355	3025	55
25 3	32	1024	1344	1764	42
26 1	76	5776	5244	4761	69
26 2	62	3844	3224	2704	52
26 3	45	2025	1125	625	25
27 1	86	7396	6794	6241	79
27 2	66	4356	4026	3721	61
27 3	38	1444	1368	1296	36
28 1	79	6241	5767	5329	73
28 2	69	4761	4278	3844	62
28 3	50	2500	2300	2116	46
29 1	82	6724	5822	5041	71
29 2	61	3721	3111	2601	51
29 3	52	2704	2288	1936	44
30 1	69	4761	4278	3844	62
30 2	54	2916	2646	2401	49
31 1	76	5776	4940	4225	65
31 2	42	1764	1470	1225	35
31 3	29	841	667	529	23
32 1	80	6400	5920	5476	74
33 1	82	6724	5986	5329	72
33 2	70	4900	3710	2809	53
33 3	36	1296	1188	1089	33
34 1	90	8100	6750	5625	75
34 2	61	3721	2562	1764	42
35 1	80	6400	4800	3600	60
35 2	72	5184	4320	3600	60
36 1	76	5776	4332	3249	57
36 2	46	2116	1242	729	27
36 3	59	3481	3127	2809	53

Appendix A

(59), continued

Subject	RPE total (Y)	Y²	YX	X²	Preliminary RPSRT(X)
36 4	62	3844	3162	2601	51
36 5	33	1089	990	900	30
36 6	45	2025	1575	1225	35
37 1	79	6241	5451	4761	69
38 1	74	5476	2812	1444	39
39 1	40	1600	840	441	21
39 2	21	441	231	121	11
40 1	43	1849	1247	841	29
40 2	29	841	667	529	23
41 1	29	841	290	100	10
	3460	225578	183957	153961	2787
	sum Y	sum Y²	sum YX	sum X²	sum X

$a_0 = 17.22078$ $n = 58$ $Y = a_0 + a_1{}^*x$
$a_1 = .88311$ $s_{y,x} = 7.8147$ $r = .9029$

(60) Calibration of the final form RPSRT (extracted scores), RPE ratings and level equivalents, overall fluency scores (see (37), (39), and footnote 34). Calculations for final form RPSRT (fifteen sentences) statistics.

Subject	RPE level score(Y)	Y²	YX	X²	RPSRT(X) (of 45)	RPE level rating	Overall fluency
19 1	78	6084	2262	841	29	3.5	4
19 2	64	4096	1984	961	31	3	3
19 3	49	2401	882	324	18	2	3
20 1	80	6400	3040	1444	38	3.5	5
20 2	65	4225	520	64	8	3	3
20 3	35	1225	70	4	2	1.5	2
21 1	83	6889	3403	1681	41	4	5
21 2	70	4900	2380	1156	34	3	?
21 3	29	841	261	81	9	1	2
22 1	74	5476	2146	841	29	3.5	4
22 3	53	2809	954	324	18	2.5	?
23 1	78	6084	2808	1296	36	3.5	?
23 2	57	3249	1539	729	27	2.5	?
23 3	46	2116	368	64	8	2	?
24 1	79	6241	2449	961	31	3.5	4

(60), continued

Subject	RPE level score(Y)	Y^2	YX	X^2	RPSRT(X) (of 45)	RPE level rating	Overall fluency
24 2	63	3969	1449	529	23	3	3
24 3	43	1849	731	289	17	2	2
25 1	78	6084	2808	1296	36	3.5	5
25 2	61	3721	1647	729	27	2.5	4
25 3	32	1024	544	289	17	1	2
26 1	76	5776	2736	1296	36	3.5	4
26 2	62	3844	1488	576	24	2.5	3
26 3	45	2025	495	121	11	2	2
27 1	86	7396	3612	1764	42	4	5
27 2	66	4356	2112	1024	32	3	4
27 3	38	1444	532	196	14	1.5	2
28 1	79	6241	3002	1444	38	3.5	4
28 2	69	4761	2346	1156	34	3	3
28 3	50	2500	1100	484	22	2	3
29 1	82	6724	2870	1225	35	3.5	4
29 2	61	3721	1586	676	26	2.5	3
29 3	52	2704	1092	441	21	2	3
30 1	69	4761	2346	1156	34	3	4
30 2	54	2916	1296	576	24	2.5	3
31 1	76	5776	2660	1225	35	3.5	4
31 2	42	1764	630	225	15	1.5	3
31 3	29	841	319	121	11	1	2
32 1	80	6400	2960	1369	37	3.5	4
33 1	82	6724	2952	1296	36	3.5	?
33 2	70	4900	1820	676	26	3	?
33 3	36	1296	504	196	14	1.5	?
34 1	90	8100	3600	1600	40	4	?
34 2	61	3721	1342	484	22	2.5	?
35 1	80	6400	2400	900	30	3.5	?
35 2	72	5184	2088	841	29	3	?
36 1	76	5776	2508	1089	33	3.5	?
36 2	46	2116	460	100	10	2	?
36 3	59	3481	1593	729	27	2.5	?
36 4	62	3844	1550	625	25	2.5	?
36 5	33	1089	396	144	12	1.5	?
36 6	45	2025	810	324	18	2	?
37 1	79	6241	3160	1600	40	3.5	?

Appendix A

(60), continued

Subject	RPE level score(Y)	Y²	YX	X²	RPSRT(X) (of 45)	RPE level rating	Overall Fluency
38 1	74	5476	1554	441	21	3.5	?
39 1	40	1600	360	81	9	1.5	?
39 2	21	441	84	16	4	.5	?
40 1	43	1849	559	169	13	2	?
40 2	29	841	319	121	11	1	?
41 1	29	841	58	4	2	1	?
	3460	225578	93544	40414	1392		
	sum Y	sum Y²	sum YX	sum X²	sum X		

$a_0 = 23.6723$ $n = 58$ $Y = a_0 + a_1 * x$

$a_1 = 1.49929$ $s_{y,x} = 7.681819$ $r = .906350$

Appendix B
Sample Score Sheet (see §2.5.5)

Name: Date of test: Location:
Age: Education: Outside travel:
Mother tongue: Other tongues: Village:

    3 points   perfect, no errors in sentence
    2 points   one error in sentence
    1 point   two errors in sentence
    0 points   three or more errors in sentence

Scoring key:

o	word omitted from sentence
s	word substituted for another
> or <	any change of word order (counts as one error)
~ ~	word garbled or distorted so as to alter meaning
+	word or phrase added to sentence
R	word or phrase repeated
w	wrong word or word ending (grammatical marker)

P1.	ɪs khʊṛki ko bʌnd kʌr do
	S O O
P2.	ziadʌ nʊqsan to nʌhī hua
P3.	ɪn tʌmam čizo̱ ko bandh kʌr rʌkh do
1.	tʊm ne hath pʌr pʌṭi kyū ba̱ndh rʌkhi̱ hɛ
2.	kyūkɪ talim hʌmare̱ mašʌre ke lie bʌhʊt zʌruri hɛ
3.	ɪs jʌdid dor mẽ talim hasɪl kʌrna bʌhʊt zʌruri hɛ
	R
4.	mæ̃ ʌb mʌzid talim hasɪl kʌrna čahta̱ hu
	R
5.	ʊn ki̱ talimat ke bare mẽ ap ka kya xɛal hɛ
	W
6.	talim hasɪl kʌrke hʌm ʌpna karobar čʌla sʌkte̱ hẽ +
	R
7.	kʌl čʌlte wʌqt mæ̃ dʌs rupe de gʌi̱ thi
8.	mæ̃ ʌpni̱ qom ki̱ xɪdmʌt ke lie pʌrhna čahta hū
	O R
9.	mera xɛal hɛ kɪ ʌb hʌme̱ ɪjazʌt dijie
10.	ye rʌsʌm lʌṛki̱ ke ghʌr ada ki̱ jati̱ hɛ
	~ ~ W
11.	talim hi hʌmare bʌhʊt se̱ mʌsail ka hʌl hɛ
12.	log gʌle mẽ phulõ ke har pɛhne̱ hue hote hẽ
13.	lʌṛki̱ wale̱ bhi laṛke ke bare mẽ malumat hasɪl kʌrte̱ hẽ
	W
14.	lʌṛke̱ ke̱ wahdæn ʌpne̱ bete̱ ke lie lʌṛki dhū̱ḍte hẽ
	R
15.	ʊs ke bad barat wapʌs dulha ke ghʌr rʌwanʌ ho jati̱ hɛ
	O S W W

Appendix C
Elaborated Transcriptions
(see §3.1.4)

(61) Urdu SRT: elaborated transcription (see §5.1)

P1. *ɪs khɪṛki ko bʌnd kʌr do*
this window to close do
Close this window.

P2. *ziadʌ nʊqsan to nʌhī̃ hua*
too much damage so not was
It wasn't very much damage.

P3. *ɪn tʌmam čizo ko bandh kʌr rʌkh do*
these all things to having tied put away
Put all of these things away.

1. *tʊm ne hath pʌr pʌṭi kyū bandh rʌkhi hɛ*
you hand on bandage why wrap have put
Why do you have a bandage wrapped on (your) hand?

2. *kyūkɪ talim hʌmare mašʌre ke lie bʌhʊt zʌruri hɛ*
because education our society for very necessary is
Because education is very necessary for our society.

3. *ɪs jʌdid dor mẽ talim hasɪl kʌrna bʌhʊt zʌruri hɛ*
this modern time in education obtain to do very necessary is
In this modern time it is very necessary to get an education.

173

4. mæ̃ ʌb mʌzid talim hasıl kʌrna čahtạ hū
   I   now further education obtain to   do   want
   I now want to get further education.

5. ʊn kị talimat ke bare mẽ ap ka kya xɛal hɛ
   his teaching about   your what opinion is
   What is your opinion of his teaching?

6. talim   hasıl kʌrke hʌm ʌpna karobar čʌla sʌkte hẹ̃
   education get   having we our business go able are
   Having gotten education, we are able to run our own business.

7. kʌl   čʌlte wʌqt mæ̃ dʌs rupe de gai thị
   yesterday go   time I   ten rupees gave
   Yesterday at leaving time, I gave (you) ten rupees.

8. mæ̃ ʌpnị qom kị xıdmʌt ke lie pʌrhna čahta hū
   I   my country's service for to study want
   I want to study for my country's service.

9. mera xɛal hɛ kı ʌb hʌmẽ ıjazʌt dijie
   my thought is that now to us permission give
   My thought is that (you) please give us permission (to leave) now.

10. ye rʌsʌm   lʌrkị ke ghʌr ada   kị jatị hɛ
    this ceremony girl's home perform is done
    This ceremony takes place at the girl's home.

11. talim   hi hʌmare bʌhʊt se mʌsaıl ka hʌḷ   hɛ
    education only our   many   problem's solution is
    Education is the only solution to our many problems.

12. log   gʌle mẽ phulọ̃ ke har   pɛhne hue hote hẹ̃
    people necks in flowers' garland wearing are
    The people are wearing garlands of flowers on their necks.

13. lʌrki wale bhi larke ke bare mẽ malumat hasıl kʌrte hẹ̃
    girl people also boy about   information obtain do
    The girl's people also gather information about the boy.

Appendix C

14. *lʌrke ke walıdæn ʌpne bete ke lie lʌrkı dhūḍte hɛ̃*
    boy's parents their son for girl search
    The boy's parents search for a girl for their son.

15. *ʊs ke bad barat wapʌs dulha ke ghʌr rʌwanʌ ho jati hɛ*
    this after procession return groom's home leave becomes
    After this the procession returns to the groom's home.

(62) Original Pashto SRT: elaborated transcription. (see §5.2)

P1. *tse e bizʌtʌ kʌre ye*
    what he scolded done
    Has he scolded you?

P2. *ta nʌ e tse jib wale de*
    you from he what pocket cut did
    Has he picked your pocket?

P3. *tʌ hʌse hʌm bazar tʌ rʌwan ye*
    you also bazaar to going
    You are also going to the bazaar?

1. *hʌlıkʌ da xʌt wa(x)la*
   boy this letter take
   Boy, take this letter.

2. *yɛrʌ ji zʌma xɛal da de*
   sir my thought this is
   This is my thought, sir.

3. *aw zʌ bazar tʌ nʌšʌm tle*
   and I bazaar to cannot go
   And I cannot go to the bazaar.

4. *da xʌt yosʌ aw ḍakxanʌ ke wʌrkʌ*
   this letter take and postoffice in give
   Take this letter and post it at the postoffice.

5. *awʌl wʌrtʌ tolıʌ wačʌwo*
   first to him towel put
   We put a towel on him first.

6. *xe kalʌre wʌrtʌ bʌnde ku*
   good collars to him tie do
   We tie his collars nicely.

7. *da lıfafʌ   yosʌ aw ḍakxane tʌ wastʌwʌ*
   this envelope take and postoffice to send
   Take this letter and deliver it to the postoffice.

8. *tʌ kʌ bʌrʌ ze no xʌfa kigʌ   mʌ da xʌt de*
   you if up go then sad become don't this letter is
   If you are going to town, (take) this letter, if you don't mind.

9. *zʌ xo ji bılkol   dʌ de xʌbʌre mʌxalıfʌt kowm*
   I well sir absolutely of this talk   oppose I do
   Sir, I am absolutely opposed to this matter.

10. *hʌlʌkʌ niazʌ tʌ rašʌ aw da čiṭʌi wa(x)lʌ*
    boy Niaza you come and this letter take
    Niaza, come and take this letter.

11. *če mʌx wʌrta post ku   no biya wʌrtʌ hejamʌt oku*
    that face him to soften we do then then him to shave we do
    After softening his face, then we shave it.

12. *aw če wixtʌ jorʌwi no raši   kʌrsʌi ta keni*
    and that hair fix   then he comes chair to he sits
    And if he is having a haircut, he comes and sits in the chair.

13. *staso bʌ ḍerʌ ḍerʌ mʌhʌrbani wi kʌ taso da xʌt*
    your will very very kindness be if you this letter

    ḍakxane tʌ oligʌlo
    postoffice to send
    It will be very kind of you if you would deliver this letter to the postoffice.

14. *aw bʌl hʌyʌ ji zmʊng dʌ jerge mʌšʌr de aw čermen de*
    and also he sir ours of jirga chief is and chairman is
    Also, sir, he is the chairman and the chief of our jirga.

Appendix C

15. ʌsʌl   ke   če   ča   kalʌj   nʌ   wi   lidʌle   no   hʌyʌ
    actually that that who college not be seen then he

    xo   bılkol   sʌbʌk   nʌ   de   wele
    well absolutely lesson not is read
    Actually, if someone has not attended college, then he hasn't had any education at all.

(63) Revised Pashto SRT preliminary form (29 sentences): elaborated transcription (see §5.3.1).

P1. taso der xʌ   xʌlɛk   yei
     you very good people are
     You are very good people.

P2. sʌwat dʌ pexawar nʌ   yʌx de
     Swat of Peshawar from cold is
     Swat is colder than Peshawar.

P3. tʌ hʌse hʌm bazar tʌ   rʌwan ye
     you also bazaar to going
     You are also going to the bazaar?

[Note: Sentences 1–15 are the original Pashto SRT as in (62)]

16. xalek pʌ žɛmi ke yanʌm kari
     people in winter in wheat sow
     People sow wheat in the winter.

17. dʌ nasim mor   hayʌ tʌ pʌ topʌi konjɛke lɛgʌwi
     of Nasim mother him to on cap shells sews
     Nasim's mother sews shells on his cap.

18. pʌ lahor ke pʌ oṛi   ke ḍɛra ziata garmi wi
     in Lahore in in summer in very much warm is
     It is very, very hot in Lahore in the summer.

19. pʌ spʌrli ke ḍer xoyesta xoyesta golun ratu kigi
     in spring in very beautiful beautiful flowers bloom become
     Many different beautiful flowers bloom in the spring.

20. dʌ axtar pʌ dwemʌ wraz pʌ pexawʌr ke ḍera yata
    of eid on second day in Peshawar in very big

   melʌ   legi
   festival happens
   On the second day of Eid, a very big festival takes place in Peshawar.

21. pʌ doršal me ila kadam ɛxɛ wo če koṭa ra   prewatʌ
    on threshhold I just step put was that room to me fell
    I had just stepped on the threshhold when the roof fell in.

22. fikʌr ke kʌm swa   larši dʌ qodrat ši   aw bɩya
    thought that some direction goes of power becomes and then

   ratlʌl tre nʌ   her   ši
   return him from forgets becomes
   Whatever direction a thought goes, it goes towards God and then forgets to return from Him.

23. če sor   pʌ učʌto zaino walaṛd wi no haywi ta har
    whoever on high places standing was then them to any

   waxt dʌ tofanuno xatra   wi
   time of storms danger is
   Those who stand on high places are always in danger from storms.

24. haya ye oguri   kʌ pʌ xpʌlʌ sʌ kawʌle ši no oyekṛi
    he   looked at if on himself what do   can then does it
    He looks at it and if he can do something about it he does it.

25. ka motʌr domra tez   nʌwe no dʌ saṛi dʌ wahʌlo
    if car   such speed if not then this man from hit

   na   mixke bʌ ye kabu kʌre we
   from ahead will   control did
   If the car was not (going) at such high speed he would have controlled it before hitting the man.

Appendix C

26. dʌ yo kas šaṛe nʌwa če biyemuntʌ no we če da
    one man blanket not when he found then said that this

    šʌl   gazʌ nʌ da
    twenty yards not is

    A man had no blanket, but when he found one he said it was not twenty yards long.

Appendix D
Sample Discrimination Index and Difficulty Level

(see §3.4.1)

182   Sentence Repetition Testing

Actual order of scores, arranged order of scores and difference, for 29
final form RPSRT

```
                Subject numbers (rater no./ratee no.)
         2041393931402320263640213633192431362722382534242923283029362633 3622
    S    3 1 2 1 3 2 3 2 3 2 1 3 5 3 3 3 2 6 3 3 1 3 2 2 3 2 3 2 2 4 2 2 3 1
         ──────────────────────────────────────────────────────────────────────
         Actual scores by each subject on the sentence
    P1   0 2 2 3 3 2 0 2 2 3 3 3 3 3 2 3 3 3 3 3 3 3 3 2 3 2 3 3 3 3 3 3 3 3
         Arranged scores according to hypothetical 'ideal'
    P1   0 0 1 2 2 2 2 2 2 2 3 3 3 3 3 3 3 3 3 3 3 3 3 3 3 3 3 3 3 3 3 3 3 3
         Difference between actual and arranged
         0 2 1 1 1 0 2 0 0 1 1 0 0 0 1 0 0 0 0 0 0 0 0 1 0 1 0 0 0 0 0 0 0 0

    P2   0 1 0 0 1 0 1 0 2 0 0 2 2 1 2 2 2 0 2 2 0 3 0 3 3 2 2 3 3 3 2 2 3 3
    P2   0 0 0 0 0 0 0 0 0 0 0 1 1 1 1 1 2 2 2 2 2 2 2 2 2 2 2 2 2 3 3 3 3 3
         0 1 0 0 1 0 1 0 2 0 0 1 1 0 1 1 0 2 0 0 2 1 2 1 1 0 0 1 1 0 1 1 0 0

    P3   0 0 1 1 0 2 2 0 2 2 2 2 3 1 2 2 2 0 2 3 0 2 2 2 3 3 2 2 1 2 3 3 2 3
    P3   0 0 0 0 0 0 1 1 1 1 2 2 2 2 2 2 2 2 2 2 2 2 2 2 2 2 2 2 2 2 2 3 3 3
         0 0 1 1 0 2 1 1 1 1 0 1 1 0 0 0 0 2 0 1 2 0 0 0 1 1 0 0 1 0 1 0 1 0

    1    2 1 1 1 3 3 3 3 3 3 3 3 3 2 3 3 2 3 3 3 3 3 3 3 3 2 3 3 3 3 3 3 3 3
    1    1 1 1 2 2 2 2 3 3 3 3 3 3 3 3 3 3 3 3 3 3 3 3 3 3 3 3 3 3 3 3 3 3 3
         1 0 0 1 1 1 1 0 0 0 0 0 0 1 0 0 1 0 0 0 0 0 0 0 0 1 0 0 0 0 0 0 0 0

    2    0 0 2 2 3 0 1 1 2 2 1 2 3 3 2 1 1 3 3 2 3 2 3 3 3 3 2 2 2 3 3 1 3 3
    2    0 0 0 1 1 1 1 1 1 2 2 2 2 2 2 2 2 2 2 2 2 2 2 2 3 3 3 3 3 3 3 3 3 3
         0 0 2 1 2 1 0 0 1 0 1 0 1 1 0 1 1 1 1 0 1 0 1 1 0 0 1 1 1 0 0 2 0 0

    3    0 0 0 0 1 3 1 2 1 2 3 1 2 1 3 2 2 3 1 2 3 2 3 2 2 3 2 2 2 3 2 2 3 3
    3    0 0 0 0 1 1 1 1 1 1 2 2 2 2 2 2 2 2 2 2 2 2 2 2 3 3 3 3 3 3 3 3 3 3
         0 0 0 0 0 2 0 1 0 1 1 1 0 1 1 0 0 1 1 0 1 0 1 0 1 0 1 1 1 0 1 1 0 0

    4    0 0 1 2 1 2 1 2 3 2 1 2 2 1 2 2 1 2 2 1 3 1 3 2 3 3 2 0 3 3 1 2 3 2
    4    0 0 0 1 1 1 1 1 1 1 1 1 2 2 2 2 2 2 2 2 2 2 2 2 2 2 2 2 2 2 2 2 2 3
         0 0 1 1 0 1 0 1 2 1 0 1 0 1 0 0 1 0 0 1 1 1 0 1 1 0 2 1 1 1 0 1 1

    5    1 1 1 1 2 0 1 3 2 2 2 2 1 1 2 2 1 2 2 1 2 2 2 3 2 2 3 3 3 3 2 3 2
    5    0 1 1 1 1 1 1 1 1 1 1 2 2 2 2 2 2 2 2 2 2 2 2 2 2 2 2 2 2 2 2 2 2 2
         1 0 0 0 1 1 0 2 1 1 1 0 1 1 0 0 1 0 0 1 0 0 0 1 0 0 1 1 1 1 0 1 0

    6    1 1 1 3 1 2 1 1 1 3 1 3 2 1 2 1 2 2 2 2 1 2 1 2 2 2 2 3 2 3 2 1 3 2
    6    0 1 1 1 1 1 1 1 1 1 1 1 1 2 2 2 2 2 2 2 2 2 2 2 2 2 2 2 2 2 2 2 2 2
         1 0 0 2 0 1 0 0 0 2 0 2 1 0 0 1 0 0 0 0 1 0 1 0 0 0 0 1 0 1 0 1 1 0

    7    0 0 1 0 0 2 2 1 2 1 1 2 3 2 2 1 1 2 1 1 3 2 2 1 2 1 1 2 3 3 2 3 3 2
    7    0 0 0 0 1 1 1 1 1 1 1 1 1 1 2 2 2 2 2 2 2 2 2 2 2 2 2 2 2 2 2 2 2 2
         0 0 1 0 1 1 1 0 1 0 0 1 2 1 1 1 1 0 1 1 1 0 0 1 0 1 1 0 1 1 0 1 1 0
```

Appendix D

sentences of the preliminary form RPSRT, to help select sentences for the

25 19 36 19 35 35 27 21 28 30 24 23 31 20 26 37 29 33 28 25 32 34 21 27			
2 2 1 1 1 2 2 2 2 1 1 1 1 1 1 1 1 1 1 1 1 1 1 1	DI	DL	Total
3 3 3 3 3 3 3 3 3 1 3 3 3 3 3 3 3 3 3 3 3 3 3 3		.09	158
3 3 3 3 3 3 3 3 3 3 3 3 3 3 3 3 3 3 3 3 3 3 3 3			
0 0 0 0 0 0 0 0 0 2 0 0 0 0 0 0 0 0 0 0 0 0 0 0	14		
3 3 3 3 0 1 3 3 3 2 3 3 3 3 3 3 3 3 3 3 3 3 3 3		.32	118
3 3 3 3 3 3 3 3 3 3 3 3 3 3 3 3 3 3 3 3 3 3 3 3			
0 0 0 0 3 2 0 0 0 1 0 0 0 0 0 0 0 0 0 0 0 0 0 0	28		
3 3 2 2 1 3 3 3 3 3 3 3 3 2 3 3 3 3 3 3 3 3 3 3		.28	126
3 3 3 3 3 3 3 3 3 3 3 3 3 3 3 3 3 3 3 3 3 3 3 3			
0 0 1 1 2 0 0 0 0 0 0 0 0 1 0 0 0 0 0 0 0 0 0 0	26		
3 3 3 3 3 3 3 3 3 3 3 3 3 3 3 3 3 3 3 3 3 3 3 3		.06	164
3 3 3 3 3 3 3 3 3 3 3 3 3 3 3 3 3 3 3 3 3 3 3 3			
0 0 0 0 0 0 0 0 0 0 0 0 0 0 0 0 0 0 0 0 0 0 0 0	8		
3 3 3 3 3 3 2 3 3 2 3 2 2 3 3 3 3 3 3 3 3 3 3 3		.21	138
3 3 3 3 3 3 3 3 3 3 3 3 3 3 3 3 3 3 3 3 3 3 3 3			
0 0 0 0 0 0 1 0 0 1 0 1 1 0 0 0 0 0 0 0 0 0 0 0	26		
2 3 3 3 3 3 3 3 3 3 3 3 2 3 3 3 3 3 3 3 3 3 3 3		.22	135
3 3 3 3 3 3 3 3 3 3 3 3 3 3 3 3 3 3 3 3 3 3 3 3			
1 0 0 0 0 0 0 0 0 0 0 0 1 0 0 0 0 0 0 0 0 0 0 0	20		
2 2 3 3 2 2 3 3 3 2 3 2 3 3 3 3 3 2 3 3 3 3 3 3		.28	126
3 3 3 3 3 3 3 3 3 3 3 3 3 3 3 3 3 3 3 3 3 3 3 3			
1 1 0 0 1 1 0 0 0 1 0 1 0 0 0 0 0 1 0 0 0 0 0 0	30		
2 1 2 2 2 2 3 3 2 3 3 3 2 2 3 2 3 3 3 3 2 3 3 3		.29	124
2 2 2 2 3 3 3 3 3 3 3 3 3 3 3 3 3 3 3 3 3 3 3 3			
0 1 0 0 1 1 0 0 1 0 0 0 1 1 0 1 0 0 0 0 1 0 0 0	26		
2 2 3 3 2 3 2 3 3 3 3 3 3 3 3 0 3 2 3 3 2 3 3 3		.29	124
2 3 3 3 3 3 3 3 3 3 3 3 3 3 3 3 3 3 3 3 3 3 3 3			
0 1 0 0 1 0 1 0 0 0 0 0 0 0 3 0 1 0 0 1 0 0 0 0	24		
3 2 2 3 3 3 2 2 2 3 2 2 2 3 3 3 3 3 3 3 3 3 3 3		.32	118
2 2 2 3 3 3 3 3 3 3 3 3 3 3 3 3 3 3 3 3 3 3 3 3			
1 0 0 0 0 0 1 1 1 0 1 1 1 0 1 0 0 0 0 0 0 0 0 0	30		

Subject numbers (rater no./ratee no.)
```
   204139393140232026364021363319243136272238253424292328302936263336 22
s    3 1 2 1 3 2 3 2 3 2 1 3 5 3 3 3 2 6 3 3 1 3 2 2 3 2 3 2 2 4 2 2 3 1
```
Actual scores by each subject on the sentence
```
 8   0 0 1 1 1 2 2 0 0 0 2 0 1 1 0 1 2 0 1 1 1 0 2 1 3 2 0 0 2 0 3 2 3 2
```
Difference between actual and arranged
```
 8   0 0 0 0 0 0 0 0 0 0 0 0 1 1 1 1 1 1 1 1 1 1 2 2 2 2 2 2 2 2 2 2 2 2
```
Arranged scores according to hypothetical 'ideal'
```
     0 0 1 1 1 2 2 0 0 2 0 0 1 0 1 1 0 0 0 1 1 0 1 0 2 2 0 2 1 0 1 0

 9   0 0 0 0 1 1 0 0 1 0 2 0 0 1 2 2 2 2 1 1 3 3 1 1 0 2 2 3 3 2 2 2 2 1
 9   0 0 0 0 0 0 0 0 0 0 0 1 1 1 1 1 1 1 1 1 1 1 1 2 2 2 2 2 2 2 2 2 2 2
     0 0 0 1 1 0 0 1 0 2 1 1 0 1 1 1 1 0 0 2 2 0 0 2 0 0 1 1 0 0 0 0 1

10   1 0 0 2 1 1 0 0 2 2 2 0 2 2 1 1 1 3 2 1 1 2 3 2 0 2 3 3 1 3 2 2 2 2
10   0 0 0 0 0 0 1 1 1 1 1 1 1 1 1 2 2 2 2 2 2 2 2 2 2 2 2 2 2 2 2 2 2 2
     1 0 0 2 1 1 1 1 1 1 1 1 1 1 0 0 1 1 0 1 1 0 1 0 2 0 1 1 1 1 0 0 0 0

11   0 0 0 0 0 0 1 0 0 0 0 0 0 0 0 1 1 1 1 0 1 1 1 0 1 2 2 2 3 2 1 3 0
11   0 0 0 0 0 0 0 0 0 0 0 0 0 0 0 0 0 1 1 1 1 1 1 1 1 1 1 1 1 1 1 2 2 2
     0 0 0 0 0 1 0 0 0 0 0 0 0 0 1 1 0 0 0 1 0 0 0 1 0 1 1 1 2 1 1 1 2

12   0 0 0 0 1 0 0 1 0 3 0 2 0 1 1 0 1 0 1 1 3 1 2 1 0 0 2 2 2 3 2 1 3 1
12   0 0 0 0 0 0 0 0 0 0 0 0 1 1 1 1 1 1 1 1 1 1 1 1 1 2 2 2 2 2 2 2 2 2
     0 0 0 0 1 0 0 1 0 3 0 2 0 0 0 1 0 1 0 0 2 0 1 0 1 2 0 0 0 1 0 1 1 1

13   0 0 0 0 1 0 0 0 0 0 0 0 0 0 0 0 0 0 0 3 1 0 0 0 1 1 3 1 0 2 1 2 2 2
13   0 0 0 0 0 0 0 0 0 0 0 0 0 0 0 0 0 0 0 0 0 0 1 1 1 1 1 1 1 1 1 2 2 2
     0 0 0 0 1 0 0 0 0 0 0 0 0 0 0 0 0 0 0 3 1 0 1 1 0 0 2 0 1 1 0 0 0 0

14   0 0 0 1 0 1 0 0 0 0 0 0 0 0 0 0 1 1 1 1 1 3 0 3 2 2 1 1 1 0 2 1 1 1 2
14   0 0 0 0 0 0 0 0 0 0 0 0 0 0 0 0 1 1 1 1 1 1 1 1 1 1 1 1 1 1 1 1 1 1 1
     0 0 0 1 0 1 0 0 0 0 0 0 0 0 0 0 0 0 0 0 0 2 1 2 1 1 0 0 0 1 1 0 0 0 1

15   0 0 0 0 0 0 0 0 0 0 0 0 0 1 1 0 1 2 0 0 0 1 0 0 0 0 1 1 0 0 2 2 0 2
15   0 0 0 0 0 0 0 0 0 0 0 0 0 0 0 0 0 0 0 0 0 0 0 0 0 0 0 0 0 1 1 1 1 1 1
     0 0 0 0 0 0 0 0 0 0 0 0 0 1 1 0 1 2 0 0 0 1 0 0 0 0 1 1 1 1 1 1 1 1

16   0 2 0 2 1 1 2 0 1 0 3 2 2 2 3 2 2 3 3 2 3 3 3 3 3 3 2 2 3 3 3 2 2 2 3
16   0 0 0 0 1 1 1 2 2 2 2 2 2 2 2 2 2 2 2 2 2 2 3 3 3 3 3 3 3 3 3 3 3 3 3
     0 2 0 2 0 0 1 2 1 2 1 0 0 0 1 0 0 1 1 0 1 0 0 0 0 0 1 1 0 0 0 1 1 1 0

17   0 0 0 0 0 0 0 2 0 0 0 0 0 0 2 0 1 1 0 0 0 1 0 0 0 1 0 0 3 1 2 2 0 2
17   0 0 0 0 0 0 0 0 0 0 0 0 0 0 0 0 0 0 0 0 0 0 0 0 0 0 0 1 1 1 1 1 1 1 1
     0 0 0 0 0 0 0 2 0 0 0 0 0 0 2 0 1 1 0 0 0 1 0 0 0 1 1 1 2 0 1 1 1 1

18   1 1 0 0 0 1 1 1 0 2 0 0 0 1 2 3 1 2 1 1 3 1 1 2 1 1 1 3 0 0 1 2 2 2
18   0 0 0 0 0 0 0 0 0 0 0 1 1 1 1 1 1 1 1 1 1 1 1 1 1 1 1 1 2 2 2 2 2 2 2
     1 1 0 0 0 1 1 1 0 2 1 1 1 0 1 2 1 1 0 1 2 0 1 0 0 2 0 0 1 0 0 1 1 2 2 1 0 0 0
```

Appendix D

```
25 19 36 19 35 35 27 21 28 30 24 23 31 20 26 37 29 33 28 25 32 34 21 27
 2  2  1  1  1  2  2  2  2  1  1  1  1  1  1  1  1  1  1  1  1  1  1  1   DI   DL  Total

 2  1  3  2  2  2  3  3  2  3  2  3  3  2  2  3  1  2  2  3  3  2  2  3        .47  93
 2  2  2  2  2  2  2  2  2  2  3  3  3  3  3  3  3  3  3  3  3  3  3  3
 0  1  1  0  0  0  1  1  0  1  0  0  0  1  1  0  2  1  1  0  0  1  1  0   36

 3  3  3  2  2  0  2  3  3  2  1  3  2  3  1  3  1  3  3  1  2  3  3  3        .44  98
 2  2  2  2  2  2  2  3  3  3  3  3  3  3  3  3  3  3  3  3  3  3  3  3
 1  1  1  0  0  2  0  0  0  1  2  0  1  0  2  0  2  0  0  2  1  0  0  0   36

 2  2  3  3  3  3  3  3  3  2  2  3  1  3  3  3  2  3  3  3  3  3  3  3        .33  117
 2  3  3  3  3  3  3  3  3  3  3  3  3  3  3  3  3  3  3  3  3  3  3  3
 0  1  0  0  0  0  0  0  0  1  1  0  2  0  0  0  1  0  0  0  0  0  0  0   30

 1  2  3  2  3  2  2  2  2  2  1  2  3  3  1  3  3  3  3  3  3  3  2  3        .53  81
 2  2  2  2  2  2  2  2  2  2  3  3  3  3  3  3  3  3  3  3  3  3  3  3
 1  0  1  0  1  0  0  0  0  0  2  1  0  0  2  0  0  0  0  0  0  0  1  0   24

 2  2  3  2  3  3  2  2  2  2  2  1  2  3  2  2  3  2  3  2  3  3  3  3        .47  92
 2  2  2  2  2  2  2  2  2  2  3  3  3  3  3  3  3  3  3  3  3  3  3  3
 0  0  1  0  1  1  0  0  0  0  1  2  1  0  1  1  0  1  0  1  0  0  0  0   30

 3  1  2  1  2  3  3  1  3  3  2  3  2  3  2  2  3  3  2  2  3  3  3  2        .56  77
 2  2  2  2  2  2  2  2  2  2  3  3  3  3  3  3  3  3  3  3  3  3  3  3
 1  1  0  1  0  1  1  1  1  1  1  0  1  0  1  1  0  0  1  1  0  0  0  1   26

 2  2  3  1  2  2  1  3  1  2  2  2  2  2  2  1  3  2  1  1  2  1  3  3        .58  73
 1  2  2  2  2  2  2  2  2  2  2  2  2  2  2  2  3  3  3  3  3  3  3  3
 1  0  1  1  0  0  1  1  1  0  0  0  0  0  0  1  1  1  2  2  1  2  0  0   28

 1  0  0  0  2  1  1  1  1  2  2  0  1  2  1  1  2  1  1  1  2  3  1  2        .75  44
 1  1  1  1  1  1  1  1  1  1  1  1  1  2  2  2  2  2  2  2  2  2  2  3
 0  1  1  1  1  0  0  0  0  1  1  2  1  0  1  1  0  1  1  0  1  1  0  1   30

 3  3  3  3  3  3  3  3  3  3  3  3  3  3  3  3  3  3  3  3  3  3  3  3        .18  142
 3  3  3  3  3  3  3  3  3  3  3  3  3  3  3  3  3  3  3  3  3  3  3  3
 0  0  0  0  0  0  0  0  0  0  0  0  0  0  0  0  0  0  0  0  0  0  0  0   20

 2  1  0  0  3  0  2  1  1  2  1  2  2  2  3  2  2  2  2  3  2  2  2  2        .66  59
 1  2  2  2  2  2  2  2  2  2  2  2  2  2  2  2  2  2  2  2  3  3  3  3
 1  1  2  2  1  2  0  1  1  0  1  0  0  0  1  0  0  0  0  1  1  1  1  1   34

 0  2  3  2  3  3  1  3  2  3  2  2  3  3  2  3  3  3  3  2  2  3  3  3        .44  97
 2  2  2  2  2  2  3  3  3  3  3  3  3  3  3  3  3  3  3  3  3  3  3  3
 2  0  1  0  1  1  1  0  1  0  1  1  0  0  1  0  0  0  0  1  1  0  0  0   36
```

```
        Subject numbers (rater no./ratee no.)
        2041393931402320263640213633192431362722382534242923283029362633 3622
S       3 1 2 1 3 2 3 2 3 2 1 3 5 3 3 3 2 6 3 3 1 3 2 2 3 2 3 2 2 4 2 2 3 1
        Actual scores by each subject on the sentence
19      2 1 0 1 1 0 3 3 1 0 1 1 1 1 0 2 1 0 2 3 0 3 0 1 3 2 3 1 1 0 2 3 1 1
        Difference between actual and arranged
19      0 0 0 0 0 0 0 0 1 1 1 1 1 1 1 1 1 1 1 1 1 1 2 2 2 2 2 2 2 2 2 2 2 2
        Arranged scores according to hypothetical 'ideal'
        2 1 0 1 1 0 3 3 1 0 0 0 1 1 0 1 1 2 1 2 1 0 1 0 1 1 1 2 0 1 1 1

20      0 0 0 1 0 0 0 0 0 1 0 0 0 1 0 0 0 0 1 0 1 2 1 0 1 2 1 1 1 1 1 2 3
20      0 0 0 0 0 0 0 0 0 0 0 0 0 0 0 0 0 1 1 1 1 1 1 1 1 1 1 1 1 1 1 1 1
        0 0 0 1 0 0 0 0 0 0 1 0 0 0 1 0 0 0 0 0 1 0 1 0 1 0 1 0 0 0 0 0 1 2

21      0 0 0 0 0 0 0 0 0 1 2 0 0 1 0 0 1 0 0 0 0 1 2 2 2 0 2 3 3 1 1 0 1
21      0 0 0 0 0 0 0 0 0 0 0 0 0 0 0 0 0 0 0 0 0 0 0 1 1 1 1 1 1 1 1 2 2 2
        0 0 0 0 0 0 0 0 0 1 2 0 0 1 0 0 1 0 0 0 0 1 1 1 1 1 1 2 2 0 1 2 1

22      0 0 0 0 0 0 0 0 0 0 0 0 0 0 0 0 0 0 0 0 0 0 0 1 1 1 0 0 1 0 1 0 1 0 0 1
22      0 0 0 0 0 0 0 0 0 0 0 0 0 0 0 0 0 0 0 0 0 0 0 0 0 0 0 0 0 0 0 0 0 0
        0 0 0 0 0 0 0 0 0 0 0 0 0 0 0 0 0 0 0 0 0 0 0 1 1 1 0 0 1 0 1 0 1 0 0 1

23      0 0 0 0 0 0 1 0 0 0 0 0 0 1 0 1 1 0 0 1 0 0 0 1 0 2 1 0 1 0 1 2 0 1
23      0 0 0 0 0 0 0 0 0 0 0 0 0 0 0 0 0 0 0 0 0 0 0 0 0 1 1 1 1 1 1 1 1
        0 0 0 0 0 0 1 0 0 0 0 0 0 1 0 1 1 0 0 1 0 0 0 1 0 2 0 1 0 1 0 1 1 0

24      0 0 0 0 1 0 0 0 0 0 0 0 0 2 0 1 0 0 0 1 0 1 0 1 0 2 1 2 2 0 1 1 1 0
24      0 0 0 0 0 0 0 0 0 0 0 0 0 0 0 0 0 0 0 0 0 0 0 0 0 1 1 1 1 1 1 1 1 1
        0 0 0 0 1 0 0 0 0 0 0 0 0 2 0 1 0 0 0 1 0 1 0 1 0 1 0 1 1 1 0 0 0 1

25      0 0 0 0 0 0 1 1 0 0 0 0 0 1 0 1 1 0 2 1 0 1 0 1 1 2 0 0 1 0 1 1 0 2
25      0 0 0 0 0 0 0 0 0 0 0 0 0 0 0 0 0 0 0 0 0 0 0 0 0 1 1 1 1 1 1 1 1
        0 0 0 0 0 0 1 1 0 0 0 0 0 1 0 1 1 0 2 1 0 1 0 1 1 2 1 1 0 1 0 0 1 1

26      0 0 0 0 0 0 0 2 0 0 0 0 0 2 0 0 1 0 0 0 0 0 0 0 0 0 0 0 0 0 0 2 0 1
26      0 0 0 0 0 0 0 0 0 0 0 0 0 0 0 0 0 0 0 0 0 0 0 0 0 0 0 0 0 0 0 0 0 0
        0 0 0 0 0 0 0 2 0 0 0 0 0 2 0 0 1 0 0 0 0 0 0 0 0 0 0 0 0 0 0 2 0 1
```

Appendix D

```
251936193535272128302423312026372933282532342127
2 2 1 1 1 2 2 2 2 1 1 1 1 1 1 1 1 1 1 1 1 1 1 1    DI   DL  Total
```

	DI	DL	Total
`1 2 0 3 3 2 3 3 2 3 2 2 2 3 3 2 3 2 3 3 3 3 3 3`		.41	103
`2 2 2 2 3 3 3 3 3 3 3 3 3 3 3 3 3 3 3 3 3 3 3 3`			
`1 0 2 1 0 1 0 0 1 0 1 1 1 1 0 0 1 0 1 0 0 0 0 0`	44		
`1 3 2 3 1 1 2 2 2 0 2 2 2 3 2 3 2 2 3 2 3 2 2 3`		.59	71
`2 2 2 2 2 2 2 2 2 2 2 2 2 2 2 2 3 3 3 3 3 3 3 3`			
`1 1 0 1 1 1 0 0 0 2 0 0 0 1 0 1 1 1 0 1 0 1 1 0`	24		
`0 2 0 3 3 3 2 3 1 3 1 2 2 3 3 3 2 2 2 3 3 3 2 3`		.56	76
`2 2 2 2 2 2 2 2 2 2 3 3 3 3 3 3 3 3 3 3 3 3 3 3`			
`2 0 2 1 1 1 0 1 1 1 1 1 1 0 0 0 1 1 1 1 0 0 1 0`	37		
`1 0 0 2 0 0 1 0 0 0 1 1 1 1 1 2 0 2 2 2 1 1 2 2`		.83	30
`0 1 1 1 1 1 1 1 1 1 1 1 1 1 1 1 1 2 2 2 2 2 2 2`			
`1 1 1 1 1 1 0 1 1 1 0 0 0 0 0 1 1 0 0 0 1 1 0 0`	20		
`1 0 2 0 1 1 1 0 1 1 2 2 2 2 2 3 1 2 3 3 0 3 3 3`		.70	53
`1 1 1 1 1 1 1 1 1 1 2 2 2 2 2 2 2 2 3 3 3 3 3 3`			
`0 1 1 1 0 0 0 1 0 1 0 0 0 0 0 1 1 0 0 0 3 0 0 0`	22		
`1 3 0 0 0 2 1 0 3 3 2 3 2 2 2 2 2 2 2 2 2 3 3 2`		.65	61
`1 1 2 2 2 2 2 2 2 2 2 2 2 2 2 2 2 2 3 3 3 3 3 3`			
`0 2 2 2 2 0 1 2 1 1 0 1 0 0 0 0 0 0 1 1 1 0 0 1`	30		
`1 1 0 2 0 3 0 0 0 0 2 1 1 0 2 2 3 3 1 3 2 2 2 1`		.71	50
`1 1 1 1 1 1 1 1 1 1 1 2 2 2 2 2 2 2 2 2 3 3 3 3`			
`0 0 1 1 1 2 1 1 1 1 1 0 1 1 2 0 0 1 1 1 1 1 1 2`	40		
`2 1 0 0 2 0 1 0 2 0 1 2 2 0 1 2 2 2 2 2 3 1 1 2`		.78	39
`0 1 1 1 1 1 1 1 2 2 2 2 2 2 2 2 2 2 2 2 2 2 2 3`			
`2 0 1 1 1 1 0 1 1 2 1 0 0 2 1 0 0 0 0 0 1 1 1 1`	26		

References

Albrechtsen, Dorte, Birgit Henriksen, and Claus Faerch. 1980. Native speaker reactions to learners' spoken interlanguage. Language Learning 30(2):365–96.

Bachman, Lyle F. and Adrian S. Palmer. 1983. The construct validity of the FSI oral interview. In John W. Oller, Jr. (ed.), Issues in language testing research, 154–169. Rowley, Massachusetts: Newbury House Publishers.

Baratz, Joan C. 1969. A bi-dialectal task for determining language proficiency in economically disadvantaged Negro children. Child Development 40:889–901.

Blair, Frank. 1990. Survey on a shoestring: A manual for small-scale language survey. Dallas: Summer Institute of Linguistics and the University of Texas at Arlington.

Bruhn, Thea C. 1990. 'Passages': Life, the universe, and language proficiency assessment. In James E. Alatis (ed.), Georgetown University round table on languages and linguistics 1989: Language teaching, testing, and technology: Lessons from the past with a view toward the future, 244–54. Washington, DC: Georgetown University Press.

Callaway, Donn R. 1980. Accent and the evaluation of ESL oral proficiency. In J. W. Oller and K. Perkins (eds.), Research in language testing, 102–15. Rowley, Massachusetts: Newbury House Publishers.

Carroll, Brendan J. and Patrick J. Hall. 1985. Make your own language tests. Oxford: Pergamom Institute of English.

Carrow, E. 1974. A test using elicited imitations in assessing grammatical structure in children. Journal of Speech and Hearing Disorders 39:437–44.

Cartier, Francis A. 1980. Alternative methods of oral proficiency assessment. In James R. Frith (ed.), Measuring spoken language proficiency, 7–14. Washington, DC: Georgetown University Press.

Casad, Eugene H. 1974. Dialect intelligibility testing. Norman, Oklahoma: Summer Institute of Linguistics.

Clark, John L. D. 1980. Toward a common measure of speaking proficiency. In James R. Frith (ed.), Measuring spoken language proficiency, 15–25. Washington, DC: Georgetown University Press.

Connell, P. J. and C. Myles-Zitzer. 1982. An analysis of elicited imitation as a language evaluation procedure. Journal of Speech and Hearing Disorders 47:390–96.

Dailey, K. and J. R. Boxx. 1979. A comparison of three imitative tests of expressive language and a spontaneous language sample. Language, Speech, and Hearing Services in Schools 10:6–13.

Dulay, Heidi, M. Burt, and S. Krashen. 1982. Language two. New York: Oxford University Press.

Educational Testing Service. 1970. Manual for Peace Corps language testers. Princeton, New Jersey: ETS.

Fasold, Ralph. 1984. The sociolinguistics of society. Oxford: Basil Blackwell.

Fayer, Joan M. and Emily Krasinski. 1987. Native and nonnative judgments of intelligibility and imitation. Language Learning 37(3):313–26.

Fishman, Joshua A. and Robert L. Cooper. 1978. In Bernard Spolsky (ed.), Papers in applied linguistics—advances in language testing series: 2-Approaches to language testing, 31–38. Arlington, Virginia: Center for Applied Linguistics.

Fraser, C., U. Bellugi, and R. Brown. 1963. Control of grammar in imitation, comprehension and production. Journal of Verbal Learning and Verbal Behavior 2:121. Reprinted in Charles A. Ferguson and Dan Isaac Slobin (eds.), Studies of child language development. New York: Holt, Reinhart and Winston.

Frith, James R., ed. 1980. Measuring spoken language proficiency. Washington, DC: Georgetown University Press.

Gallimore, Ronald and Roland G. Tharp. 1981. The interpretation of elicited sentence imitation in a standardized context. Language Learning 31(2):369–92.

Gass, Susan and Evangeline Marlos Varonis. 1984. The effect of familiarity on the comprehensibility of nonnative speech. Language Learning 34(1):65–89.

Grimes, Barbara F. 1986. Evaluating bilingual proficiency in language groups for cross-cultural communication. Notes on Linguistics 33:5–27.

———. 1987. How bilingual is bilingual? Notes on Linguistics 40:3–23.

References

Hallberg, Calinda E. and Clare F. O'Leary. 1991. A sociolinguistic survey of the Gujari language. ms.

Hamayan, Else, Barbara R. Markman, Susanne Pelletier, and G. Richard Tucker. 1978. Differences in performance in elicited imitation between French monolingual and English-speaking bilingual children. International Review of Applied Linguistics 16(4):330–39.

Hatch, Evelyn, and Hossein Farhady. 1982. Research design and statistics for applied linguistics. Rowley, Massachusetts: Newbury House Publishers.

Hendricks, Debby, G. Scholz, R. Spurling, M. Johnson, and L. Vandenburg. 1980. Oral proficiency testing in an intensive English language program. In J.W. Oller and K. Perkins (eds.), Research in language testing, 77–90. Rowley, Massachusetts: Newbury House Publishers.

Henning, Grant. 1983. Oral proficiency testing: Comparative validities of interview, imitation and completion methods. Language Learning 33(3):315–32.

Ingram, Elizabeth. 1978. The psycholinguistic basis. In Bernard Spolsky (ed.), Papers in applied linguistics—advances in language testing series: 2-Approaches to language testing, 1–14. Arlington, Virginia: Center for Applied Linguistics.

Jones, Randall L. 1975. Testing language proficiency in the United States government. In Randall L. Jones and Bernard Spolsky (eds.), Testing language proficiency, 1–9. Washington, DC: Center for Applied Linguistics.

Kamp, Randy. To appear. Inherent intelligibility, bilingualism, or both? In Eugene H. Casad (ed.), Windows on bilingualism and other matters.

Lee, L. 1970. A screening test for syntax development. Journal of Speech and Hearing Disorders 35:103–12.

McDade, H. L., M. A. Simpson, and D. E. Lamb. 1982. The use of elicited imitation as a measure of expressive grammar: A question of validity. Journal of Speech and Hearing Disorders 47:19–24.

Menyuk, Paula. 1964. Comparison of grammar of children with normal and deviant speech. Journal of Speech and Hearing Research 7:109–21.

———. 1969. Sentences children use. Cambridge, Massachusetts: MIT Press.

Miller, Jon F. 1973. Sentence imitation in pre-school children. Language and Speech 16:1–14.

Milroy, Lesley. 1987. Observing and analysing natural language. Oxford: Basil Blackwell.

Naiman, N. 1974. The use of elicited imitation in second language acquisition research. Working papers on bilingualism 2:1–37.

Natalicio, Diana S. and Frederick Williams. 1971. Repetition as an oral language assessment technique. Austin, Texas: Center for Communication Research, School of Communication, University of Texas at Austin.

———. 1975. What characteristics can "experts" reliably evaluate in the speech of Black and Mexican-American children? In Leslie Palmer and Bernard Spolsky (eds.), Papers on language testing 1967–1974, 164–71. Washington, DC: Teachers of English to Speakers of Other Languages.

Norman, Donald A. 1976. Memory and attention. New York: John Wiley and Sons.

Oller, John W., Jr. 1979. Language tests at school—A pragmatic approach. London: Longman Group.

——— and Kyle Perkins, eds. 1980. Research in language testing. Rowley, Massachusetts: Newbury House Publishers.

Oskarsson, Mats. 1981. Subjective and objective assessment of foreign language performance. In John A. S. Read (ed.), Directions in language testing—Selected papers from the RELC seminar on "evaluation and measurement of language competence and performance", Singapore, April 1980, 225–39. Singapore: Singapore University Press.

Palmer, L. 1973. A preliminary report on a study of the linguistic correlates of raters' subjective judgments of nonnative English. In Roger W. Shuy and R. W. Fasold (eds.), Language attitudes: Current trends and prospects, 41–59. Washington, DC: Georgetown University Press.

Perkins, Kyle, Sheila R. Brutten, and Paul J. Angelis. 1986. Derivational complexity and item difficulty in a sentence repetition task. Language Learning 36(2):125–41.

Politzer, Robert L., Mary Rhodes Hoover, and Dwight Brown. 1975. A test of proficiency in Black standard and nonstandard speech. In Leslie Palmer and Bernard Spolsky (eds.), Papers on language testing 1967–1974, 91–100. Washington, DC: Teachers of English to Speakers of Other Languages.

Prutting, C. A., T. M. Gallagher, and A. Mulac. 1975. The expressive portion of the NSST compared to a spontaneous language sample. Journal of Speech and Hearing Disorders 40:40–48.

——— and J. E. Connolly. 1976. Imitation: A closer look. Journal of Speech and Hearing Disorders 41:412–22.

Quakenbush, John Stephan. 1986. Language use and proficiency in a multilingual setting: A sociolinguistic survey of Agutaynen speakers in Palawan, Philippines. PhD. dissertation, Georgetown University.

Radloff, Carla. 1991. Avenues of acquisition of Urdu proficiency for Hindko-speaking women of Hazara division (Pakistan). In Gloria E. Kindell (ed.), Proceedings of the Summer Institute of Linguistics

References

International Language Assessment Conference, Horsleys Green, 23-31 May 1989. Dallas: Summer Institute of Linguistics.

——— and David Marshall. 1986. Sentence repetition—A pilot study. ms.

Read, John A. S., ed. 1981. Directions in language testing—Selected papers from the RELC seminar on "evaluation and measurement of language competence and performance", Singapore, April 1980. Singapore: Singapore University Press.

Rensch, Calvin R. 1987. Patterns of language use among the Kohistanis of the Swat Valley (Pakistan). ms.

———. 1988. The language environment of Hindko-speaking people (Pakistan). ms.

———. To appear. Developing community profiles. In Eugene H. Casad (ed.), Windows on bilingualism and other matters.

Richards, Jack C. 1970. A psycholinguistic measure of vocabulary selection. International Review of Applied Linguistics 8(2):87–102.

Shavelson, Richard J. 1988. Statistical reasoning for the behavioral sciences. Boston: Allyn and Bacon.

Showalter, Catherine J. 1991. Getting what you ask for: A study of sociolinguistic survey questionnaires. In Gloria E. Kindell (ed.), Proceedings of the Summer Institute of Linguistics International Language Assessment Conference. Horsleys Green, 24–31 May, 1989. Dallas: Summer Institute of Linguistics.

Showalter, Stuart D. 1989. Alternative bilingualism measures for rural African settings: A field test report. Paper presented at the International Language Assessment Conference. Horsleys Green, 24–31 May, 1989.

Summer Institute of Linguistics. 1987. The SIL second language oral proficiency evaluation. Notes on Linguistics 40A:24–54.

Simons, Gary F. 1983. Language variation and limits to communication. Dallas: Summer Institute of Linguistics.

Slobin, Dan I. 1973. Introduction to studies of imitation and comprehension. In Charles A. Ferguson and Dan Isaac Slobin (eds.), Studies of child language development, 462–65. New York: Holt, Reinhart and Winston.

——— and C. Welsh. 1968. Elicited imitations as a research tool in developmental psycholinguistics. Working paper 10. Berkeley: Language-Behavioral Research Laboratory, University of California, Berkeley.

Smith, Larry E. and John A. Bisazza. 1982. The comprehensibility of three varieties of English for college students in seven countries. Language Learning 32(2):259–69.

Spiegel, Murray R. 1972. Schaum's outline of theory and problems of statistics. London: McGraw-Hill.

Spolsky, Bernard, Penny Murphy, Wayne Holm, and Allen Ferrel. 1975. Three functional tests of oral proficiency. In Leslie Palmer and Bernard Spolsky (eds.), Papers on language testing 1967–1974, 75–90. Washington, DC: Teachers of English to Speakers of Other Languages.

Stevick, E.W. 1976. Memory, meaning and method. Rowley, Massachusetts: Newbury House Publishers.

Streiff, Virginia. 1978. Relationships among oral and written cloze scores and achievement test scores in a bilingual setting. In J. W. Oller and K. Perkins (eds.), Language in education: Testing the tests, 65–102. Rowley, Massachusetts: Newbury House Publishers.

Swain, Merril, Guy Dumas, and N. Naiman. 1974. Alternatives to spontaneous speech: Elicited translation and imitation as indicators of second language competence. Working papers on bilingualism: Special issue on language acquisition studies 3:68–79.

Valette, Rebecca M. 1977. Modern language testing. New York: Harcourt Brace Jovanovich.

Wardhaugh, Ronald. 1986. An introduction to sociolinguistics. Oxford: Basil Blackwell.

Wilds, Claudia P. 1975. The oral interview test. In Randall L. Jones and Bernard Spolsky (eds.), Testing language proficiency, 29–44. Washington, DC: Center for Applied Linguistics.

Woods, Anthony, Paul Fletcher, and Arthur Hughes. 1986. Statistics in language studies. Cambridge: Cambridge University Press.

www.ingramcontent.com/pod-product-compliance
Lightning Source LLC
Chambersburg PA
CBHW051811230426
43672CB00012B/2691